W9-AJX-956

ALSO BY DAVID ROBERTS

ONCE THEY MOVED LIKE THE WIND:

COCHISE, GERONIMO, AND THE APACHE WARS

MOUNT MCKINLEY: THE CONQUEST OF DENALI

(with Bradford Washburn)

ICELAND: LAND OF THE SAGAS

(with Jon Krakauer)

JEAN STAFFORD: A BIOGRAPHY

MOMENTS OF DOUBT

GREAT EXPLORATION HOAXES

DEBORAH: A WILDERNESS NARRATIVE

THE MOUNTAIN OF MY FEAR

EXPLORING THE ANASAZI WORLD OF THE SOUTHWEST

DAVID ROBERTS

In Search of the Old Ones

SIMON & SCHUSTER

NEW YORK LONDON TORONTO SYDNEY TOKYO SINGAPORE

SIMON & SCHUSTER
ROCKEFELLER CENTER
1230 AVENUE OF THE AMERICAS
NEW YORK, NY 10020

DESIGNED BY KAROLINA HARRIS

MANUFACTURED IN THE UNITED STATES OF AMERICA

10 9 8 7 6 5 4 3 2 1

LIBRARY OF CONGRESS
CATALOGING-IN-PUBLICATION DATA
ROBERTS, DAVID, DATE.
IN SEARCH OF THE OLD ONES ; EXPLORING
THE ANASAZI WORLD OF THE SOUTHWEST /
DAVID ROBERTS.
P. CM.
INCLUDES BIBLIOGRAPHICAL REFERENCES AND INDEX.
1. PUEBLO INDIANS—HISTORY. 2. PUEBLO INDIANS—
ANTIQUITIES. 3. SOUTHWEST, NEW—ANTIQUITIES.
I. TITLE
E99.P9R537 1996
979'.004974—DC20 95-46218 CIP
ISBN 0-684-81078-6

Contents

Land of the Anasazi

LAND OF
UTAH
MESA VERDE ANASAZI
River
Blanding
Montezuma Creek
MOQUI CANYON
GRAND GULCH
PRIMITIVE AREA
KAIPAROWITS
PLATEAU
HOVENWEEP
N.M.
Halls
Crossing
CEDAR MESA
Cortez
San
Juan
Bluff
Lake Powell
Rainbow Bridge
Navajo Mountain
UTE
MOUNTAIN
INDIAN
RES.
River
Colorado
TSEGI
CANYON
NAVAJO
RESERVATION
NAVAJO
N.M.
Keet Seel
Betatakin
Kayenta
KAYENTA ANASAZI
CANYON
DE CHELLY N.M.
Chinle
ARIZONA
Little
NAVAJO
RESERVATION
Colorado
Sichomovi
Kykotsmovi
Hano
Oraibi
HOPI
RESERVATION
Walpi
Gallup
River
Flagstaff
Zuni
ZUNI
INDIAN RE
LITTLE COLORADO ANASAZI

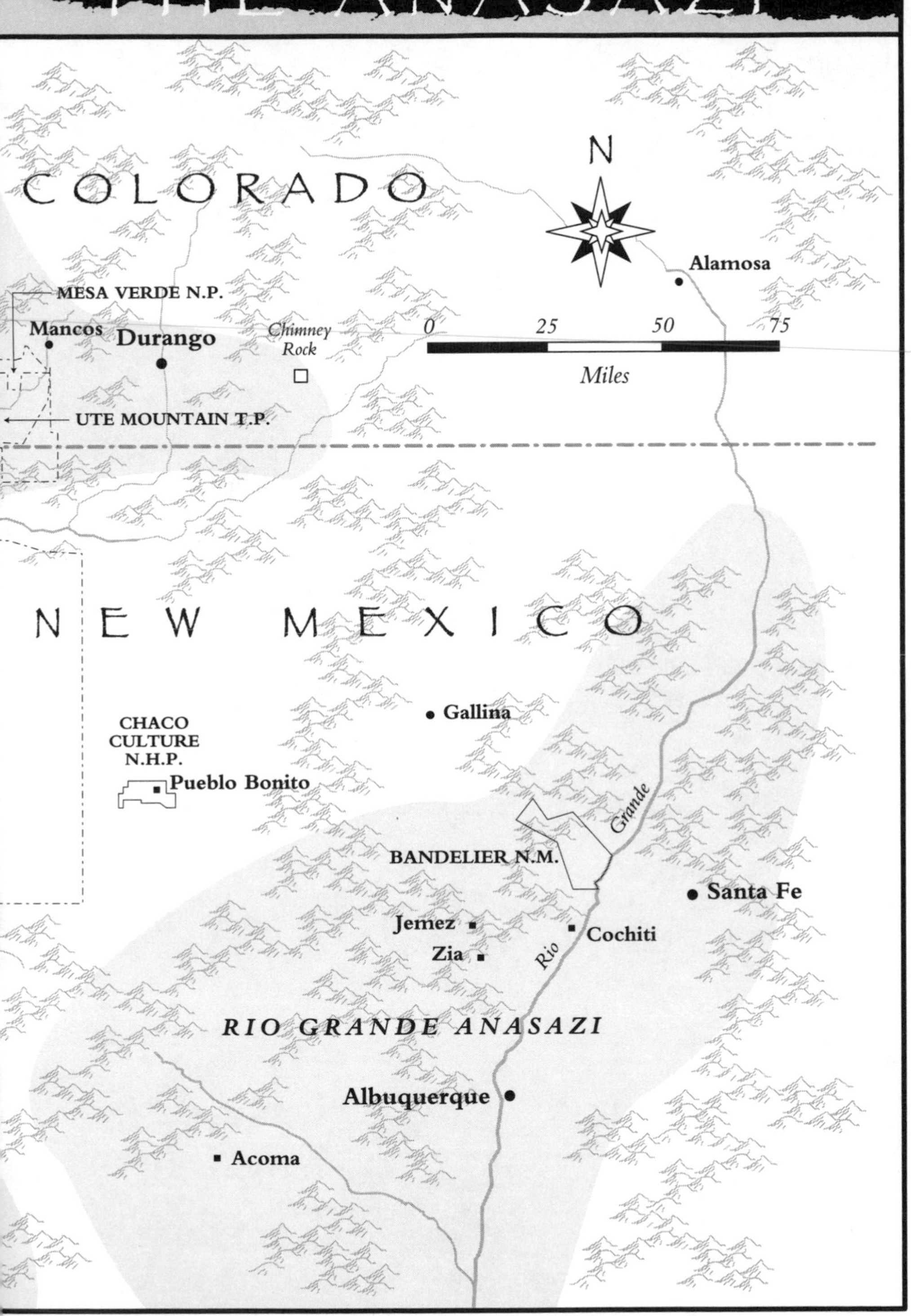

THE ANASAZI
COLORADO
N
Alamosa
MESA VERDE N.P.
Mancos
Durango
Chimney Rock
0
25
50
75
Miles
UTE MOUNTAIN T.P.
NEW MEXICO
Gallina
CHACO CULTURE N.H.P.
Pueblo Bonito
Grande
BANDELIER N.M.
Santa Fe
Jemez
Cochiti
Zia
Rio
RIO GRANDE ANASAZI
Albuquerque
Acoma

Author's Note

THE term *Anasazi*—a Navajo word meaning "ancestral enemies"—has been standard archaeological usage for the prehistoric people with whom this book deals since 1936, when it was proposed by Alfred V. Kidder. The term has always been offensive to the Hopi and other Pueblo Indians who are the descendants of the Anasazi. The word the Hopi use for their ancestors—*Hisatsinom*—is, however, different from the ancestral term in use at the Pueblo town of Zuni, which in turn is different from that used at the Pueblo town of Acoma, and so on.

In recent years, there has been a movement among younger archaeologists and some Pueblo people to substitute "Ancestral Puebloans" for "Anasazi." This book resists that nomenclature on several grounds. Whatever its faults, *Anasazi* has been a well-defined archaeological term for almost sixty years (to distinguish that culture, for example, from the contemporary Hohokam to the south or Fremont to the north); *Puebloan* derives from the language of an oppressor who treated the indigenes of the Southwest far more brutally than the Navajo ever did; and, at book length, repeated again and again, "Ancestral Puebloans" is a cumbersome mouthful.

It may be germane to point out that no term embodies a more

egregious misnaming than Columbus's "Indians," yet "Native Americans" has yet to supplant it—even among American Indians themselves, who are still more likely to call themselves Indians than Native Americans.

Prologue

I WOKE at dawn, as alpenglow painted the sandstone wall behind my tent a lurid reddish orange. A film of ice had formed inside my water bottle; I shook it loose and took a cold drink. White rafts of cumulus clouds sailed across the sky out of the northwest, where the subarctic fronts came from. It would be windy up on the canyon rim.

I put on all the clothes I had and crawled out of the tent. The seat I had built of three flat stones was cold to the touch, so I laid my day pack across it before I sat down. The butane stove fired at the touch of a match, its dull roar erasing the silence of the canyon. On the stove I placed my smaller pot, filled the night before with water dipped from a bedrock pool down in the canyon bottom. The skim of ice on the surface melted in patches.

The date was October 29. It was my third day alone in the obscure canyon in southeastern Utah. During those forty-some hours, I had seen no one else. My voice felt rusty with disuse, for I am not the sort of solo vagabond who talks to himself for company.

Tiny bubbles were forming on the bottom of the pot. I spooned freeze-dried coffee into my metal cup and thought about the discoveries of the previous day. Joyous though my long prowl under the late-autumn sun was, I had been acutely aware all day of my vulnerability as I scrambled through a slickrock wilderness far from any trail. In the night I had wakened with a jolt at 2 A.M., then lain for two hours in my sleeping bag without a hint of drowsiness, watching through the transparent roof of my tent as the moon slid west above the canyon rim. Eventually the prickles of anxiety ebbed, and sleep filled my head.

Now I waited for the sun to rise in the *V* notch on the horizon, fifteen degrees south of east. I had chosen the campsite by compass, counting on that earliest possible sunrise, but now the sky abruptly darkened and a chilling rain began to fall. I hurried through breakfast—coffee, a packet of sugary instant oatmeal, dried apricots. Just as I zipped closed the tent and hoisted my day pack, the rain stopped and patches of blue poked through the streaming clouds.

The day before, from the rim across the canyon to the south, I had spotted a small ancient ruin tucked under the mesa top, visible from few vantage points. With binoculars I had invented an approach route, memorizing landmarks that would look a lot different when I was upon them. The ruin stood only a quarter mile east of my camp, four hundred feet above it. But I couldn't see it from camp, and I knew that a direct approach would be stymied by overhanging bands of rock.

I was off at 9 A.M. Eighty feet below camp, on the canyon floor, ice glazed the pothole pools. Here, thanks to the vagaries of the jutting skyline, the sun would not rise till about eleven, more than four hours after its rays found my tent. Most hikers in canyon country regard the ideal campsite as a sandy bottom bench under the limbs of some generous cottonwood, close to the trickling water. Not me—and not the Anasazi, whose lives were woven tight into the wheeling circles of the sun.

On a bedrock of blue Halgaito shale, I hiked back upstream, retracing the path by which I had entered the canyon two days before. At the first north tributary, I veered right into a short, steep draw, then zigzagged upward among the ledges. The brown soil froze my footprints; I plucked sagebrush leaves, rubbed them, and breathed the bursting scent—essence of the desert Southwest. Just below the rim, I had to climb a ten-foot wall. *Be careful, this could be trouble,* nagged the fussy worrier in my head—the one whose doubts had kept me awake in the night. *Big deal, it's easy,* answered his cocky antagonist. A right hand jammed in a crack to pull on, a small hold high for the left foot, and I was up.

The wind hit me as I emerged on the rim, tearing my eyes. I pulled the hood of my jacket over my head and stood facing south, away from the wind. There across the canyon, silhouetted like a cardboard cutout beneath the sun, was the dizzy peninsula of stone that it had taken me the whole previous day to explore. Far to the east, dull brown in the low sun, heaved the humpbacked domes of the Comb Ridge. At that moment, was there another living person in the sweep of cosmos I surveyed?

I set off east across the mesa. Pausing on a point of rimrock, I gazed down into the canyon, searching for the yellow dot of my tent. It took a while to find it, and when I did, I was impressed by how lost, how obscure my camp seemed in the context of the intricate canyon. A helicopter flying over, searching for an overdue hiker, might easily miss that yellow dot. A ground team, pushing down the canyon, would have no clue of the camp hidden on a ledge eighty feet above.

Soon I recognized the ovoid boulder, the pair of piñon pines I had memorized the day before. I looked for a way to clamber down under the mesa rim and found, after a search, the devious zigzag that must have been the ancient inhabitants' only approach route.

Eighty feet beneath the rim, I headed back west on a good ledge and turned a corner. All at once, the ruin stood before me, half hidden under a five-foot-high overhang. Five rooms had been built here, side by side, sharing common walls. The two on either end had fallen to pieces, but the central three were exquisitely preserved, the worked sandstone slabs laid horizontal, mortared in place with brown mud, in which I could see the press marks of patting fingers.

Before the ruin, scattered in the dirt, I found scores of broken potsherds. Some of them were decorated with jagged designs in the distinctive style called Mesa Verde black-on-white. Those sherds and the masonry of the rooms told me that the Anasazi had built here during the Pueblo III period, sometime between A.D. 1150 and 1300. I knew that by the latter date they had left for good; for the whole of the Colorado Plateau—on which my Utah canyon was but a tiny wrinkle—had been abandoned just before the onset of the fourteenth century.

I lingered for more than an hour at the site, gobbling an early lunch of chocolate, cheese, and crackers. Below the rim I was out of the wind; the facing sun was so warm I took off my jacket and hat. For the same reason the Anasazi had preferred such a site: no angle of a twisting canyon trapped and held the winter warmth so effectively as a high south-facing ledge beneath the rim.

The doorways to the conical rooms, so small I could not squeeze through them without causing them harm, gaped as rounded rectangles in the stonework, the edges smoothed with mortar, a peeled stick serving as lintel above each. I stuck my head inside each room and waited for my eyes to adjust to the darkness. One room had a hearth made of shaped stones on the floor, tucked under the east wall; another was full of small corncobs, plucked clean of every kernel. The ceilings of all three rooms were black with cooking-fire soot. From the pattern of their shared walls, I could discern the sequence of building: the central room first, the adjoining pair next, and the outliers—so thoroughly destroyed they must have been deliberately taken apart—last.

On the underside of the overhang that formed the ceiling of the shelter, I found a smooth, cream-colored panel of sandstone that had served as canvas for an Anasazi brush: on it were several zigzag snakes in brown paint and a number of brown handprints. As I sat before the ruin, basking in the sun, I tried to imagine the family that had built and lived here.

The site seemed to my modern sensibility blissful and serene, a lordly nook in a wilderness that made the heart soar. But the Anasazi would have regarded it chiefly in practical terms, and by that reckoning, the dwelling place must have seemed marginal. It was a long, hard way to water: indeed, the circuitous route by which I had gained the site, climbing a five-hundred-foot slope out of the canyon and traversing the rim, must have been the path by which, every day, women had carried their jars to fill from the trickle in the canyon floor. There was arable land closer by, on the mesa top behind the rim; but in earlier epochs, the Anasazi had lived beside their fields, right on that mesa top, not hidden beneath the rim.

There were only two real advantages to the site. It gathered the heat of the sun in winter, and in summer the overhang provided cooling shade. Even more important, the site was supremely defensive. Its only approach from the rim was the tricky scramble down I had just made—a route that could be guarded by a single sentinel. From below, the dwellings were impregnable.

Like so many other ruins I had explored that also date from the Pueblo III period, just before the abandonment, this one raised an age-old question—a question archaeologists still have not definitively answered, even though it may be the most fundamental of all concerning the Anasazi.

What were they afraid of? Who were the enemy?

Before climbing back up to the rim, I chose to follow the ledge east as far as I could. It turned corners, growing narrower. I knew from binocular inspection the day before that the ledge eventually blanked out in overhang: that was part of the natural defenses of the site. I walked a hundred yards, then fifty more; at one point I had to sidle delicately around a boulder that leaned close to the precipice. I was about to give up when I turned the last corner.

The vocabulary of astonishment is an impoverished one, heavy with clichés like, "I felt a chill crawl up my spine." Yet in that moment, as I stopped walking and stood in my tracks, I was aware of a tingling of the skin, a suffusion of pleasure with overtones of shock, that began in the middle of my back and rose slowly, settling in my shoulders.

As I had followed the ledge eastward, the recessed stratum in which the ruin was built had steadily dwindled, until now, on my left, it amounted to a two-foot-high continuous niche. A crumbly band of red rock, sandwiched between solid gray brows of sandstone, hinted at the geological anomaly that produced the niche.

There before me, tucked into that two-foot aperture, a few yards short of where the ledge blanked out, sat an intact Anasazi pot. Slowly I approached. A branch of dead juniper had fallen to the ledge, close to the pot; now it guarded it like a fence. I got on my knees to peer close.

The pot was brownish red, decorated in the style called corrugated, used only for cooking. The Anasazi potter, having coiled and scraped the pot to its basic shape preparatory to firing it, had taken a tool and poked every inch of the pot's surface below the rim with bands of sharp triangular dents.

The pot was a big one: I estimated it at fourteen inches tall by fourteen inches wide. It would have held, I suppose, four or five gallons of water. As I peered at the pot from all angles, I detected its only blemish: a hairline crack zigzagging from the lip a few inches down one side—the kind of crack an accident of firing makes, not a cook who drops the pot. The crack was so fine that water would not have leaked from it.

The reddish marl of the crumbly stratum had collapsed and drifted around the pot over the centuries, imbedding it to a depth of six inches at the back. To try to pull the pot loose would be to destroy it. I was afraid even to touch it.

The pot, it was clear, had been cached in this arcane spot by someone who hoped to come back to retrieve it. Perhaps it had been placed here late in the 1200s by some Anasazi woman whose people had seen yet another harvest fail and had decided to move elsewhere for a year or two. The pot was too big to carry, too valuable to throw away. Hide it away on this ledge where the wrong ones would not find it, then come back soon and use it again. . . .

But they never came back. For at least seven hundred years the pot had rested in its niche, saved from the weather by the overhang above, preserved by the dry desert air. During those centuries of gnawing time, how many human eyes had gazed on the pot between the last Anasazi's and mine?

FOR a decade and a half I have sought out Anasazi ruins in the Southwest; during the last five years, my curiosity about those prehistoric agriculturalists has grown to become a passion. Like most devotees of the Anasazi, I began with the national parks and monuments: Mesa Verde, Canyon de Chelly, Chaco Canyon, Hovenweep, Montezuma Castle, Pecos, Bandelier.

In 1987, on a three-day hike into Utah's Grand Gulch, for the first time I came across Anasazi ruins in the backcountry—unexcavated, unrestored, with potsherds and corncobs still strewn in the dirt where the last dwellers had left them. I camped on alluvial benches where the ancients had once planted their crops; I drank from the springs that had sustained them. That trip changed everything for me: a passive admiration for the Anasazi, of the sort one feels in a museum, turned into something like a quest.

A quest—but a quest for what?

That late October day, alone in the wilderness, as I stumbled upon the corrugated pot—the first intact Anasazi vessel I had ever found—a glimpse of the answer came to me. I was no pothunter: it was not treasure I sought. I felt not even a moment's impulse to dig the pot out and take it home (quite apart from the fact that to do so would be to violate a federal law). The pot belonged where I found it, where its owner had hidden it in the thirteenth century.

My travels in Utah, Arizona, New Mexico, and Colorado have nonetheless been, in some sense, a pursuit of that very pot. Not of the pot itself, not of a ceramic object, however beautiful. What I sought instead was some connection with the Anasazi that I could feel beneath my fingertips as well as in my mind. The pot I looked for was—though I hesitate to use the word, with its facile evocation of the spiritual—a pot of communion.

You cannot, of course, set out to find such a pot. It must burst upon you by accident, when you expect nothing but another corner in the sandstone. And yet you must prepare yourself to find it; you must read the driest archaeological monographs and hike through the starkest badlands to reach the ledge where the pot awaits.

In the last analysis, the most impressive thing about the Anasazi is not their dazzling achievements at Cliff Palace, Pueblo Bonito, Hovenweep, and other storied cities of the dead. It is their thorough permeation of a country so difficult to travel in today that most of it remains uninhabited. Yet everywhere you go, in the most remote and unpromising corners of that country, you find a scattering of flint flakes here, a sherd or two of gray utilitarian cookware there, to testify to the passage of the ancients.

For all the pitiless rigor of that desert land, the Anasazi Southwest forms the most compelling landscape I know of in the world. The chapters that follow are an attempt to trace my meanderings in recent years across that landscape, sometimes in the company of various friends and acquaintances, sometimes alone. And if my erratic journey deserves after all to be called a quest, then it is a quest that I doubt I shall ever finish.

1

The Cowboy Who Found Cliff Palace

I PULLED my rental car into a slot between a Winnebago and a Mountain Aire, parked, and got out. A scent, heavy in the air—pine sap on a May breeze—carried me instantly back into the past. As a boy of twelve, car-camping with my family, I had first come to Mesa Verde, in southwestern Colorado, in the mid-1950s. For two days, we had toured the ruins: with my younger brothers and sister, I had climbed in and out of subterranean kivas, crawled through small portals into dark rooms, stood on high ledges and leaned over ancient walls masoned at the very edge of the precipice.

My father, an astronomer, had told me the two most important things he knew about the Anasazi, both considered, in the scientific optimism of the fifties, solid fact. They were, moreover, the kind of truths a boy with a restless spirit could never forget. A terrible drought in the late 1200s, my father said, had driven the Cliff Dwellers out of Mesa Verde, never to return. But before that, they had built their houses beneath the arching sandstone overhangs, in "caves" where no rain or snow could fall, chiefly because of the climatic advantage: the shelters were warm in winter, cool in summer.

Later, when my father hired a contractor to build an extension to our house on Bluebell Avenue in Boulder, he himself designed a roof that overhung our new living room at precisely the angle of the sheltering brow of certain Mesa Verde ruins. And it worked: to the marvel of the neighbors, our living room, with its floor-to-ceiling windows facing south, was full of sun in December, cool and shadowy in June.

In my memory, at Mesa Verde in the 1950s, we had been free to prowl and clamber through the ruins almost at will. Much had changed in the decades since. Now, on my ninth or tenth visit to the national park, I joined the crowd at the asphalt-paved overlook and waited for the four o'clock tour of Cliff Palace. It was May 1994. Of the six hundred Anasazi cliff dwellings in the park, only two were at the moment open to the public: Spruce Tree House and Cliff Palace. For the first season ever, Cliff Palace—the largest Anasazi cliff dwelling ever built—could be seen only on a ranger-led hourly tour. You had to get a ticket at the visitor center, four miles away, and the tours were limited to sixty people each.

As we waited, the ranger—identified as James on his name tag—explained the new regimen as a response to burgeoning tourism. "Yeah," he said, "Cliff Palace's been taking a beating." But I knew that visitation at Mesa Verde had held steady, just under seven hundred thousand per annum, for the last several years; 1993 had actually seen fewer tourists than the year before.

On the hour, the forty-five visitors in our group trooped slowly down the paved trail to a point short of the ruin itself, where James parked us in the shade. It was a cool afternoon, and after fifteen minutes many in our group were shivering, but James had his spiel to give. He seemed defensive about the new restrictions. "The Park Service has a twofold mission," he recited. "One is to serve you, the public. The other is to preserve the ruins."

James, I thought, was a sympathetic enough fellow: he looked like a Park Service lifer, and he was a Westerner through and through, who pronounced the place "Mesa Vurduh." I could hardly blame the ranger for his rote, mechanical delivery. How many tours a week was he charged with processing through the ruin?

But I wondered if he cared about the misinformation he was dishing out—or even knew that much of what he said was wrong. Chaco Canyon, James told us, "is in the middle of the Navajo Reservation." (Chaco lies east of the reservation.) "The Anasazi were the first people in North America to build permanent stone structures." (Had James heard of Chichén Itzá, Palenque, Bonampak?) "The Anasazi," claimed James with a hint of fervor, "actually did better than the Egyptians who built the pyramids—and they did it without the horse and the wheel and slave labor." (Not a single horse or wheel or slave helped build the pyramids.)

No one in our shivering group, myself included, raised a peep. The kids, bored with the lecture, played with stones or their shoelaces. Opposite us, gleaming in the sun, stood Cliff Palace; but it was like a slide projected on a screen.

With half our precious hour gone, James at last herded us over to a restored kiva, where we sat and listened as he resumed his lesson. The ranger was no mere automaton: in some sense, he cared deeply about Mesa Verde and the Anasazi. But when he expressed that enthusiasm, it came out in clichés. "Mesa Verde is like a large puzzle," he proposed, "like that TV show *Unsolved Mysteries.*"

All too soon, it was time to file out of Cliff Palace. I loitered at the back of the group, then, when James wasn't looking, poked my head inside the ground-level window of a remarkable four-story square tower, craned my neck, and stared once more at the vivid red paintings on the inner walls at the third-story level. In recent years archaeologist Kim Malville, of the University of Colorado, has shown that these pictographs demonstrate an Anasazi awareness of the arcane astronomical phenomenon called the lunar standstill.

Only two or three years earlier, when you could still wander into Cliff Palace on your own and stay till the 6 P.M. closing, the ranger on duty had encouraged visitors to look at the pictographs inside the square tower. Now, with a group of forty-five, doing so was too much of a bother.

A few members of our group paused at the outskirts to snap a last photo of Cliff Palace shining in the late sun. "Take your picture quickly," James urged, " 'cause we have to get out of here before the next tour comes in." Indeed, the five o'clock bunch were at the moment settling down for their own lecture in the shade.

At the time of my visit, the Park Service employed about 30 full-time rangers at Mesa Verde. In summer, the peak season, that number swells to 100. The park concessionaire, ARA, has some 150 employees working in May, 250 during the summer.

At Mesa Verde in May, you can stay in the park motel, called Far View Lodge, or camp in the campground; you can eat in four different restaurants, buy supplies in two groceries, browse through four different gift shops; you can gas up at two filling stations, or peruse brochures and watch a slide show at the visitor center. But in May you can walk through only two cliff dwellings, and you can visit the finest of them all only with a ticket, as part of a horde of forty, fifty, or sixty.

It is not, in the last analysis, tourist impact on the ruins that has turned Mesa Verde so restrictive. It is bureaucracy on the rampage. The more "services" a national park offers, the more snags and hassles the overworked rangers confront. And their bosses, rather than pare back a gift shop here, a snack bar there, shut down the ruins instead. Already there is doleful talk that in the next few years the Park Service may close Cliff Palace altogether, confining visitors to the distant overlook.

When I was twelve, Cliff Palace had sung to my spirit. Four decades later, the place was dead for me. During my regimented hour under the tutelage of James, the predominant emotion I had felt was vexation. Only my furtive glimpse of the hidden pictographs inside the square tower had touched me with the breath of wonder.

Yet Cliff Palace—despite the paved trails, the roped-off "no entry" precincts, the crude overreconstruction by archaeologists in the 1920s, and the rangers' canned talks today—remains a remarkable place. One way or another, I thought, it was worth the effort to see Cliff Palace afresh . . . to see it as Richard Wetherill had, that December day in 1888.

BENJAMIN WETHERILL, patriarch of a steadily growing clan, had led his family on an erratic pilgrimage through the Midwest, homesteading in Wisconsin, Iowa, Kansas, and Missouri before fetching up in 1880 in southwestern Colorado. On the Mancos

River, a few miles downstream from the frontier town of the same name, Wetherill built his Alamo Ranch, taking the cognomen from the Spanish word for "cottonwood."

Years of farming and prospecting had broken the old man's health. During the 1880s, his five sons took over the running of the ranch. Eldest of the five was Richard, barely twenty-two when the Alamo was being built. Thin, strong, five feet eight, his hair already turning gray, Richard was a man of few words. "He kept his eyes fixed," writes his biographer, Frank McNitt, "unblinking and often quizzical, upon those he was addressing. Some of his friends have said they had a nervous feeling that he gazed right into their minds."

His formal education limited to high school, Richard nonetheless was a bookworm with a driving curiosity. In the coming years, he would gain a proficiency in both the Ute and Navajo tongues. And though the ranch demanded most of his time, at heart Richard Wetherill was an explorer.

In the 1880s, the town of Mancos lived in constant fear. The Utes upon whose land the pioneers had infringed were not happy about the trespass; without warning, they would raid and burn isolated homesteads or attack travelers passing through. The women and children of Mancos felt an edgy apprehension even in their own backyards, and the Mancos men rode everywhere armed.

The Wetherills, however, were Quakers. Although all five sons became crack shots, they sometimes left their guns at home when they rode into the backcountry. Perhaps their faith gave them added courage, for almost alone among the Mancos ranchers, they prowled at will downriver, into the canyon-thronged heartland of the Ute Mountain Utes.

The Indians took notice. The daring of the Wetherills gained them a wary respect: within a few years, ill or hungry Utes felt safe showing up at the Alamo Ranch, and in turn they let the Wetherills graze their cattle in canyons that were off-limits to all other Anglos.

Directly west of the Alamo Ranch, plunging the valley year-round into early sunset, loomed the vast, high tableland of Mesa Verde. In the 1880s, the mesa remained terra incognita to white settlers. Yet as they pushed their cattle into the side canyons of the

Mancos south of the plateau, the Wetherill brothers began to discover small cliff dwellings ensconced in south-facing sandstone alcoves. They were not the first Anglos to do so: as early as 1874, the great photographer William Henry Jackson, exploring for the Hayden Survey, had found and recorded a nine-room ruin that he called Two Story House in Mancos Canyon.

Digging among the ruins, taking home curios, the Wetherills developed a part-time hobby to leaven the heartless toil of ranch work. Meanwhile, they befriended the Ute chief, Acowitz. One day, twenty miles down the Mancos from the ranch, Acowitz walked up to Richard Wetherill as he stared at the twisting bends of Cliff Canyon, where he had never been.

At that moment, Acowitz chose to tell his cowboy friend something he had told no other white man. Far up Cliff Canyon, near its head, he avowed, stood many houses of the ancient ones. "One of those houses," said Acowitz, "high, high in the rocks, is bigger than all the others. Utes never go there. It is a sacred place."

Richard pleaded to be guided to the site, but Acowitz warned him that he too should avoid the ruin. "When you disturb the spirits of the dead," the chief insisted, "then you die too." Richard filed away the tantalizing information.

Almost two years passed. On a bitter day in December 1888, with snow on the wind, Richard and his brother-in-law Charlie Mason rode horseback along the rim of Mesa Verde above Cliff Canyon, tracking cattle that had strayed far from their usual pastures. Twenty-five miles from the Alamo Ranch, the cowboys knew they faced a cold bivouac under the pines before they could bring the cattle in.

A looping track drew the two men near the mesa's edge, where a cliff dropped sheer to the talus below. They dismounted, walked to the rim, and gazed east across the head of Cliff Canyon. Suddenly Richard blurted out a cry of astonishment.

Half a mile away, in the cliff forming the canyon's opposite wall, loomed an overhang that sheltered a natural cavern fully four hundred feet long by ninety feet deep. Inside it stood the pristine ruins of an ancient city, more than two hundred rooms built back-to-back of stone and mud, dominated by a round three-story tower. So this was the place Acowitz had told Richard about! "It looks just like a palace," murmured Mason.

Either then or shortly after, Wetherill named the ruin Cliff Palace. The brothers-in-law forgot about their cattle. Roping together dead trees with their lariats, they improvised a ladder to descend the cliff, then scrambled down through the piñon pines to the canyon floor and up the opposite slope to enter the majestic ruin.

It was as if the vanished inhabitants had walked off a few hours before, leaving everything in place. The rooms were strewn with intact ceramic pots sitting in the dust. On one floor the ranchers found a heavy stone axe, still hafted to its wooden handle. A perfunctory dig in the rubble uncovered three skeletons.

Wild with the passion of discovery, the men split up to search for other ruins in the few hours of daylight they had left. Wetherill headed northwest across the mesa top and stumbled upon another great ruin, which he named Spruce Tree House. He rejoined Mason at dusk; the men built a campfire and talked into the night.

In the morning, the pair found yet a third village, whose most startling feature was a soaring four-story tower. Square Tower House was the obvious name.

Today, Cliff Palace and Spruce Tree House are the only cliff dwellings in Mesa Verde National Park open year-round. Visitors peer from a lookout point down on Square Tower House, whose fragility has caused it to be closed to the public. Meanwhile, Cliff Palace has become the best known of all Anasazi sites, one of the most famous ruins in the world.

After his discovery had brought Richard Wetherill a modest celebrity, his brother Al—second in the line of five sons—complained that he had glimpsed Cliff Palace a year before Richard had found it, in fading light from half a mile below the site. Magnanimously, both Richard and Charlie Mason granted the younger brother's claim.

Many years later, Al Wetherill described that fugitive glimpse:

> In the dusk and the silence, the great blue vault hung above me like a mirage. The solemn grandeur of the outlines was breathtaking. My

mind wanted to go up to it, but my legs refused to cooperate. At the time I was so tired that I thought later would be the time for closer investigation.

The discovery of Cliff Palace was the turning point in Richard Wetherill's life. A part-time hobby became a passionate obsession as Richard sought to transform himself into a self-taught archaeologist. During the next few years, the Wetherill brothers found ruin after ruin on Mesa Verde—182 sites in all. They dug at will among the dwellings and carted out not only pots and stone axes and jewelry, but skeletons and skulls.

Hoping to arouse public interest and sell the relics they had dug, the brothers organized exhibitions of their booty in Durango, Pueblo, and Denver. The shows were utter failures; their reception, as Al later put it, amounted to "indifference verging on ridicule." Then Charlie Mason and Clayton Wetherill (fourth of the five brothers) discovered an exquisitely preserved mummified child. Where old pots and burnished arrowheads had failed, the mummy prevailed: in Denver it became a cause célèbre, and the brothers sold their first collection to the State Historical Society.

By his own later admission, when he began digging in the ruins, Richard Wetherill was little more than a pothunter. For that matter, in 1888 true archaeology had scarcely been practiced in the United States, and many a professional in Wetherill's time excavated as crudely as he did.

Gradually, however, Richard realized that science would better be served if the intact collections could find their way into museums. Instead of well-heeled curio hunters, he began to search for altruistic patrons.

One of the first was a young Swedish baron, Gustaf Nordenskiöld, who was traveling across the West in search of a cure for tuberculosis (from which he would die at the age of twenty-six). University trained in geology, Nordenskiöld had visited digs in Italy and was aware of the best European techniques. Hiring Richard Wetherill to supervise ambitious excavations at Mesa Verde in 1891, he taught the cowboy to use a trowel instead of a shovel and stressed the importance of written and photographic documentation.

Wetherill was an eager student. Soon he had devised his own field-note forms, and the records he kept grew more and more detailed and precise. The judgment of posterity lay always heavy in his thoughts. As he wrote a later patron, "This whole subject . . . is in its infancy and the work we do must stand the most rigid inspection, and we do not want to do it in such a manner that anyone in the future can pick flaws in it."

Eventually, vast collections of Anasazi artifacts assembled by Wetherill would anchor the Southwest holdings of half a dozen major institutions, including the Field Museum in Chicago, as well as the American Museum of Natural History and the National Museum of the American Indian in New York City. Although Nordenskiöld's assemblage—the only Wetherill collection to leave the country—finally found its way to the National Museum of Finland in Helsinki, in 1891 the Durango sheriff, prompted by local outrage, arrested the Swedish aristocrat in an attempt to keep the relics in the United States. (He was freed when it was learned that no law forbade the export of ancient artifacts; the Antiquities Act would not be passed until 1906.) Nordenskiöld's seminal report, *The Cliff Dwellers of the Mesa Verde,* published in Stockholm in 1893, was the first scholarly monograph ever written about the Anasazi.

The passion intensified. Led by Richard, all five brothers and Charlie Mason, along with a handful of cronies, began to push their explorations far beyond Mesa Verde. Richard found a series of patrons to bankroll these excursions—most fruitfully, Talbot and Fred Hyde, near millionaires from New York who were heirs to the Bab-O soap fortune. In the virtually unknown wilderness of southeastern Utah, Richard found canyon after canyon spangled with Anasazi ruins. In one of them, in December 1893, he made his greatest discovery.

At the dawn of serious study of the Cliff Dwellers—the term "Anasazi" did not become current until 1936—remarkably little was known of these ancients. No one could say whether their lost cities were five hundred or three thousand years old. A prevalent assumption held that they were the work of Aztecs from Mexico:

whence such place names as Montezuma Creek, Utah; Cortez, Colorado; and Aztec, New Mexico.

Most crucial, no one yet recognized any developmental stages in the culture of the vanished ancients. The various ruins and artifacts were tacitly regarded as the product of a uniform people, changeless over time.

Richard Wetherill's great discovery changed all that.

ON that December day in 1893, Wetherill dug beneath an unprepossessing ruin in a small alcove, turning up a familiar scatter of Anasazi pots and tools. A few feet down, he hit a layer of sterile soil. Normally, Richard would have quit at this point, assuming the ruin had yielded its secrets, but a hunch of his brother Al's made him keep digging.

Five feet beneath the surface, he began to uncover remarkable things. The cave was riddled with bottle-shaped pits that had been used as burial cists. Eventually Wetherill unearthed more than ninety skeletons in the alcove. Some four-fifths of them showed evidence of violent harm, and scattered among the bones were many deadly flint points, including one embedded in a backbone. Was this the site of some prehistoric battle or mass execution?

The importance of Wetherill's discovery, however, lay not in the damaged skeletons per se. Almost at once, the rancher-turned-archaeologist made an acute observation. These deep-buried human remains and artifacts differed in important ways from the kind he had dug at Mesa Verde. The people he uncovered five feet under had no pottery; they used the atlatl, or spear-thrower, rather than the bow and arrow; they made superb baskets of yucca, willow, and squawbush, some woven so tight they could hold water; they were slightly taller than the Cliff Dwellers of Mesa Verde; and they had round skulls, rather than the flattened crania nearly all the skeletons he had previously dug had borne. (The flattening is now known to have been caused by the use of hard cradle boards in infancy).

Wetherill was convinced he had found a different people from the Cliff Dwellers. In a letter to his patron Talbot Hyde, he proposed the term "Basket People" (soon standardized as Basketmakers). What was more, Wetherill deduced that the Basket People had lived in an earlier age than the Cliff Dwellers.

This simple conclusion involved a great intellectual leap. No one in North America had previously correlated depth in the soil with prehistoric age. Six decades later, the great archaeologist Alfred V. Kidder tipped his hat to the Mancos rancher: "[Nels] Nelson and I have often been credited with doing the first stratigraphic work in the Southwest, but Richard, in recognizing the greater antiquity of the Basketmakers than that of the Cliff Dwellers, used the method many years before anyone else in that field." Wetherill was wrong about the Basketmakers being a separate people: they turn out to be the ancestors of the Cliff Dwellers. Yet the distinction between the Basketmaker and the Pueblo phases of Anasazi culture—with the transition taking place around A.D. 750—has become one of the cornerstones of Southwest archaeology.

Whenever Wetherill shipped a collection of artifacts to an Eastern museum, he sent along his field notes as well. Over the years, however, these records were sometimes misinterpreted, ignored, or even misplaced. In a perverse twist, such curatorial carelessness contributed to the cowboy archaeologist's lingering reputation as a mere pothunter.

In the 1980s, a loose band of Westerners—nearly all of them amateurs in archaeology, as Wetherill had been—launched what they called the Wetherill–Grand Gulch Research Project. Their central figure is Fred Blackburn, a wilderness guide and educator who lives in Cortez, Colorado. In the 1970s, Blackburn had served as a Bureau of Land Management ranger in Grand Gulch, where Wetherill had pursued some of his boldest digs. Blackburn became obsessed with retracing the cowboy's footsteps across the Southwest.

After visiting several museums, Blackburn and his colleagues realized that in most cases, not only did Wetherill's notes still exist, but so did scores of glass-plate photos he had exposed. The team believed that it might be possible to relink the artifacts in the museums with their proveniences—their contexts in the original sites. This sort of reverse archaeology—the term is Blackburn's coinage—

could hold a vast potential for rejuvenating "dead" collections. The Wetherill Project, its members hoped, might serve as a model by which archaeologists could wring new insights out of old artifacts. And along the way, the team sensed, they might do much to rehabilitate Wetherill's reputation.

Though by 1893 the cowboy was keeping careful notes of his excavations, he tended to be cavalier about geographical position—perhaps because the wilderness, in all its intricacy, was so clear in his head. The site of his discovery of the Basketmakers he had named simply Cave 7. After his death, the location of the alcove became muddled. In Frank McNitt's excellent biography, *Richard Wetherill: Anasazi,* published in 1957, one of Wetherill's photographs of Cave 7 appeared with a caption erroneously placing it in Grand Gulch—twenty-five miles southwest of its true location.

One of the Wetherill Project's finest accomplishments was to rediscover Cave 7. The search took two years. The sleuths had only a few tantalizing clues: a sketch map and description of the site among Wetherill's notes, a pair of photos, and the heading of the letter in which the cowboy excitedly described his find to Talbot Hyde: "First Valley Cottonwood Creek 30 Miles North Bluff City."

In June 1993, Blackburn took me on a hike into Whiskers Draw, a minor tributary of Cottonwood Wash, some ten miles west of Blanding, Utah. Joining us was project member Winston Hurst, a freelance archaeologist who lives in Blanding. Hurst had spearheaded the search for Cave 7.

Blackburn is a stocky fireplug of a man, with red hair, a flamboyant moustache, a battered old brown cowboy hat, and a slow, tired voice that breaks without warning into streams of obscenity. He manages, as I soon saw, to meld a wry sense of humor with a permanent chip on his shoulder against bureaucracies—particularly federal agencies charged with caretaking the backcountry.

Hurst, on the other hand, is a tall, rail-thin melancholic of quiet disposition. A Mormon by upbringing, he pulls off the neat trick of working as an archaeologist in the very town that may be home to the nastiest and most serious pothunters in the West.

As Hurst and Blackburn led me into Whiskers Draw, I could appreciate what a needle in the haystack the search for the ordinary-looking cave must have been. It was a blazing day in the nineties; bull flies stung our legs, while tamarisk thickets lashed our faces as we bushwhacked up the draw. The country for hundreds of square miles around us was crisscrossed with mazes of similar side canyons.

A crucial hint had come in an oral history transcript from a Mormon pioneer named Albert Lyman—ironically, Hurst's great-uncle. Another clue lay in the dated signatures Wetherill and his friends were wont to scrawl in charcoal or scratch with a bullet cartridge on the cave walls. To later generations, these inscriptions have often seemed offensive graffiti. Yet in the 1890s, to leave one's name on an archaeological site was the normal practice followed by professional excavators and government explorers alike. The deed amounted to no mere braggart "Kilroy was here"; it was instead an integral part of the documentation of the dig.

As Hurst's team searched the tributaries of Cottonwood Wash, the dates got warm, clustering within days of December 17, 1893—the date on Wetherill's letter to Talbot Hyde. But as it turned out, the real Cave 7 was the very last of all the possible rock shelters Hurst and his colleagues looked into. As we bashed our way through the stand of tamarisk fronting the cave, I asked Hurst what he had felt that day in September 1990. "As soon as I was fifty feet away," he said, "I shouted out, 'Shit! This is it!'"

Now I had my own epiphany of recognition. With the photo from McNitt's book in hand, I stood on the exact spot where Wetherill had exposed the glass plate in 1893. The crumbling Pueblo wall on the left still stood, albeit more ravaged than a century before. In the old photo, Basketmaker skulls litter the floor of the cave. Now I could see the deep depressions in the dirt, a mute memorial to the ninety-some skeletons Wetherill had extracted.

Before relocating Cave 7, Hurst and Christy Turner, of Arizona State University, an expert on prehistoric human remains, had traveled separately to the American Museum of Natural History, to which Wetherill had sent the materials he dug in 1893. There both scholars were able to examine the very bones and projectile points Richard Wetherill had found in Cave 7 nearly a century before.

Reintegrating the site and the artifacts, Hurst and Turner demonstrated that Cave 7 had been the scene of a wholesale massacre more than fifteen hundred years ago: the carnage involved stabbing by daggers, shooting with atlatl darts, bludgeoning, scalping, and possibly even torture.

Hurst and Turner's work represents a major step in revealing what some have called the dark side of Anasazi culture. Since it was first proposed more than a century ago as a possible cause of the abandonment of the Colorado Plateau around A.D. 1300, violence and warfare among the Anasazi have been scantily documented. As Hurst and Turner write in a recent paper, the evidence from Cave 7 "document[s] yet another example of our species' strange capacity for both terrible destructiveness and the creation of beautiful works of art."

A FEW days after our hike into Whiskers Draw, Blackburn and I spent three days in Grand Gulch, site of two of Wetherill's most ambitious expeditions, in 1893–94 and 1897. These jaunts, like nearly all the brothers' archaeological excursions, took place during the winter, the only season they could spare from ranch work. The sheer logistics of Wetherill's toil in Grand Gulch—up before dawn, working long into the night, camping in snowstorms, packing artifacts by horseback more than a hundred miles back to Mancos—testify to his diligence.

On our first day we were joined by Marietta Davenport, an archaeologist employed by the U.S. Forest Service, who happens to be Richard Wetherill's great-granddaughter. All through college and graduate school, she had to endure professors casting aspersions against her forebear. "I wouldn't say anything in class," she remembered. "Afterwards I'd go up to the professor and say, 'Wait a minute, let's talk about this.' I wouldn't let on right away that Richard was my great-grandfather."

In 1987, I had hiked into Bullet Canyon, Grand Gulch's main tributary, from its headwaters near Utah State Highway 261. This time, guided by Blackburn, we set off south across the mesa from a trailhead at Sheik's Flat. On this very route, exactly a hundred years before our visit, in 1893, Richard Wetherill had discovered a shortcut into Bullet and built a horse-packing trail down it.

We came to the rim of Bullet Canyon. Four hundred feet below us, the stream snaked among bright green cottonwoods. Blackburn had rediscovered Wetherill's old trail: now, as we zigzagged down the steep, rocky slope, he pointed out cairns and trail-improving cribwork built by the rancher a century before.

At the superb site called Perfect Kiva, which I had first visited in 1987, I recognized that a Richard Wetherill signature I had seen then had since been rubbed smooth—probably by an ecologically minded hiker. When I mentioned this to Blackburn, he unleashed a streak of profanity, then told me stories about many another effaced Wetherill inscription.

We hiked on to Jailhouse Ruin, one of the eeriest of all Anasazi sites in Grand Gulch, where huge, baleful "full-moon" pictographs dominate an airy, masoned ledge. It was a glorious hot afternoon, with canyon wrens singing on the breeze. As we sat on the bedrock sandstone below the ruin, Davenport said quietly, "It's pretty exciting for me to visit a site he dug. It's a very powerful thing."

We camped out that night, then, minus Davenport, headed the next morning down Sheik's Canyon, a Grand Gulch tributary. Some hiker had built small but unnecessary cairns to mark the route here, where the only path possible was the creek bed. As he walked past each cairn, Blackburn kicked it to pieces, muttering once or twice, "Read the goddamn map." Blackburn knew every wrinkle of his old stomping grounds, and though I had hiked the canyon before, he showed me things I had failed to see, such as a panel of petroglyphs (rock engravings) with three ithyphallic renderings of Kokopelli, the hunchbacked flute player.

In one unremarkable bend of the canyon, Blackburn stuck his hand into a hole in the cliff and pulled out five tin cans. He had discovered them in 1985 and concluded from the soldered seals on the lids that the cans may well have been Wetherill's. Inside one can, I found Blackburn's own eight-year-old note begging passersby to leave the relics in place. As I held the battered, rusty can in my hand,

I felt a frisson of contact with the man I was coming to venerate.

By midday we reached Green Mask Spring, a Basketmaker site so profusely decorated with pictographs that in four hours of staring I could only begin to sort out the enigmatic paintings. Here Wetherill had camped in January 1897. His second expedition into Grand Gulch proved even more arduous than the first: nine of his forty horses perished by falling off cliffs or breaking down and being abandoned on the pack trip in.

As dusk approached one evening, Wetherill dug a likely spot behind some rocks against the cliff at Green Mask. The burial he uncovered, working into the night by lantern, would be the single most striking find in all his years of Anasazi work. A five-and-a-half-foot-wide basket covered another basket; beneath them lay a turkey-feather blanket decorated with bluebird feathers and another blanket spangled with yellow canary spots. A final basket covered the perfectly mummified head of a woman. Her body was painted yellow, her face red.

The stunned archaeologist nicknamed his discovery the Princess. Never did he excavate a mummy more carefully or pack one more delicately to be carried out of Grand Gulch, back to Durango and the railroad east.

Using Wetherill's field notes and photographs, Blackburn's team had been able to pinpoint the pit at Green Mask Spring from which the Princess had been removed. Now I stood on the spot and pondered a pair of haunting pictographs that had been painted directly above the grave. The anthropomorphic figures in white, decorated with red circles covering their breasts, stood solemn and rigid side by side, almost like some bridal couple.

Here was another tantalizing promise spun out of Blackburn's reverse archaeology. Almost nowhere in the world has rock art been convincingly associated with burials. Yet if these pictographs commemorated the woman buried beneath them, then the paintings themselves might tell us more about the Princess—and vice versa. In particular, it has long been argued that the Anasazi were an intensely egalitarian people, with no royalty, perhaps even no chieftains. Yet the lavish and beautiful burial of the Princess, as well as the regal-looking paintings that stare down upon her grave, might constitute evidence to the contrary.

BENJAMIN WETHERILL, the ailing patriarch, died in 1898. Meanwhile, the brothers' pursuit of their new avocation had become so absorbing that they tended to neglect their ranch work. By 1898, thanks also to drought and early frosts, the Alamo was in trouble.

To eke out extra income, the brothers began guiding Eastern visitors through the ruins they had discovered. For a three-day tour of Cliff Palace, Spruce Tree House, and Square Tower House—grub, horses, and camping gear included—the boys charged twenty dollars. Some found their rates exorbitant. Gustaf Nordenskiöld, the Swedish aristocrat, grumbled that the three dollars a day he paid John Wetherill (third of the brothers) to organize his dig was almost as much as a professor made back home.

Among the Wetherill clients in 1895 was a family of traveling musicians from Kansas. Richard fell deeply in love with the eighteen-year-old harpist and soprano, Marietta Palmer. With the family, Wetherill made his first trip to Chaco Canyon in New Mexico, then so remote as to be all but unknown to white explorers. On the way back from their two-month outing, Marietta was the only passenger who dared ride the wagon as Wetherill forced it through a perilous ford of the swollen San Juan River.

On the far bank, both drenched, Richard looked hard at Marietta and asked, "Were you frightened?"

"Why sure," she answered. "I was scared to death."

"Where do you put your fear?"

"I guess I swallowed it. I couldn't say anything."

"No, you didn't say a word. Will you marry me?"

So Marietta recalled many years later. Abandoning any hope of a civilized life back in Kansas, she became Richard's wife, staying at his side through the last fourteen eventful years of his life. Yet she never called him by his first name: he remained "Mr. Wetherill" throughout their marriage.

In her old age, Marietta became the most important source for

McNitt's biography, and she left many hours of tape-recorded reminiscences that have been edited as a book-length memoir (*Marietta Wetherill*). Unfortunately, by then she had become a great fabulist and romanticizer, and her tales are unreliable in the extreme.

In her memoir, Marietta did leave a fresh description of the cowboy who wooed her in 1895:

> He had a moustache. His hair was black and slightly gray in the temples and his eyes were black and penetrating. He looked a hole right into you. He wasn't a big man, about five feet nine or ten [actually five eight], and never fat. He didn't have time to put any fat on.

Although Wetherill became a good photographer in the service of his archaeology, he was camera-shy himself. The best surviving picture of the man, taken at the Saint Louis World's Fair in 1904, demonstrates that piercing gaze, even while the mouth-guarding moustache and the somber mien bespeak a deep taciturnity.

Wetherill was miserably insecure about his shortcomings as a scholar: writing a patron in 1896, he confessed, "Some time in the future I hope to do something in the way of putting my work in book form. But first I must be educated. This is rather a slow process." Yet Richard's letters reveal a frank, clear prose that many an academic might emulate.

Year by year the fortunes of the Alamo Ranch declined, and in 1902 the family bowed to the inevitable and sold out. Meanwhile, Richard and Marietta and their infant son had already moved to Chaco Canyon, where the cowboy built a trading post back of Pueblo Bonito. No archaeologist had ever touched this colossal ruin of some eight hundred rooms. Constructed in the shape of a massive capital *D,* masoned with the finest Anasazi stonework ever seen, Pueblo Bonito, we know today, incorporates astronomical alignments and stands at the hub of a mysterious network of far-reaching Anasazi roads.

Here Wetherill went to work with a will, not only digging in the ruin but filing for homestead rights on the ground that surrounded it. By now, the cowboy had incorporated his patrons' continued sponsorship as the Hyde Exploring Expedition. Under this aegis, Wetherill dug 190 rooms at Pueblo Bonito over four years and shipped ten thousand pieces of pottery, five thousand stone implements, and one thousand bone and wooden objects to New York, where the Hydes donated the material to the American Museum of Natural History.

The Hydes' patronage was a mixed blessing. Anxious to cover the digging at Pueblo Bonito with the cloak of academic legitimacy, Talbot Hyde sought out the august Frederick Ward Putnam at Harvard, one of America's leading archaeologists. Putnam cavalierly dispatched a twenty-three-year-old student named George Hubbard Pepper to superintend the work.

Pepper was a self-important dandy, who would later arrogate nearly all the credit for Wetherill's Chaco discoveries while doing the collections themselves a grave disservice. Richard found him worthless in the field, insensitive to the Navajos he hired as diggers, too effete to labor in the hot sun himself, pompously dictating orders to the man who knew Anasazi ruins better than perhaps anyone else alive.

Inevitably, Wetherill's one-man monopoly of what was coming to be recognized as the most important Anasazi site in the Southwest aroused professional attention. A campaign to halt his unsupervised research was launched by Edgar L. Hewett, president of New Mexico Normal University and an archaeologist who had his own eye on Chaco. Decrying Wetherill's work as mere "vandalizing," Hewett persuaded the General Land Office to launch an investigation of the cowboy's doings. The upshot of the prolonged inquiry was dramatic: in 1902, Richard Wetherill was forbidden to dig at Chaco. For the last eight years of his life, the self-taught archaeologist turned not another shovelful of Anasazi soil.

A WEEK after visiting Grand Gulch, and ninety-six years after Wetherill dug up the Princess, I went to New York City to look for her. The mummy had been donated to the American Museum of Natural History (AMNH), but now I learned that she rested in a sealed case not at that museum but at the National Museum of the American Indian (NMAI).

Over the next few days, with the help of Ann Philips, another member of the Wetherill Project, I discerned the bare outlines of a turn-of-the-century scandal. A few years after clashing with Wetherill at Pueblo Bonito, George Pepper landed a job at the AMNH. Here, too, he quarreled with his colleagues, until the museum fired him in 1908. At some point, Pepper was hired by millionaire George Heye—probably the most rapacious collector of Indian artifacts in American history—to serve as curator of his new NMAI.

On leaving the AMNH, Pepper had somehow managed to take with him roughly half of the Wetherill collections from the AMNH, including all the most spectacular objects—and the Princess. For eight years, this booty lay in storage in Philadelphia. Now, in 1916, the Wetherill materials were carted back to New York to form the backbone of the NMAI's Southwestern holdings. To make the deal marginally legal, Heye and Pepper bought out Talbot Hyde with sweet talk and a lump-sum payment.

As preparation for my visit to the NMAI, I had negotiated for four months with its staff, who seemed leery of my intentions. Now I was told that the Princess, along with other mummies excavated by Wetherill, could not be viewed by anyone, even professional researchers.

"What, then, is the ultimate fate of the Princess?" I asked Duane King, director of the museum. "To be locked up forever?"

He answered in a roundabout fashion, alluding to the board of directors. The Princess's fate, he ventured, had "yet to be determined."

Later, under tightly controlled conditions in the museum's research branch, a grim brick fortress in the East Bronx, I was allowed to view some of the artifacts Wetherill had dug. On the surfaces of several, I was intrigued to detect faint traces of the original AMNH accession numbers, which had been rubbed off and superseded by new accession numbers when the NMAI got hold of the relics. The new catalogue entries were vague in the extreme. For example:

Pottery Disc. Drilled.
Grand Gulch
Utah
Collected by Richard Wetherill
Mrs. Thea Heye Collection.

Needless to say, Pepper's bootlegging had played havoc with the provenience of the objects.

At the AMNH, I got a warmer reception. Senior technician Anibal Rodriguez opened many drawers of Wetherill materials: I saw splendid Chaco black-on-white pots, intricately woven baskets, atlatls and cradle boards and wooden clubs for killing rabbits.

The next day, Jaymie Brauer, scientific assistant for anthropology, showed me Cut-in-Two Man, a mummy every bit as startling as the Princess must have been. (In Grand Gulch a week earlier, Blackburn had guided me to Wetherill's Cave 12/19, the Basketmaker alcove out of which the mummy had been excavated. The gloomy shelter was not easy to climb up to. As an experienced mountaineer, I volunteered to lead, then belayed Blackburn with his own hemp lariat. "It's not me having trouble with this goddamn move," he inveighed, struggling with a steep section, "it's Baby Joey"—Blackburn's name for the generous stomach he carried before him. Once we had entered the alcove, Blackburn led me to a nook high against the back wall. Beneath us a faint depression in the dirt was all that showed of the spot where, as Blackburn had painstakingly deduced, Wetherill had made his bizarre find in January 1894.)

Now Brauer lifted the mummy out of its storage locker and laid it on an antiseptic table. Though I had read Wetherill's own description of Cut-in-Two Man, I gasped when I saw him. The lower part of the body had been cleanly severed from the upper by a sharp cut straight through the hips and abdomen (no entrails remained). Astonishingly, the two halves had been prehistorically sewn back together with an eighth-inch-thick twine made of braided human hair.

Wetherill had thought Cut-in-Two Man must have suffered some mortal wound with a flint knife and that the sewing was a desperate surgical attempt to save him. "It seems most horrible to me," he wrote Talbot Hyde. "The face seems to indicate pain."

"All mummies look like that," said the iconoclastic Brauer. "The skin stretches tight over the bones after death. And I don't think the man could have survived the injury. I'd guess the sewing was done posthumously."

For various reasons, it has been Richard Wetherill's fate to be blamed for the misdeeds of the different museum staffs who later mishandled his collections. After my trip to New York, I visited the Colorado Historical Society in Denver, for which Wetherill had gathered a major Anasazi collection in 1892. The Colorado state archaeologist, Susan Collins, guided me through the collection, now housed inside a glass display room. "I don't think Wetherill was a very good archaeologist," she said, "because we've had a great deal of trouble linking the proveniences of these artifacts with the sites." Later, however, within the CHS archives, I found internal memos from several decades earlier admitting that Wetherill's catalogue had been lost and that some identification tags had been inadvertently separated from the artifacts.

WITH the selling of the Alamo Ranch in 1902, the once tight-knit Quaker clan dispersed. Al Wetherill left the Southwest entirely, drifting to Arkansas and Oklahoma, working as a postmaster and storekeeper. Nostalgia for the landscape of his boyhood, however, brought him back to New Mexico, where he settled in Farmington. Late in life, he wrote a rambling, wistful memoir full of his own cowboy poetry, posthumously published as *The Wetherills of Mesa Verde*.

John Wetherill struck out for northeastern Arizona, where he became a Navajo trader in the midst of wilderness no other Anglos dared inhabit. For the rest of his life—he died in 1944—he explored the Anasazi country and guided visitors into all-but-unknown canyons. (Over the years of my own prowlings through the Four Corners, I actually have found more cave-wall inscriptions from John Wetherill than from Richard.)

In 1909, aided by a Paiute guide, John led a team of archaeologists over incredibly rough country to make what may have been the Anglo discovery of Rainbow Bridge, the largest natural arch in the world. Later John guided such luminaries as Teddy Roosevelt and Zane Grey to the bridge. In 1934, John's wife, Louisa, collaborated with a writer to produce an evocative memoir called *Traders to the Navajos.*

Richard Wetherill, alas, never wrote a memoir of his own. Forbidden to pursue his archaeological passion, he stayed on at his Chaco trading post after 1902. No white settlement in the United States lay farther from the beaten path. For Marietta, these were hard years, but Richard was in his element. He spoke good Ute and Navajo, and now, as he traded regularly with the Chaco Navajos, he got to know these former nomads better than any white man ever had.

Trouble struck one day in June 1910. Wetherill had hired an assistant named Bill Finn, a tight-lipped gunslinger with icy blue eyes and a dubious past. The biographer Frank McNitt was able to discover that Finn's real name was Joe Moody, that he had been a cattle rustler in New Mexico, and that he had escaped a posse that had captured his partner.

According to McNitt, Wetherill sent Finn out that June day to take back a black colt he had given his daughter, which a Navajo had stolen and badly abused. Finn found the supposed offender, brutally pistol-whipped him, and left him unconscious. In revenge, another Navajo, Chiishch'ilin Biye', lay in ambush that evening as Finn and Wetherill drove cows along the Chaco Canyon wash. The Indian fired at both men, struck Wetherill through the chest, then taunted the fallen man before he blew half his face away with another bullet.

There are other sides to this tragic tale. According to Chaco Navajos, Chiishch'ilin Biye' was the brother-in-law of Finn's victim; the colt was a horse belonging to this man, who hoped to sell it to Wetherill; and the fatal encounter was a gun battle provoked by Wetherill, not an ambush. Moreover, tensions had become strained by Wetherill's habit of seizing Navajo livestock when their owners failed to pay off trading-post debts.

The plot grows even thicker in light of the possibility that Marietta may have been having an affair with Finn. After Wetherill's death, she moved with Finn to the remote hamlet of Cuba, New Mexico. Though she explicitly denied the fact in her memoirs, several Wetherill descendants confirm that Marietta married Finn. Some observers have even speculated that it was Finn, not the Navajo, who killed Wetherill. (The blue-eyed gunslinger died of influenza in 1918. Chiishch'ilin Biye', who pleaded self-defense, eventually served three years in the state penitentiary, gaining early parole when it was learned he had tuberculosis.)

IN the history of the Southwest, no scholar ever found or discovered more sites, or more important sites, than Richard Wetherill—not even his indefatigable brother John. One might expect that Richard's achievement, which rivals those of Heinrich Schliemann at Troy and Hiram Bingham at Machu Picchu, should be hailed as a landmark in American archaeology. But the cloud of controversy that shadowed his work from start to finish has never entirely lifted. Schliemann and Bingham had their own critics, to be sure, but the places of both men in the pantheon of prehistoric discovery are secure. Wetherill's is not.

At Mesa Verde, ambivalence toward the cowboy-turned-savant remains the most acute, as I found during several recent visits. There, Wetherill's nemesis became Jesse Nusbaum, himself a pioneer in Anasazi archaeology as well as the superintendent of Mesa Verde National Park from 1921 through 1927. It is a truism in archaeology that each generation deplores the fieldwork of its predecessors. Even so, Nusbaum's animus toward Wetherill, whom he never met, is hard to account for.

To the end of his life, Nusbaum dismissed Wetherill's work at Mesa Verde as "ravaging and looting" and as "commercial exploitation" of the ruins. Performing his own excavation at Step House in the park in 1926, he claimed that the Wetherill crew had "churn[ed] up most of the undisturbed debris, skim[med] the cream of the early material," and "toss[ed] out on the fill" sandstone slabs that were parts of ancient buildings. He insisted that the Wetherills had used dynamite to open another ruin at Mesa Verde (no evidence of such a practice has ever been produced). Nusbaum even denied Wetherill credit for discovering Cliff Palace.

At the park headquarters, district interpreter Linda Martin admitted to me, "There's long been a controversy within our staff over Wetherill. Personally, I think hindsight tends to be better than foresight. What Wetherill did here a hundred years ago is what I would have done."

Research archaeologist Jack Smith was more critical. "I can't condemn the Wetherill brothers, but I can't praise them either," he said. "It's hard not to conclude that their excavating techniques were pretty brutal. I've seen three backcountry sites where somebody has used [Anasazi] roof beams as levers to tear out the back walls of the ruins. At these sites, you find Wetherill's signature scrawled on the cave walls. Yes, that's only circumstantial evidence, but I think it's convincing."

As I took the group tour of Long House, I heard the ranger repeat an old canard against the Wetherills: "Some of the early cowboys got cold and burned the roof timbers." Later, a seasonal ranger who had been on the job only two weeks told me, "I got the feeling when we were in training that the Wetherills were bad guys. No one suggested to us that Richard Wetherill might have been an archaeologist. I thought he was a pothunter who burned the timbers."

In 1993 the park museum devoted a gallery to Gustaf Nordenskiöld's pioneering work in the ruins. The exhibit hailed the young Swede as "far ahead of any contemporaries" in the field. The Wetherills, who taught Nordenskiöld all about the Anasazi, were barely mentioned. (Al Wetherill remembered the Swedish youth as "helpless as a babe when it [came to] camp work.") A pair of photos taken at Step House in 1891 and 1991 inadvertently revealed that the carved signature of Clayton Wetherill had been effaced by rangers. Meanwhile, in the official brochure, the site marker a few feet away, "N. 21" of Nordenskiöld, carved in large characters into a slab beside ancient axe-sharpening grooves, was pointed out proudly.

At Chaco Culture National Historical Park, despite Edgar Hewett's antipathy to the rancher, today Wetherill's memory is honored. The trail guide to Pueblo Bonito grants that the cowboy "contributed immensely to the early archaeology" of the canyon. Chief of interpretation Kim McLean told me, "As far as archaeology is concerned, Wetherill's work was as good as or better than that of many of the professionals of his day."

The work of the dedicated amateurs who make up the Wetherill Project has begun to win the cowboy a new respect. And the strictures of Nusbaum, Hewett, and other professionals are balanced by the praises of some of the Southwest's leading archaeologists. Earl Morris, who made pioneering digs at Canyon de Chelly and Aztec Ruin, wrote of his predecessor, "In [Wetherill's] exploration, or exploiting, if one wants to call it that, of the ruins, [he] did no more, nor differently than I think I would have done under like circumstances." In 1946, John Otis Brew, of Harvard's Peabody Museum, hailed the sum of Wetherill's work as "the most far-reaching single event in Southwestern archaeology." Last year Jeffrey Dean, of the Laboratory of Tree-Ring Research in Tucson, told me, "Wetherill was a far better archaeologist than [Dean named a famous name] who's sort of regarded as a god around here."

In June 1993, I met Al Wetherill's grandson Tom Wetherill, a sixty-three-year-old contractor living in Farmington, New Mexico. Together we traveled to the Alamo Ranch, now owned by a family named Jankowski. Nothing remains of the original farmhouse, but the stately Pennsylvania Dutch barns with their zinc-plated roofs and wooden-pegged joints and ventilation cupolas still grace the acres of nearby pasture. "I get a tingle every time I come here," said Tom as we stood by the corral and looked west, where the sun was setting in a blaze of orange clouds behind the high plateau of Mesa Verde.

Then Tom told me a doleful story. In 1946, when he was seventeen, Tom and his brother took Pop, as they called their grandfather, back to Mesa Verde. What should have been a proud walk through a landscape of memory turned to ashes as the eighty-four-year-old man stood in a crowd of tourists at Cliff Palace and heard the ranger hurl pejoratives at the Wetherill brothers. "Tell him, Pop. Set him straight," Tom pleaded. But Al Wetherill could not bring himself to speak up. "It's no use," he mumbled to the boys.

"It was so sad," Tom told me now, shaking his head. "Heartbreaking, really."

Later on the same trip, in Denver, Al and his grandsons visited the Colorado Historical Society in Denver. "We asked to see the Wetherill collection," Tom recalled, "but they refused us. The stuff was all in boxes in the basement. They said it was just too much of a hassle."

A few days before, at Chaco Canyon, I had visited Richard Wetherill's grave. Though it lies less than a quarter mile from Pueblo Bonito, no signs indicate its whereabouts, at the end of a weedy path. The site is a depressing one, a patch of scrubby ground surrounded by a chicken-wire fence. Wetherill's small gray headstone leans at an angle. His last name is misspelled "Wetherell," as it was constantly during the cowboy's life. Yet I saw that other visitors had come to pay homage to the pioneer: although gathering Anasazi potsherds is illegal in the park, someone had scattered a handful of them across the mound beneath which Wetherill's body lies.

A week later, I hiked with Fred Blackburn to Sandal House. It was here, a dozen miles down the Mancos River from the Alamo Ranch, that the brothers found their first ruin, several years before the discovery of Cliff Palace. Naming the site after the scores of yucca sandals they unearthed, the Wetherills here caught the bug of Anasazi exploration. And here, in the summer of 1895, the Palmer family camped in a box elder grove for two weeks, while Richard, too shy to declare his affection, kept showing up around supper time. "Just riding by," he always said; "thought I would stop and see how you folks are fixed."

Sandal House lies only five miles east of thronged Cliff Palace; yet it is in the Ute Mountain Tribal Park, can be approached only with a Ute guide, and is almost never visited. Blackburn himself had never been there.

Our guide was Tommy May, a young man from Towaoc, Colorado, who had taken a keen interest in Anasazi matters. Sketch pad in hand, Blackburn was in a state that can only be described as rapture. He had found on the cave's walls the signatures or initials of four of the five Wetherill brothers: no other site had yielded so many. And he had found his first "Mamie Palmer"—Marietta's maiden name—carved in neat capitals that summer when she first got to know the gruff cowboy who stayed for supper.

After two hours of sifting our way through the jumbled ruin, Tommy May found a very faint inscription, written in pencil on a stone in a kiva wall. Blackburn's ecstasy turned up another notch as he squatted in the rubble, flashed mirrored light across the evanescent message, and puzzled it out. After half an hour, his notebook bore the following:

R Wetherill
Sept 28. 88
3½ P.M
1-3 gal Jar
return for it
about Oct. 2

The note, which meant little to me, was ringing bells of correlation in Blackburn's brain. Wetherill had found a big Anasazi pot, which he was caching in the ruin and would return to retrieve in four days. Blackburn paused in his labor, wiped his sweaty brow with a bandana, and said to no one in particular, "This is as close as we're ever going to get to talking to him."

2

Moqui Canyon

THE youngest of the five Wetherill brothers and the one least devoted to prowling through the backcountry in search of Anasazi ruins was Winslow, known as Win. Nonetheless Win's son Milton became a professional archaeologist. Late in his career at the Museum of Northern Arizona in Flagstaff, Milton remarked that it was his life's ambition to discover an Anasazi site that had not already been visited by one of his uncles.

For Richard Wetherill in 1893, Grand Gulch was a very long haul from the Alamo Ranch. Just getting from Mancos, Colorado, to Bluff, Utah (the last Anglo outpost), required a minor expedition in its own right. From there, as Richard wrote in his laconic way, "to enter the cañon [Grand Gulch] a party must be equipped with suitable pack animals and expect to spend 3 days on the road from Bluff."

Road, indeed! The astounding Hole-in-the-Rock trail, carved in 1880 by Mormon homesteaders sent out by Brigham Young to establish Bluff and forestall the Gentiles who were trickling into southeast Utah, covered part of that dusty trek. But Cedar Mesa, from the heart of which Grand Gulch snakes southwest sixty miles to the San Juan River, remained virtually terra incognita. The gulch itself, claimed Richard, was "the most tortuous cañon in the whole of the South West."

Yet beyond Cedar Mesa to the west lay even more remote canyons, most of them angular tributaries of the Colorado River. One of them caught Richard's fancy in 1897, no doubt because of its name, probably slapped on the place by prospectors or cowboys. The name of Moqui Canyon alludes to the Hopi people, who live 120 miles to the south, on the points of three mesas slanting sunward above the parched Arizona desert. The Hopi, as we know now, and as many Anglos guessed in the 1890s, are descended from the Anasazi. The term *Moqui* (or *Moki*), of obscure, possibly Spanish origin, rings derisive in the Hopi ear; but Wetherill would have known that a place with such a name must shelter Anasazi ruins.

Obsessed that spring of 1897 with Basketmaker burials, Richard sent his brother Clayton off on a foray to Moqui Canyon, along with two cronies and a month's supply of food. Clate pulled off the demanding trip with the usual Wetherill panache. He returned to report that he had found Basketmaker burial sites with their bottle-shaped cists, but that the graves had already been dug and looted, perhaps by the same nameless pioneers who had put the canyon on the map.

Nothing is known of the fate of the relics wrenched from those sites. Almost nothing is known of Clate's reconnaissance into Moqui Canyon: Frank McNitt devotes a dry three sentences to it in his biography of Richard Wetherill.

In June 1993, I spent five days in Moqui. By now the canyon is no longer remote: it twists west to its junction with the Colorado only a few miles north of State Highway 276, which links Natural Bridges National Monument with Hall's Crossing, a busy marina on Lake Powell. Yet I had reason to believe that Moqui was seldom visited. The canyon bisects open range, grazed by cattle, guarded by no state park or national forest. The guidebooks to hiking in Utah barely mention the canyon.

My companion was Irene Spector, a photographer and old friend with whom I had traveled on magazine assignments to Newfoundland and Alaska. Irene wangled a commission to write and shoot a short travel piece for *The Boston Globe.* For her, however, the jaunt loomed as no mere lark: she had never backpacked in the canyon country before, and for all my reassurances about the beauty of the Southwest and the ease of camping there, she hoisted her pack that hot June morning with a certain trepidation.

The proximate nudge for my outing had come in the form of a monograph published by the University of Utah in 1963. In the late 1950s, when the conservationists led by David Brower had conceded bitter defeat in their crusade to stop the building of Glen Canyon Dam, a gang of Southwestern archaeologists sprang into action. Like the Aswan Dam in Egypt, Lake Powell would drown hundreds of ancient sites that had never been dug or even surveyed. For eight summers, even as the waters crept slowly up the myriad side canyons of the Colorado, these scholars fanned out in a desperate effort to salvage what they could of the incalculable prehistoric heritage that would be lost forever beneath the reservoir, whose raison d'être was to furnish power to the air conditioners and water to the swimming pools of Phoenix.

There was no hope, for the most part, of careful excavation: simply to record, in mute dots on the map, the habitations and burial sites of the Old Ones was the most that could be done. The labor of those scores of field-workers from 1956 to 1963—one of the most heroic campaigns in American archaeology—remains an untold saga.

Moqui Canyon, the salvagers recognized early on, was among the richest tributaries of all in terms of Anasazi presence. Two summers of hasty reconnaissance led to a third, full-bore field season. From early June to late August 1961, a small team led by Floyd Sharrock, Kent Day, and David Dibble spent eleven weeks in Moqui Canyon. By the time they were done, they had identified one hundred Anasazi sites ranging in time from before A.D. 400 right up to the abandonment, just prior to 1300. None of the sites was very large; none was spectacular. But across the span of at least a millennium, Moqui Canyon had been home to hundreds of men, women, and children.

Though by now the lake has swallowed the lower six miles of the canyon, some twenty miles stand high and dry upstream. Accessible though it is from the highway, Moqui Canyon is not easy to get into.

For most of its twenty-six-mile course, the south wall of the canyon blanks into sheer, even overhanging, precipice. The only weakness in its defenses lies in four giant sandslides—dunes that the winds of the centuries have piled five hundred feet high against the south wall, so that they smother the vertical cliff and form sandy ramps.

In 1961, the Utah crew had trucked their gear across the mesa to a depot near the easternmost (and easiest) of the four sandslides. From there, they had horse-packed in broad zigzags down the dune, then pushed downcanyon three miles to set up base camp under a stately cottonwood tree, opposite a small side valley that they called, appropriately, Camp Canyon. For eleven weeks they had poked and scrambled up- and downstream, venturing into every side canyon, to find their hundred sites. To an Anasazi archaeologist, "site" means anything from a handsome cliff dwelling to a single petroglyph to a mere assortment of flint flakes discarded in the dirt (known in the trade as a lithic scatter).

It was June 3 when Irene and I set out. On the mesa top, a southerly breeze tempered the seventy-five-degree heat. I carried about fifty-five pounds in my pack; Irene, forty—more than she had ever lugged before. From the car we navigated north by compass. A desert mesa can bewilder the traveler: each sandstone knob looks like a dozen others; you walk in circles without suspecting it; and the horizon yields no clues—indeed, trudging across a seemingly limitless plain, you find it hard to believe there *is* a canyon ahead.

Suddenly we hit the rim. Five hundred feet below us, a serpent of green—cottonwoods and tamarisk—slithered from right to left, defining the watercourse. Peering through binoculars, I was relieved to see a small flowing stream. The previous winter had witnessed one of the heaviest snowfalls in decades; in April the San Juan had raged above its banks. It was a good thing, for many a desert stream dries up entirely by June, not to resume until the thundershowers of August drench the caked and cracking soil.

For two miles we rim-walked east, admiring the deep overhangs in the red Navajo sandstone that punctuated the opposite wall a mile across the canyon. Especially in the Pueblo III period, from A.D. 1150 to 1300, the Anasazi had thronged to such shelters to build their huddled room blocks. Each one promised us a discovery.

We stumbled across a lithic scatter. Beneath our feet, scores of worked flakes—ruddy flint, gray and creamy chert, black obsidian (sharper by twenty times than the sharpest metal surgical knife)—lay gleaming on the ground. It seemed significant to me that a bedrock pothole filled with many gallons of rainwater lay only a few yards away. We picked up flakes and fondled them with our fingertips. Someone had carried the priceless lumps of flakeable stone many miles from their sources to this open-air workshop. But unless he is a true lithic expert, even a good archaeologist can tell little about the date of a lithic scatter. These jagged pieces of semitranslucent stone could have been knapped loose by Archaic hunters making spear points to thrust into the sides of mammoths long before the birth of Christ, or by Basketmakers honing blades to tip the atlatl darts they would fling at bighorn sheep around A.D. 300, or by Pueblo III craftsmen making cunning tiny arrowheads to shoot at rabbits in the hard times of 1250.

We came to the big sandslide, four miles downstream from the one the Utah team had used to enter the canyon. The dune was deep orange, with spindly weeds growing out of it and clumps of white flowers here and there. At once I started plunge-stepping recklessly down the forty-degree slope, sliding with the sand. As pleasant as the descent proved now, it would be onerous climbing out four days hence. I turned to look for Irene. Unfamiliar with such a freak of nature as the dune, teetering under her unaccustomed load, she was stepping carefully, her knees bent, as if afraid the whole mountain of sand would collapse underfoot. "Ski it!" I yelled.

Once on the canyon floor, we entered a world of searing heat and stifling closeness. The streambed was choked with ten-foot-tall tamarisks. Like several other of the most ubiquitous and nasty plants in the Southwest—notably the Russian thistle, or tumbleweed, and the thorny Russian olive—the tamarisk is not indigenous to North America. All three were brought over from the Old World, most likely as seeds in the hair coats of horses, cows, and sheep stowed in the holds of Spanish galleons.

Bashing through trackless thickets of tamarisk, we made pitifully slow progress. The flash floods of March and April had left monstrous tangles of branches, bark, and leaves that we had to climb over like boulders. Soon I was bathed in sweat and cursing out loud. To make matters worse, we were wearing shorts and T-shirts: the scratchy tamarisk tore at our skin, but in the heat it seemed too great an effort to change to long pants and long-sleeved shirts.

The stream itself, only inches deep, was muddy and warm to the touch. In beat-up running shoes, we splashed our way upriver. When we broke free of the tamarisk, the deerflies descended, worse than I had ever seen. Their sting is sharp and infuriating, almost as painful as the tsetse's. We applied mosquito repellent and the much-touted Avon Skin-So-Soft (supposed to be the only prophylactic against gnats and no-see-ums); neither discouraged the deerflies one whit. For some reason, the buzzing creatures bit only our legs, leaving our arms unscathed. I broke off a tamarisk branch and developed a technique for whacking my own legs as I strode along cursing. One branch lasted about a quarter mile before being reduced to tatters.

June, I had known, was too late for the canyon country. Besides the problems of water, no-see-ums, and deerflies, the sunlight turns flat and harsh overhead, the antithesis of the glancing, evocative rays of March or October. But our schedules had dictated the visit, and in a perverse way, I wanted to see just how bad the going was in summer, the season in which, thanks to the academic year, nearly all the field teams of Anasazi archaeologists had prosecuted their toil over the last fifty years.

At the first clearing of any size, four miles in, opposite the mouth of a wrinkled tributary called Dry Canyon, we set up camp. The vague sense of disappointment I had felt since reaching the canyon floor lingered. Moqui, I had to admit, was not nearly so beautiful a place as Grand Gulch. A claustrophobic pall hung over my spirit. The walls were too close, cut out too much of the sky. In a canyon, I prefer to camp, as the Anasazi did, on a shelf above the valley floor, with a better view and more hours of sunlight. Here that was impossible: instead, we pitched the tent on a sandbar beside the stream.

We tried to hike up Dry Canyon but were stopped almost at once by a deep plunge pool, a sump of water that had collected beneath the spout of a pourover forty feet up, a lip of overhanging sandstone that, when the stream flowed, would issue a freestanding waterfall. The walls on both sides were too sheer to climb. The pool, only thirty feet across, was deeper than head high. Having never learned to swim, I let Irene flail her way across the dark water. On the far side, she could not climb out, so smooth was the arching stone.

Somehow the Utah team had found a way up Dry Canyon, for their sketch map indicated two Anasazi sites just a few hundred yards above the pourover. But it might well have been the work of days, circling far up- or downstream, climbing to the north rim, then back into the side canyon from above. We would leave Dry Canyon for another trip.

Back in camp we hung our shoes and socks on bushes to dry, pumped stream water through a filter to purify it, and started cooking powdered onion soup. The sun, long hidden below the arching cliff in the west, cast a soft yellow light on the highest promontories. Zephyrs of cool air shook the cottonwood leaves.

Gradually the canyon transformed itself. The deerflies vanished—did it take a certain temperature to launch them on their mad quest for human blood? The claustrophobic sense of being caught at the bottom of a pit dissolved into a cozy contentment. We built a small fire of cottonwood twigs; the heat was superfluous, but some genetic link to our hunter-gatherer ancestors made the dancing flames warm our souls. A mourning dove presided over our grove.

At dusk I examined closely, for the first time, the flowers at the tip of a tamarisk bough. For hours I had flailed and crashed through these noxious bushes: now I let myself study them. From two feet away, I saw only a pale, pinkish lavender fuzz. Up close, each inch-and-a-half-long tendril revealed itself to be made of forty or fifty tiny, perfect bell-shaped blossoms. A single branch bore a thousand flowers. It was these exquisite plumes I had beaten to shreds as I switched the deerflies off my legs.

The next day we pushed upstream, covering only three miles each way, but taking nine and a half hours to do so (such is the nature of hunting for ruins). The Utah map showed thirteen numbered dots along the floor of Moqui Canyon within those three miles. Most of the sites we never found: some might have washed away in the floods of the thirty-two years between the Utah survey and our own cursory search. But we found the Bernheimer Alcove and lingered there for almost two hours.

After Clate Wetherill's 1897 jaunt into Moqui, a quarter century passed before the next archaeologically minded visitor arrived. In 1923, on assignment for *National Geographic,* Neil Judd spent several autumn weeks crisscrossing the wilderness cradled between the San Juan and Colorado Rivers. His guide was John Wetherill.

Judd was one of the finest archaeologists of his day; in retrospect, his work in the Southwest stands up better than that of all but a few of his contemporaries. (Ironically, at Chaco Canyon, it was Judd who picked up the research torch two decades after Richard Wetherill had been forbidden to continue digging there in 1902. Through seven field seasons, from 1921 to 1927, with National Geographic Society support, Judd excavated Pueblo Bonito. The reconstructed ruin that visitors tour today owes its look chiefly to Judd, and the foundation of our understanding of Chaco comes from his work.)

In the fall of 1923, Judd, John Wetherill, and two companions set out with twelve mules and a month's food to explore a blank on the map that Judd thought the least-known region in all the Southwest. Of that triangle between the San Juan and the Colorado he later wrote:

> Here, in an area larger than the State of Connecticut, there resides no living soul. The silence hangs heavily. Roving, four-footed beasts of the desert are rarely seen. . . . Even the birds seem to have deserted this strange country.

Judd and Wetherill recruited two Navajos to guide them into the unknown; both deserted before the party left Wetherill's trading post at Kayenta, Arizona. A third recruit stuck out the voyage but spent the weeks in a state of constant apprehension. Even the Indians regarded the blank region as a place of harm.

After crossing Grand Gulch, where Wetherill had dug almost three decades before, the team traversed the Clay Hills and entered Moqui Canyon by one of its giant sandslides. Before they were finished, the explorers covered eighteen miles of the canyon. When the mules balked at boulder-choked narrows, Wetherill and Judd plunged on by foot. They found a number of Anasazi sites, including the jewel of the canyon, later called Bernheimer Alcove. Yet Judd never shook a feeling of malevolence about the place. The many quicksand bogs, which Wetherill deftly scouted, filled Judd with terror. In "Beyond the Clay Hills," he wrote:

> Moki Canyon, place of the dead! Like the Venus flytrap (*Dionaea muscipula*), whose sticky leaves fold down upon the fluttering wings of a careless insect, the quicksands of Moki Canyon patiently wait to embrace the blind or heedless passer-by.

Six years later, John Wetherill came back to the canyon. By now he was sixty-two years old, but still as tough and resourceful as the leanest Navajo. "Guide extraordinary and master of the whole plateau country," Judd called him. "I knew the mettle of the man. Where he started, there he went, if humanly possible to do so."

Wetherill's client in 1929 was one Charles Bernheimer, a New York businessman who had made his fortune from a company called Bear Hosiery. An amateur explorer and archaeologist, he had fallen in love with the Southwest, through which he had pushed bold excursions almost every summer since 1915. Though he wrote articles for *National Geographic* and *Natural History,* as well as a charming book called *Rainbow Bridge,* Bernheimer never pretended to be an expert at either archaeology or wilderness travel. In a "Dramatis Personae" in the front of his book, he identifies himself as "Tenderfoot and cliff dweller from Manhattan."

Wetherill took Bernheimer to the alcove that would be named by the Utah team in honor of the tenderfoot. In 1929, Bernheimer's team was the first to dig in the alcove. Just as Richard Wetherill had at Cave 7 in 1893, when he had made his discovery of the Basketmakers, Bernheimer dug beneath the surface remains from the

Pueblo III period to strike Basketmaker II burials, perhaps a millennium older.

Irene and I had learned from our first day's folly: now we wore long pants, which kept the deerflies at bay. The canyon wound and warped, never opening up; but we bashed through no thickets of willow or tamarisk as bad as the previous day's. The wet spring had given the wildflowers a longer lease: still in full bloom were patches of red penstemon, white morning glories, tiny purple asters.

Two miles upcanyon we came to Bernheimer Alcove. From the valley floor, it was all but invisible, hidden on a southeast-facing ledge 130 feet above the stream. Out of the back wall of the deep overhang jutted the ruins of six masoned Pueblo III rooms. What seized my eye, however, was a swath of pictographs ranging across a hundred feet of smooth sandstone above the site. Yellow handprints, tiny white stick figures, abstract red blobs . . . The crowning glory of the site was a pair of large white-and-red anthropomorphs—as the rock-art experts call them, for fear of leaping to the conclusion that what look like paintings of human beings actually represent humans.

These were classic Basketmaker II figures. It is all too easy to slip into the lazy habit of seeing history as progress: the bow-and-arrow as an improvement on the atlatl, ceramic vessels as more versatile than baskets. The pinnacle of Anasazi rock art, however, comes in the Basketmaker II epoch, as early as several centuries before Christ and no later than A.D. 500. By Pueblo III, a grand artistic tradition had degenerated into—in the mordant phrase of Polly Schaafsma, the leading expert on Southwestern rock art—"mere doodling."

The two anthropomorphs at Bernheimer Alcove faced me straight on, frozen in rigid severity. From broad shoulders, vestigial arms dangled straight down, and the bodies tapered in powerful triangles to a blank below the pelvis. Most beguiling to my eye was the conjunction here of pictographs and petroglyphs—of painted outlines and pecked-out symbols; one rarely finds them mixed in a single design anywhere in the Southwest. In lieu of facial features, one anthropomorph bore two pecked ovoids where nose and forehead would have been; the other had four pecked ovoids descending like breastplates from neck to groin. The head of the latter was rendered as a featureless crescent. Experts have speculated what the Basketmaker II crescent heads signify: clouds, helmets, trance states? What, in general, the haunting, magisterial art of these preceramic seminomads is all about, no one has the foggiest idea.

Puttering around the alcove, we came across a flat boulder resting near the outer lip of the ledge. On top, I was excited to find a neatly chiseled inscription:

J.W.
10-26-23
6-11-29

Beside it:

Bernheimer Expd.
6-11-29

No one dug at Bernheimer Alcove during the thirty-two years between the Manhattan tenderfoot's excavation and the Utah team's in 1961. The latter party was surprised to find that the place was far from cleaned out. In the withering heat of July, they unearthed a rich assemblage of Basketmaker II artifacts: coiled baskets of yucca, belts made of human hair, rabbit-fur blankets, a three-colored sandal made of braided yucca, soft cradle boards (as distinct from the later, hard-backed ones that flattened infants' skulls), ornaments of shell, bone, and stone, and a bizarre leather-wrapped pad used apparently to preserve an infant's umbilical cord. They also uncovered the burials of five children, ranging from newborn babies to a mummified seven-year-old. There was no mistaking the ancient sorrow that had laid these doomed children so carefully in the dirt.

At last we pushed on. In the alcove, the deerflies had left us alone; down in the streambed again, they swarmed about our legs, frenzied at the mammalian feast so near and yet, thanks to our trousers, so inaccessible. Just this side of a tributary called Blocked Draw we found a cribworked livestock trail switchbacking its way up to the north rim. The cottonwood and juniper logs bore the gouges of a metal axe, but the trail was old. It was the first possible route out of Moqui Canyon on either side upstream from the sandslide by which Irene and I had entered. Perhaps the trail had been built by an early Mormon rancher, perhaps by Indians—for in 1923, Judd had found Paiute and Navajo hunting trails in Moqui, the only human vestiges since the Anasazi abandonment.

It was bliss to climb out of the canyon, to see all the way to the horizon again, to bask in a heat-cutting breeze. I lay down on a smooth slab and fell asleep. Despite the claustrophobic tightness of the canyon, once I had entered Moqui I had felt utterly at peace. For Irene, however, the canyon was so unlike any landscape she had ever hiked in that a tense watchfulness had seized her spirit. She had slept poorly on the sandbar. As she later wrote in her diary, "Not that I didn't enjoy being down there . . . but [I was scared] that I couldn't physically do it, that I couldn't keep up with David, that maybe I'd be in a situation where I'd have to get out alone."

That night the moon was full. Though it rose at sunset, our camp lay so far underneath the arching rim that not until eleven-thirty did the moon climb over the cliff and flood our clearing with silver light. Watching the moon rise in binoculars, I saw, in the instant before its disk broke the horizon, distant cliff-top junipers ablaze with light as if on fire. I slept till morning, but Irene, restive once more, got up at 4 A.M. to see moonbeams from the west casting leaf shadows on the tent, and Venus high in the east.

On our third day we headed downstream, into the heart of the Utah discoveries. I was obsessed with the need to see as much of the canyon as daylight allowed, and my impatience daunted Irene. As she wrote in her diary,

> David was always about 20–30 yards ahead of me, never inclined to wait or let me catch up, always on his own agenda. I got used to this attitude—he wasn't there to baby-sit me or coddle me and he just expected me to pull my own weight. Sometimes it annoyed me . . . yet on the other hand he was treating me like just another friend or chum who was along with him, an equal, not a sissy girl.

In ten hours of hard pushing, I managed to visit five intriguing sites and to see three others that looked fiendishly difficult to get to. We covered twelve miles and climbed more than a thousand feet up and down from the various sites.

The most interesting of the five, called Rehab Center, lay inside a huge cave 250 feet above the stream. The Utah team, observing a long practice of giving Anasazi sites whimsical names, here commemorated the relief from the July heat that the cave's shadowy, sixty-foot-deep interior afforded. At the back of the alcove, a pool of clear water caught the seepage from a flowing spring, the finest I had ever seen in an Anasazi cave. Lush green canes and grasses fringed the pool's banks. For weeks, the Utah team had drunk the spring untreated. I might have, too, but for noticing that, remote though it seemed, the cave had been camped in in recent years by ranchers: cow pies and horse dung lay in desiccated lumps among the ruins.

It will be decades yet before the old hard-bitten Western cowboys learn to treat Anasazi sites with the care they deserve. Waiting out August thunderstorms or November blizzards, the ranchers had built campfires of Gambel oak branches inside the shelter, using shaped Anasazi building stones for their fire ring. The 1961 report had a good photo of Structure 1—a long, four-foot-high wall full of "loophole" apertures, punctuated in the middle by a classic Pueblo III *T*-shaped doorway. To my shock, I realized that half the wall was gone—leveled to the ground since 1961. Had horses or cows milling in the shade simply knocked it to pieces? Or worse—had some idiot vandalized it for fun?

Here, too, the Utah team had found Basketmaker II burials beneath Pueblo III remains: infants, again, one in a basketry tray, the other wrapped in a woven shroud. Many of the details the team had noted were impossible for me to find. I felt a glum discouragement: if thirty years of relatively light visitation could wreak such havoc, what hope did such fragile sites have in the future?

Yet of all the sites we would visit in Moqui Canyon, Rehab Center was Irene's favorite. Scanning the back wall to discern the traces of faint pictographs, she discovered an even fainter charcoal inscription. I asked her to copy it in my notebook. A florid Victorian hand had scrawled "Geo. W. Dunn," next to the date "Sept. 20th, 1894."

Earlier even than Clayton Wetherill! Later I consulted that connoisseur of Southwestern inscriptions, Fred Blackburn. He had never heard of Dunn but guessed the man must have been one of the prospectors working the Colorado River who had ventured far up a side canyon. Perhaps Dunn had dug some of the graves here in Rehab Center that Clate Wetherill had found looted in 1897.

We pushed on downstream, bushwhacking for a mile through willow thickets made even nastier by beavers that had felled young cottonwoods to build their dams. The canyon grew deeper and more convoluted. We were so dehydrated that we each drank three quarts of water. By early afternoon, we neared the lake. I climbed to another high site, while Irene pushed on to the lake, hoping for a swim. Envisioning a deep, sparkling bay, she was disappointed to find only a knee-deep trough of weed-choked water. She plunged in and hiked on, but the water stayed knee deep. Taking off her clothes to bathe, she was swarmed by deerflies. She gave up and turned around.

On the way back to camp, despite my weariness, I was determined to find a site the Utah team had called Red Ant Kiva. I had seen no trace of it on the way downcanyon. Irene begged off, stumbling back to camp on her own.

It took an hour of vigorous searching to find Red Ant Kiva, but it was worth the effort, for I had never seen anything like it. The discovery and excavation of the site in 1961 had represented perhaps the Utah team's finest work. At this point in Moqui Canyon, the streambed lies at the bottom of a deep arroyo—a veritable gorge of mud so hard it forms nearly vertical walls 125 feet high. In the early thirteenth century, the canyon had had no arroyo: a plain of fertile alluvium had stretched from one wall to the other, across which the stream meandered gently.

An arroyo is created when the normally slow process of erosion suddenly goes wild. In relatively few years, the stream carves a deep canyon in the alluvial terrace, and the water table of the surrounding soil plunges as well. Once fertile fields turn barren. An agricultural haven transforms into a place where no corn or squash can grow. Arroyo cutting remains a mysterious geological phenomenon: no one can be sure even today what triggers it. Yet we know that a fierce cycle of arroyo cutting set in all over the northern Southwest about the middle of the thirteenth century and that it may have contributed to the abandonment.

We know also that after 1880 a new cycle of arroyo cutting, apparently similar to the one in the thirteenth century, seized the Southwest. The recent cycle, which continues today, may have been launched by herds of cattle and sheep overgrazing the land: fields chewed to stubble are far more vulnerable to flash floods than ones lush with knee-high grasses.

In 1961, a Utah archaeologist hiking the canyon noticed a barely perceptible fragment of an Anasazi wall protruding from the bank of the arroyo, seventy-five feet up. It was a lucky find, for here was almost the last place one would look for ruins. Climbing the bank by chopping steps in the steep mud and belaying with ropes, the team reached and eventually excavated the finest kiva they found in Moqui Canyon.

Among all Anasazi structures, kivas are the most provocative for archaeologists. They do not appear until about A.D. 750, at the beginning of the Pueblo I period. Unlike the square aboveground room blocks that make up the habitation units of a Pueblo Anasazi village, kivas are usually subterranean, round, and entered only through a hole in the roof.

The first Anglo explorers in the Southwest called these kivas *estufas,* Spanish for "steam rooms," on the assumption that they were like the sweat-bath lodges observed among living (mostly Plains) Indians. By the 1890s, however, the first serious students of Southwestern prehistory called them kivas, because they had concluded that Anasazi culture led in an unbroken line to the Pueblo Indians of today.

At Hopi, windowless chambers entered by ladders through a hole in the roof were called kivas. Hopi men gathered there (women were not allowed) both to indulge in social discourse and to perform religious ceremonies. Though it might have given observers pause that Hopi kivas were built above ground and were square, after 1890 the term "kiva" was nevertheless applied to the round underground chambers found at so many Anasazi sites.

It was Edgar Hewett (Richard Wetherill's antagonist at Chaco Canyon, who launched the investigation that shut down the cowboy's digging) who pounded home, in the 1930s, the idea that Anasazi kivas served ceremonial and religious functions.

For almost seven decades, the idea went unchallenged. If you tour a national park such as Mesa Verde today, the rangers will recite Hewett's formula and even point out the *sipapu,* a cup-shaped hole in the floor that, by analogy with Hopi kivas, supposedly represents the mythical hole through which the People emerged into this, the Fourth World, from their underground Third World.

In 1988, Stephen Lekson, until recently director of the Crow Canyon Archaeological Center, published a small paper in a journal called, ironically, *Kiva.* Lekson questioned the whole idea that Anasazi kivas were religious or ceremonial places. How do we know, he asked, that they were not used for domestic purposes? The paper caused a furor. Many dismissed Lekson's argument out of hand as the mischief of a born iconoclast. Within the next seven years, however, Lekson won over a number of influential colleagues.

Lekson's attack raised a number of other basic questions. On the unthinking assumption that kivas were ceremonial, archaeologists had built complicated edifices, arguing, for instance, from the ratios of living rooms to kivas that certain sites were ceremonial centers serving far-ranging populations. And Lekson's stab cast a skeptical light on the validity of Pueblo oral tradition. Yes, he said implicitly, the Hopis are descended from the Anasazi; but that does not mean that we can count on living informants to interpret what the ancients were doing.

All of which only makes the study of kivas all the more interesting. At Red Ant, the Utah team found a kind of time capsule, for they deduced that shortly after the abandonment, dirt had filled and buried the kiva, keeping it intact until the 1961 excavation uncovered it. Digging slowly on their precarious perch, the team found, exquisitely preserved, many of the classic kiva features: a stone bench running along the inner walls, two pilasters on which a cribbed-log roof would have rested, a ventilator shaft through which smoke escaped, a deflector slab to keep the fire from blowing across the floor.

In the early 1960s, archaeologists evaluated Glen Canyon sites as a dispersal from two great heartlands: Mesa Verde to the east and the Kayenta region to the south, in Arizona. By counting potsherds and analyzing masonry styles, the experts gauged the relative weight of Mesa Verde versus Kayenta influence. On the whole, they concluded, the Glen Canyon tributaries owed more to Kayenta culture than to Mesa Verde. Moqui Canyon was the exception: here the Mesa Verde influence predominated.

Implicit in this analysis was the idea that the Glen Canyon Anasazi were a frontier folk, marginal—hillbillies, in a sense. Yet Moqui Canyon, and Red Ant Kiva in particular, threw a monkey wrench into this intellectual machine. Of all the structures excavated throughout the Glen Canyon area by the scores of workers from 1956 to 1963, Red Ant Kiva had the purest stamp of the Mesa Verde style. What was more, it was a masterpiece: those who had built it were not hillbillies. The dwellers in Moqui Canyon may have lived on the fringe of the Anasazi world, but they spoke the language of its culture as fluently as the priests of Cliff Palace or Keet Seel.

At last I spotted Red Ant Kiva, not from below but from a narrow ledge fifty feet above. I carried with me a Xerox copy of the Utah team's photograph of the excavated kiva. Now, thirty-two years later, I stared in shock at what was left. The arroyo had cut back so much farther that only the innermost corner of the kiva remained. Building blocks had peeled loose from the structure and hung, teetering, above the seventy-five-foot drop: a touch would set them loose. With delicate steps, I could have scrambled down the fifty feet to examine the kiva up close; but in doing so I might have kicked loose stones that would have wiped out whole sections of the remaining walls. I kept my distance and stared. Red Ant Kiva, possibly nine centuries old, had only a few years of existence left. Perhaps I was the last visitor who would ever see it.

Irene and I spent our final full day in Moqui probing to the head of Camp Canyon, at the mouth of which the Utah team had pitched its base camp. In seven hours we found only a few vestigial sites, but I was delighted by the strangeness of the place. Camp

Canyon is a short, branching defile choked by sand. Orange dunes towered everywhere, pushing us into weird and arduous scrambles. At one point we walked in a streambed only three feet wide, in a canyon of sand, between steep slides towering three hundred feet on either side.

And here we found the quicksand that had so addled Neil Judd and that had caused the Utah team a great deal of trouble. A sheer rock wall on the left and a steep arroyo bank on the right forced us to wade straight through the gooey muck if we wanted to proceed. Because of their weight and their relatively slender legs, cows and horses can indeed get inextricably mired in quicksand. The stuff will not, however, swallow humans in the fashion so memorably depicted in old Western movies.

As I waded in, Irene balked. She had never before dealt with quicksand, and those movies were vivid in her mind. I coaxed her on. She waded ankle-, then knee-deep, then panicked, as most do on their first try: she lurched and reeled and nearly fell in her desperation to extricate her legs from the sucking slime. I confess that I laughed and took pictures before coaching her to move slowly, to pull each leg loose with a patient effort before surrendering it again to the ooze.

For me the quicksand was sloppy play; for Irene, even after she realized she would survive the ordeal, the oily muck retained a tinge—as it evidently had for Judd—of the nightmarish.

On the morning of June 7, we packed up and headed out. The five-hundred-foot sandslide, as I had expected, was an awful climb. It was like hiking uphill in new powder snow with a heavy pack, slipping a foot back for every two feet gained. As Irene wrote later:

> I tried to walk in David's trail but sometimes I lost it and had to forge my own way. . . . Panic set in several times, either that I'd lose my balance and fall and go tumbling down, or that it would just get too hard and I'd want to give up. But of course I had no choice.

At last we gained the rim. Striding along the edge, we looked down at the sites we had explored two days before. In five days in

Moqui Canyon, we had seen no other people, not even, except on Irene's approach to the lake, a human footprint. Irene was happy to be out: already she looked forward to the motel in Blanding, a hot shower, dinner in a restaurant. I felt a familiar depression, the sorrow at leaving a special place that I had just begun to know.

At the end of their 1961 work, the Utah team had come to some interesting conclusions about the place of Moqui Canyon in the scheme of Glen Canyon. Of all the left-bank tributaries north of the San Juan, Moqui offered the Anasazi the best hunting and gathering and the best planting. Recognizing its well-watered fertility, the ancients had moved in at least as early as Basketmaker II times, before A.D. 500. Inexplicably, however, they had vanished from the canyon for six centuries, from 500 to 1100. What had seemed wrong about the place during that long skein?

At the end of Pueblo II, after A.D. 1150, the Anasazi had come back. Red Ant Kiva was one of the first structures they had built upon their return. The population had swelled through Pueblo III, reaching a peak shortly before 1300. Then once more the canyon, along with the rest of the northwestern half of the Anasazi domain, had been abandoned for good. Never again, but for the odd hunter on some daring quest far from home, would the Anasazi enter Moqui Canyon.

The 1961 team's solid work, in conjunction with their colleagues' surveys all up and down the Colorado River, had laid the groundwork for a grand regional synthesis. But thanks to Lake Powell, that synthesis would never be written. For every question the teams had answered between 1956 and 1963, they had raised a half-dozen new ones. For the most part, they had had too little time to dig and no time to put together a comprehensive research plan. As Alexander Lindsay, one of the leading scholars in the Glen Canyon mission, had told me, "Eighty percent of what we saw is under water."

Even if ecoterrorists inspired by novelist Edward Abbey's brash polemics were someday to blow up Glen Canyon Dam, the sites will never be recovered. The water has done its work, washing the masoned walls to rubble, scouring the alcoves of all they held.

As we unlocked the car and dumped our packs in the trunk,

however, I was not done with Moqui Canyon. I had one more item on what Irene called my agenda. The numbered Utah map made it clear that twenty-three of the sites the 1961 team had investigated now lay beneath the surface of Lake Powell. I wanted to drive to Hall's Crossing, rent a motorboat, and cruise up the six drowned miles of Moqui, just to glimpse the shadow of what had been lost.

In all my years of traveling in the Southwest, I had never before visited Lake Powell. The place for me, as for other devotees of the Anasazi, has the aura of a blight upon the earth. It seemed almost a matter of honor not to patronize the Glen Canyon National Recreation Area. When my twenty-eight-year-old nephew, who had grown up in Albuquerque, once told me that his idea of a perfect vacation was to get a bunch of buddies together, rent a houseboat, and head out on Lake Powell for a week of sunbathing and beer drinking, I felt like delivering him a stern lecture.

After five days of peace and silence, Hall's Crossing jangled my nerves badly. The marina was swarming with college kids in swimsuits, with families gobbling Coke and hot dogs, with crew-cut employees cracking jokes as they pumped gas into boats. The whine of engines filled the air. I muttered dark imprecations, and for once Irene abandoned her gentle manner and scolded me. Later she wrote: "David's mood grew surly and hostile, which really annoyed me—he can be such a snob and difficult at times."

We rented a basic skiff and motored north to the mouth of Moqui. Speedboats plowed grooves in the water and bounced us in their wakes; water-skiers wove reckless loops nearby; fishermen sat on their houseboats and drank Budweiser as they dangled their lines.

As we started up Moqui, Irene drove the skiff while I correlated the Utah map with the USGS quadrangle. We passed houseboats called *Anasazi Nights* and *Mansion Moki*. At my urging, Irene took us close to the north wall. The upper ten feet of what I knew must have been a huge alcove protruded above the water, bleached pale by the reservoir's bathtub ring. I read the dry but eloquent report of the Anasazi prodigy that had once stood a hundred feet below us. At that moment a motorboat hot-rodded by, and a water-skier cut a turn ten feet from our skiff. I felt like screaming.

At the head of navigation, we tied off our boat. Two parties of picnickers had claimed the shore. One group sat in lawn chairs beside their canvas tent, cocktails perched on a folding table. A blonde in a bikini lay asleep atop an air mattress, floating among the tips of drowned tamarisks. From above I heard a shout and saw two guys scrambling awkwardly toward a cave, kicking rocks loose as they went.

In the weeds I stepped across a scotch bottle and a potato chip bag. Irene lingered, hoping still for a swim, while I hiked up to the two nearest Anasazi sites. One, called Copter Ledge by the 1961 team, had once been so remote that its first visit by Anglos had been accomplished by helicopter in 1955. There I saw, beside a set of Anasazi pictographs, a chalked cartoon of a stick-figure Tonto with feathered headdress shooting a bow and arrow. At the other site, someone had scratched on the wall above a pair of fragile Anasazi granaries, in big block letters, C. JACK WAS HERE WITH THE CREW.

On our way out, we poked up North Gulch, also known as Secret Gulch for its erstwhile inaccessibility. The Utah team had found seven sites here; all were now under water. My mood was black. As Irene held the tiller, I pointed to one corner of the sandstone after another, intoning pedantically, "That was Site 605. Over there was Site 734."

I was beginning to think the half-day boat ride was a mistake. I had expected to be appalled, but the desecration I had seen and, perhaps even worse, the blithe, uncaring ignorance of the tourists all about me threatened to ruin the memory of our five good days in Moqui. Yes, I was a snob. As the frat boys zipped by, whooping with macho joy, I wanted to shout at them, "You're water-skiing in a cathedral! Stop it!"

Then, in a relatively quiet bay far up North Gulch, I saw something that momentarily raised my spirits. High above the shore, facing south, on a freestanding pillar of sandstone turned black with the patina of desert varnish, I saw the patterns of tall petroglyphs. It was a perfect spot for the Anasazi to carve their enigmatic runes.

I raised my binoculars and realized my error. The petroglyph was a peace symbol, spray-painted on the rock in big white strokes, a hippie's proclamation from the early 1970s. The symbol was riddled with bullet holes. Over the years, good old boys had used it for target practice.

"Let's head for Blanding," I told Irene. She nodded and turned the skiff south.

3

Fault Lines

IT is one thing to scout out Anasazi ruins, to finger potsherds, to stare at pictographs. It is another to imagine the lives—the hopes and fears, the joys and sorrows, the methods of grasping the universe—of those ancients whose skeletons, recumbent on their sides, knees flexed against chests, lie mute beneath the dirt. Archaeology at its most magisterial can only begin to elucidate the passions that grip the heart of a civilization.

From my first foray into the Anasazi backcountry, in 1973, onward, I asked myself what it was about this ancient civilization that so fascinated me. Glimpsing them through their ruins and artifacts, I tried to divine their way of life. To do so requires fending off all kinds of romantic impulses. The abandonment, in particular, has lent itself to much facile hokum about "vanished" and "mysterious" tribes. With respect to the Anasazi, a treacly vein of Southwestern gothic runs through such potboilers as Louis L'Amour's *The Haunted Mesa* and even Willa Cather's otherwise remarkable *The Professor's House.*

Archaeologists are so tired of this sentimental claptrap that some of them go out of their way to deny that there is anything mysterious about the Anasazi. (Yet, regardless of the scholars, the abandonment remains a true mystery.) And living Puebloans are fed up with the notion that their ancestors vanished. In 1991, Leigh Jenkins, a

Hopi who serves as his people's cultural preservation officer, told me about a recent Four Corners conference focusing on the abandonment. "They invited me at the last minute," he said in his prickly way. "All these professional archaeologists were debating the question 'What happened to the Anasazi? Where did they go?' I said, 'They didn't go anywhere. They're still around. I can tell you exactly where.'"

For four years, from 1989 through 1992, I had crisscrossed another part of the Southwest—a huge region lying south of the Anasazi domain, spilling across the Mexican border into Chihuahua and Sonora—in quest of the sites that had mattered most to the Chiricahua Apache. The travel was research for a book about Cochise, Geronimo, and the tribe that had fought the last all-out Indian war in the United States.

It was obvious why the Chiricahua way of life appealed to me. In their fierce resistance to the armies of two nations, from 1861 to 1886, the Apache honed to a fine edge their skills of ambush, raiding, lightning attack, and flight. The ultimate nomads, they thought nothing of riding a hundred miles a day or walking and running seventy-five. They went days without food and found water where Anglos died of thirst.

In my twenties and thirties, nothing had been more important to me than the ascent of unclimbed peaks and routes in the Alaskan wilderness. Mountaineers think of themselves as explorers: explorers fancy themselves latter-day nomads.

Yet the Anasazi who had built the dwellings I pushed into the backcountry to find had been farmers. Every time I discovered a metate (one of those stone grinding basins, scalloped with decades of toil) or a mano (the smoothed stone that did the grinding), I was obliged to picture women on their knees scraping corn kernels to powdered meal day after drudging day. Every ceramic bowl in a museum—indeed, every broken potsherd in the dirt—betokened a kindred slavery to domestic routine: fetching and boiling water, sorting and storing beans and piñon nuts.

How could the daily rounds of the farmers of Cliff Palace ever inspire me to envious identification, as the headlong flight of Geronimo's warriors into their stronghold in the Sierra Madre had? Part of the answer was that the Anasazi penchant for cliff dwellings—for cliffs themselves—lay close to my affinity for rock climbing. Over the years, I had come across many an Anasazi hand-and-toe trail, a line of shallow steps gouged in a precipice by some ancient artisan wielding only a quartzite pounding stone, that I found too daunting to follow, even with rock-climbing shoes on my feet. (The archaeologists attribute the present difficulty of these trails to erosion over the centuries, but I wonder. Sometimes you can feel the grooves of individual fingerholds in the sandstone, and if the dwellings themselves have stayed pristine for more than seven hundred years, why not the hand-and-toe ladders?)

Without question, the Anasazi were the finest prehistoric climbers ever to inhabit the United States. The Navajo, arriving on the Colorado Plateau more than a century after the abandonment, were so dazzled by the vertical skills of their predecessors that they attributed their technique to magic. The cliff dwellings, said Navajo sages, had been built by Anasazi who could fly, or who had special sticky feet, or who used shiny stones to slide up and down rock walls; the lizards of today, scuttling up and down the cliffs, are the descendants of the Anasazi, punished thus for having displeased the Holy Beings. (These glimmerings are recorded in Robert S. McPherson's *Sacred Land, Sacred View,* the best account yet written of the Navajo perception of the Anasazi.)

Yet I also had to recognize that cliff dwellings were not the Anasazi norm: far fewer than 10 percent of all their habitations, from the Archaic period through Pueblo III, were built on ledges above the void. Much more typical over the centuries was a room block standing by itself in the middle of a flat mesa top, or a collection of pithouses dug in a grassy bench beside some stream. Only in the last half of the thirteenth century did cliff dwellings predominate, and then, as experts are beginning to prove, almost surely as a response to stress and threat. As beautiful as the tourist of today finds a cliff dwelling such as Betatakin (one of the three jewels of Navajo National Monument, in northeastern Arizona), the men and women who lived there must have sensed its cramped confinement as a compromise, an uneasy solution to a world torn by fear and hunger.

In my predilection for the vertical, I was hardly alone. It is no accident that most of the Anasazi sites hallowed as national parks and monuments are cliff dwellings: Cliff Palace, Spruce Tree House, and other ruins at Mesa Verde; Betatakin and Keet Seel at Navajo National Monument; the cliff-edge towers of Hovenweep; Antelope, White, and Mummy Houses at Canyon de Chelly; the towering, cave-hung ruin called Montezuma Castle; the gloomy, cozy warrens carved into tuff cliffs at Bandelier. (The notable exception is Chaco Culture National Historical Park, in western New Mexico, whose fourteen "Great Houses" stand aloof on the floor of a shallow canyon or atop the broad surrounding mesas.) So fixed, in fact, is the association of the Old Ones with cliffs, that even today, if you mention the term "Anasazi" to a traveler unfamiliar with the Southwest, you are likely to draw a blank, whereas the passé Victorian "Cliff Dwellers" still does the trick.

So the Anasazi had been climbers as well as farmers. Surely there was more to my fondness for the ancients than that. Throughout the course of their existence, most archaeologists conclude, the Anasazi were a supremely egalitarian people. They may have had chiefs, but nothing like royalty or a stratified class system. The evidence is simple and persuasive: nearly every ruin, no matter how large, is made up of rooms more or less equal in size; and there is a dearth of status burials, rich in the grave goods that among other cultures demarcate kings or high priests. (The great exception to this general rule, which erupts at Chaco between A.D. 900 and 1125, is a phenomenon scholars are only beginning to fathom. Of this, more below.)

Who among us does not approve, in principle, of a democratic rather than a hierarchical society, either in prehistory or on earth today? On a magazine assignment, I once spent two months in Egypt pondering the pyramids and tombs of the Old Kingdom (2700–2150 B.C.), a culture whose titanic energy was marshaled to a single end: the worship of its pharaohs, living and dead. No more top-heavy, socially stratified, undemocratic regime ever claimed the earth. After two months of gaping at pyramids, of admiring magnificent bas-reliefs in tombs, of regarding the chants and boasts carved in limestone hieroglyphs, I still felt a certain chill in my heart as I contemplated the Old Kingdom. Yet in southeastern Utah, a single potsherd painted with black-and-white hatches warmed my fingers as I held it.

The third source of my affinity was Anasazi art—particularly the vast corpus of pictograph and petroglyph panels scattered all over the Southwest, of which no traveler in his lifetime can hope to behold more than a fraction. There are many different styles over the centuries, categorized by experts such as Polly Schaafsma and Sally Cole under such rubrics as San Juan Anthropomorphic and Glen Canyon Linear. To my eye, what they all have in common is a rigid, formal, stylized severity. The anthropomorphs stand facing you, features and bodies reduced to simple triangles and lines, limbs vestigial or missing. Even bighorn sheep seen in profile have a frozen simplicity. In Anasazi rock art, there is virtually no effort to render motion or life: the naturalistic virtuosity that graces the paintings of animals in such Paleolithic caves as Lascaux or Altamira is wholly absent in the Southwest.

Yet formal severity is my cup of tea. Anasazi rock art dances in my eye with intimations of an invisible power, much as the counterpoint of Bach rings in my ear. Form blurring into abstraction, a stern sense of fate framed by symmetry—here, for me, lies a lucidity beyond words. I once spent a month traveling across Catalonia seeking out remote Romanesque churches (many in ruins) and the peeling frescoes anonymous artists had painted on their walls in the eleventh and twelfth centuries. I was alone, with only a few words of Spanish and none of Catalan; but I was tranced with the passion of discovery. Those staring black-eyed saints; that Christ in majesty blessing the world with impossibly crooked fingers; those garments zigzagged into ornamental borders; those chimeric, ravaging monsters carved on the capitals of marble columns . . . Romanesque art, once sneered at as crude and primitive, virtually ignored by the art-loving public, moved me more than all the frescoes and panels of Giotto and Cimabue, where tentative Romanesque gropings had supposedly come to glorious Gothic fruition.

Something akin to that bold, blank, impersonal dignity leaps out at me from the sandstone panels of the prehistoric Southwest. The very rigidity of the beasts, men, and spirits figured by the Anasazi epitomizes some formal truth. Though life itself is transitory, the hunt has its eternal plot.

So the Anasazi were climbers, democrats, artists; still, the center of their lives after about A.D. 500 had been the tedious tilling and harvest of fields of corn, squash, and beans. Could I admire and identify with that?

The first effort by an Anglo writer fully to imagine the Anasazi life remains one of the most curious books ever written about the Southwest. Adolf Bandelier was a Swiss-American from Illinois who became a self-taught archaeologist and ethnographer in the 1870s. Eventually he spent thirty years prowling across the Southwest, covering thousands of miles on foot in his search for ruins and insinuating himself deeply into several New Mexican Pueblo villages. Bandelier National Monument, west of Santa Fe, commemorates the man who laid the groundwork for all subsequent research on the prehistory of the northern Rio Grande.

With his restless, obsessive curiosity, Bandelier had always seemed to me the type of the nomad-vagabond. His partner and protégé, Charles F. Lummis, himself as restless and obsessive as they come, apotheosized Bandelier thus: "Like John Muir, it was not physical strength that carried him—either would take a crust of bread, and a pinch of tea, and go like a cat over cliff and crag, a day's trip no mere athlete could follow."

In 1890, Bandelier published *The Delight Makers,* a 490-page novel that realizes the author's fantasy of Anasazi life in Frijoles Canyon, at the heart of today's national monument. Bandelier wrote the book out of a fear that scientific treatises would never capture the lay reader's attention. "By clothing sober facts in the garb of romance," he claimed in his preface, "I have hoped to make the 'Truth about the Pueblo Indians' more accessible and perhaps more acceptable to the public in general."

A strange book, dated today not only in style but by the discoveries of a century of further research on the Anasazi. I know of more than one archaeologist who sheepishly admits to never having been able to plow his way through the book.

The Delight Makers is bound by Victorian conventions not only of fiction but of ethnography. "Whatever there is in nature which the Indian cannot grasp at once, he attributes to mysterious supernatural agencies," writes Bandelier with the sweeping condescension of his day. Despite that smugness, the author is at pains to dignify the Anasazi in an age when natives were assumed to rank lower on the evolutionary scale:

> If the Indian is not an ideal being, he is still less a stolid mentally squalid brute. . . . His senses are very acute for natural phenomena; his memory is excellent, as often as he sees fit to make use of it. There is no difference between him and the Caucasian in original faculties, and the reticence peculiar to him under certain circumstances is not due to lack of mental aptitude.

Bandelier's dialogue, as wooden as Fenimore Cooper's or Zane Grey's when rendering Indian conversation, mixes chivalric cadences with homegrown epithets in an unintentionally humorous manner: "'Lay down your club, you dirty ear of corn,' replied the maiden, 'or you will fare badly.'"

Two things, in the long run, redeem *The Delight Makers,* saving it from its own tedious verisimilitude. They are the dramatic plot, which hinges on war between Pueblo tribes spurred by a woman's being accused of witchcraft; and Bandelier's deep understanding of the people of Cochiti Pueblo, among whom he had lived. The scholar had deduced—correctly—that the Cochiti were the descendants of the ancients who had lived in Frijoles Canyon. In effect, then, he simply translated Cochiti life as he knew it in the 1880s backward into his prehistoric drama. The alien words and names sprinkled through the book are taken directly from the Keresan tongue spoken at Cochiti.

Granting Bandelier the assumptions and conventions of his day, I still cannot take *The Delight Makers* seriously. I do not want a writer to invent prehistoric dialogue for me. Even at its best—Jean Auel dramatizing Cro-Magnon France, Jane Smiley in medieval Greenland—what might be called the ethnographic historical novel leaves me cold. I would rather do my own imagining. I would rather read a statistical analysis of the ratios of Kayenta- to Mesa Verde–style potsherds in Moqui Canyon than have a writer guess for me what an Anasazi hunter dreamed of.

In Bandelier's day, forty years before the discovery of tree-ring dating, no expert had any idea how old Anasazi ruins might be. That they must date from before Coronado was evident, for the conquistador had encountered Puebloans on the first European *entrada* into the Southwest. In the absence of any coherent sequence of phases of Anasazi culture—by 1890, Richard Wetherill was still three years from making his profound distinction between the Basketmakers and the Pueblo people who succeeded them—most researchers, Bandelier included, uncritically took the Pueblo ways of his day as virtually identical to those of the ancients. What he saw going on at Cochiti he assumed had gone on in Frijoles Canyon before the Spanish had arrived.

The 1880s, 1890s, and 1900s were great decades for ethnography in the Southwest. Such savants as Jesse Walter Fewkes and Matilda Coxe Stevenson wrung from their Pueblo informants a store of secret and sacred knowledge that later anthropologists would envy and that the Puebloans themselves would come to rue having shared. For the most part, these scholars believed in the literal truth of myths and oral traditions, and they freely asked Puebloans to interpret Anasazi sites and rock art. At Zuni, Frank Cushing went native so far as to dress in Pueblo garb, to take part in raids against the Apaches, and possibly to kill and scalp an Apache so that he could participate in the Zuni Scalp Dance.

The credulous divulgence of so much secret lore on the part of the Puebloans is understandable. For more than two centuries, they had suffered under Spanish tyrants who violently eradicated every trace they could find of Pueblo religion, condemning it as blasphemy and idolatry. Now came these gentle Americans who professed to admire that religion, who were avidly curious about every detail of dance and rite. The Puebloans had no way of foreseeing the impact on their own way of life that scholarly books published between gray covers in Washington, D.C., might one day have. In the

1990s, the Pueblos bear the brunt of that disclosure almost daily. One of the most grievous abuses of their sacred lore comes at the hands of New Age gurus who ransack the old Bureau of American Ethnology reports in order to hold workshops in which they teach their clients the karmic benefits of, for example, making their own Hopi *pahos* (prayer sticks) and altars.

In the 1920s, a professional reaction against the blithe assumptions of the likes of Fewkes and Cushing set in. The new skepticism, spearheaded by Alfred V. Kidder, one of the greatest figures in Southwestern archaeology, was a much-needed corrective to the old, uncritical acceptance of whatever Pueblo informants told their auditors. Kidder and his cronies demanded a more rigorous standard of truth, and they sought it in the dirt of excavation, not in the tales of Zuni elders.

The unfortunate by-product of Kidder's rigor was a tendency during the next four decades to ignore living Puebloans altogether. By the early 1960s, though he would most likely not have said so out loud, the typical Anasazi archaeologist believed in his heart that oral tradition was all but useless. In the interim, tree-ring and carbon 14 dating had revealed the great span of Anasazi occupation in the Southwest, stretching back into the dim epoch before the birth of Christ. What good would it do to ask a Hopi shaman what the Basketmakers might have been up to nearly two thousand years ago?

With the liberalism of the 1970s and a new sensitivity to Indian culture, yet another counterreaction set in. Anasazi archaeology today is caught on the horns of a fierce dilemma. A younger generation of researchers, championing the Indian right to repatriate artifacts and human remains gathered in museums over the last century, insists that Pueblo oral tradition is every bit as valid as the most rigorous archaeology. The most extreme among these younger scholars argue that there is no excuse any more ever to dig an Anasazi site, unless it is irrevocably threatened by the building of a highway or a shopping mall. Some of them, Anglo archaeologists working *for* the various Pueblos, try to reconcile objective scholarship with the passionate advocacy of land claims and Indian rights their bosses hired them to perform.

Their opponents, many of them the leading scholars of the previous generation, men and women now in their fifties and sixties, resist this trend, seeing in it a new sentimentality not far from Cushing's. They retain Kidder's skepticism about the worth of oral tradition. Since their views place them now on the wrong end of the "politically correct" spectrum, they tend to voice their qualms in muted tones.

In the 1990s, this dilemma is a brushfire raging through archaeology all over the globe, though nowhere does it burn hotter than in the Southwest. As I sought a firsthand understanding of the ancients who built such prodigies as Betatakin and Spruce Tree House, I had to confront my own ambivalence about the living Pueblos and to make my own judgments about the worth of oft-told tales.

In August 1994, I attended my first Pecos Conference, held in the campground at Mesa Verde. This chummy and informal gathering of Southwestern archaeologists, founded by Kidder in 1927, takes place every summer in a different locale. One of the highlights of the 1994 conference was a mass firing of pots, orchestrated by a man named Clint Swink.

On a Thursday night, 116 pots of various shapes and sizes—handled mugs, shallow bowls, tall pitchers, sturdy ladles, and duck-effigy vessels—were laid atop sandstone slabs resting in a bed of coals within an eighteen-foot-long open trench. Each of the pots had been decorated with a white slip and black designs drawn in paint made from Rocky Mountain bee plant or tansy mustard. Perhaps a dozen different potters had shaped the vessels from local clay. Swink's charge to each of them was to imitate, as closely as possible, the style and shape of Mesa Verde black-on-white—the ceramic standard throughout the thirteenth century across a huge swath of the Colorado Plateau. Now the green (unbaked) pots were covered with thin protective sherds; then a bonfire of juniper and piñon boughs was set atop the assemblage. The fire burned for four hours as a sweet smell—bee plant and tansy mustard baking—permeated the air. Finally the trench was smothered with dirt.

Twenty hours later, on Friday afternoon, just after a violent lightning storm had swept the plateau, Swink led the unveiling. The dirt and ashes were cleared off the trench, the cover sherds removed. All at once the crowd watching the ceremony burst into murmurs and applause. Resting among still-warm embers, the pots gleamed black-and-white in the setting sun. A few were broken; others had hairline cracks; but most were intact, and the colors looked right, largely free of the dark smudges caused by hot spots. Swink lifted a vessel he had molded, grinned broadly, and told the crowd: "I want to congratulate everybody on the first Mesa Verde black-on-white firing of this magnitude since thirteen hundred A.D." The crowd cheered once more.

One thing struck me as particularly curious about this scene. None of the dozen-odd potters was an Indian. In fact, not one person among the sizable gathering was a Puebloan. The rediscovery of Mesa Verde black-on-white was a project perpetrated entirely by Anglos.

On many occasions, I had toured Pueblo villages where women stood behind rickety card tables selling their ceramic creations. Sometimes I was invited into a potter's home, where I watched an expert dip a split yucca leaf in a black paste of bee plant and trace a deft design—"just as our ancestors did a thousand years ago," I would be told.

Such an illusion, of the ancient continuity of craft passed on from mother to daughter over the generations, lies at the heart of the Indian art market. In 1982, *National Geographic* published a stunning foldout chart illustrating the evolution of Anasazi pottery from the first crude efforts such as Lino black-on-gray, around A.D. 500, all the way to current Pueblo styles such as Acoma polychrome. By implying a steady, smooth progression over the centuries, the chart fostered the same myth I was being fed in the potters' homes.

The fact is, not a single living Puebloan today knows how to make Mesa Verde black-on-white pottery. It is not simply a matter of design styles: the very firing technique was forgotten long ago. Until the last few years, despite the tens of thousands of Anasazi vessels unearthed all over the Southwest, no archaeologist had yet found an Anasazi kiln. By now, three dozen are known: nine came to light all at once on Mesa Verde during recent excavation in the path of a water-line project. The kilns surprised everyone: they lay nowhere near Anasazi villages, they preserved a unique orientation perpendicular to long slopes (presumably to control the flow of air), and the oblong trenches looked nothing like the kilns Pueblo potters use today.

Even with the discovery of the kilns, it took years of trial and error on the part of Clint Swink (who is an artist, not an archaeologist) to begin to produce well-fired pots in the Mesa Verde black-on-white style. The fine points of his technique will someday fill a weighty volume. But, as I learned at the Pecos Conference, Swink's work leads to some fascinating conclusions. As one archaeologist mused, "It turns out that anybody can make a pot, but it takes a real expert to fire it right." Perhaps for this reason the kilns lay not within villages, but in places where several villages might meet for a grand ceremonial event. Perhaps the magical rite of firing itself, superintended by specialists, drew disparate peoples together.

It seemed obvious to me that we were dealing with a lost tradition. But at Pecos, when I uttered those words, several archaeologists (of the left-leaning, younger sort) jumped down my throat. "It may not be a lost tradition," one told me, "but a freely abandoned one. When you go somewhere else, as the Anasazi did in thirteen hundred, you need a new tradition. You have new clay sources, and you adapt the technology to the clay."

Yes, but . . . the best of today's Pueblo potters turn out exquisite vessels. A style such as the black ware produced at Santa Clara and San Ildefonso Pueblos—so chic and pricey in the Santa Fe galleries—corresponds, however, to nothing the Anasazi ever made. For centuries, the Puebloans have used cow and sheep dung to fire their kilns, and metal grates to set the pots on. Both innovations came as a result of the Spanish *entrada*.

It is hardly surprising, then, that the old technique might have been lost. For all I know, my own ancestors a mere three hundred years ago included tinkers, coopers, and cobblers, but I haven't the slightest idea how to mend tin pans, or turn boards into barrels or cowhide into shoes.

Clint Swink hopes soon to present his findings to a gathering of

Pueblo potters, but he recognizes that that transaction could be fraught with tension. Who is this Anglo artist to tell a Pueblo people how their ancestors once made pots? Swink has already been cautioned by Jody Folwell, an articulate Santa Clara woman and master potter, that the making and selling of replicated Mesa Verde black-on-white ware smacks for her of nascent racism.

Two months after the Pecos Conference, at Jemez Pueblo, forty miles north of Albuquerque, I witnessed another provocative colloquium in the rediscovery of a lost art. On a frosty October morning, a group of ten men sat on the ground before a small bonfire in front of the Jemez visitor center, pounding stones together and sending chips flying. Nine of the men were from Jemez or nearby Zia Pueblo. The tenth was Bruce Bradley, an archaeologist from Crow Canyon Archaeological Center in Cortez, Colorado.

What I was seeing was a seminar in the ancient art of flint knapping, the process by which shapeless chunks of chert, obsidian, and flint are reduced to slender arrowheads and sleek dart points. It was Bradley who was doing the teaching. Like most American Indians, the Jemez and Zia men no longer know how to make arrowheads. Why should they bother to retain that arcane skill, when for a century the most effective way for them to hunt deer or elk has been with rifles?

Bradley had learned his flint knapping during twenty years of experimenting and under the tutelage of a French archaeologist named François Bordes, who had set out to replicate the stone tools found in Paleolithic European sites. There were significant differences, Bradley learned, between Old and New World flaking stones. "Bordes was a power flaker," Bradley told me, "which doesn't work with obsidian. Obsidian flakes easily, but it's 'cheap'—fickle, brittle, unforgiving. Bordes liked to say, 'Flint, she is a woman; obsidian, she is a whore.'"

The Pueblo men had showed up that October day not so much because they hankered to reclaim their heritage as because they had formed an archery club. In effect, they were cultivating a hobby. And Bradley had eased his way into their midst only after years of making friends among the Zia. His sympathy for the Puebloans goes so far that he refuses to read the turn-of-the-century ethnographic works that contain so much of their secret knowledge—despite an intense curiosity about that lore. Among the Zia, as he put it, "I never ask questions. When they're ready to tell me something, they'll tell me."

Now I listened as Bradley tried to explain his craft to his Puebloan students in terms that sounded to me like sheer mysticism. "You have to isolate a platform," he said, and "Do it from this side if you don't want it to dive," and "I want to get this edge cleaned up and release this."

In an hour and a half, knocking with quartzite pounders, then pressure-flaking with an elk antler, Bradley turned a fat block of creamy gray chert into a perfect Clovis point, identical to the blades Paleo-Indians had attached to their spears nine thousand years before Christ. One of the Zia men held the point and murmured, "It's almost like a miracle, to see that rock before lunch and see it now."

Later we all drove to the community center, where Jemez women served us a robust dinner of corn bread, enchiladas, and salad. Good feeling wafted through the room on waves of jokes, some of them in the Jemez tongue. I had never been more hospitably treated. It was easy to feel good about this rare rapport between an archaeologist and his Pueblo hosts. Only a few years ago, Jemez had been one of the Pueblos most tightly closed to outsiders. Virtually no photography was allowed within the village, and tourism was not encouraged.

Yet the flint-knapping workshop had served to remind me once more of the wholesale acculturation Anglos had wrought upon the Pueblo world and, in turn, to reinforce my skepticism about oral tradition. If such basic crafts as pot firing and arrowhead making had been lost over the centuries, what sort of drift from the truth had legends and migration stories undergone?

A few years ago I had raised this question with Jeffrey S. Dean, a veteran archaeologist who works at the University of Arizona's Laboratory for Tree-Ring Research. Unlike Bradley, Dean is of the old school. We had been talking about Hopi stories. "I don't think the Hopi oral traditions are worth the paper they're written on," he said in a blunt and memorable oxymoron.

"The standard view," Dean went on, "is that contact with the

Spanish, beginning in fifteen forty, was so disruptive, it laid a great fault line across the oral record. I think there were two fault lines, the earlier one occurring in the fourteenth century, after the abandonment—exactly why, we don't know. I think the Hopi are almost as far removed from the Anasazi of Pueblo III as we are."

Unlike Bradley, I had never felt entirely comfortable visiting a Pueblo village. Each such encounter set my mind racing with a hundred questions: the links with the Old Ones, so tenuous yet so visible, spoke in every masoned doorway and path grooved in the bedrock. Yet the deep reticence of the Pueblos daunted and frustrated me. It was not in my temper to follow Bradley's axiom of never asking questions. Several years ago, touring the Hopi village of Walpi, I had been galvanized when our guide pointed out the site on the plain below, where according to old stories the village that preceded Walpi had stood, whose name meant "the place left in ashes." When I pressed her for its Hopi name, she turned evasive.

Gazing down at the vanished town, I stupidly asked, "Has anybody done archaeology there?"

"No," said my guide. "The Hopi don't like archaeology very much."

Of all the Pueblo legends I had ever heard, the one that most haunted me came from Acoma in western New Mexico. It had to do with a startling sandstone butte, seven hundred feet high, that lies three miles northeast of the Sky City of Acoma. The People call it Katzimo; to the Spaniards, it was Mesa Encantada; today's road maps call it Enchanted Mesa.

Clinging to Katzimo with a millennial tenacity, an old tale persists in Acoman memory. It was first reported in 1885 by that champion of Indian rights Charles F. Lummis, Bandelier's protégé. Lummis claimed to have heard it straight from the mouth of Martin Valle, the aged governor of Acoma.

Long, long before the advent of the Spanish, the legend had it, even before the coming of the Navajo and Ute and Apache, the Acomans all lived atop Katzimo. A great leaning slab of rock, on the side facing present-day Acoma, offered the only access to the summit. One day all the people but three women were down on the plains, tending to their fields. An unprecedented violent rainstorm suddenly struck, unleashing floods all over the region. The farmers crawled under ledges to wait out the deluge.

When the rains stopped, the people discovered to their horror that the leaning slab, undercut by floods, had fallen away. They could never regain their village. One of the three trapped women threw herself off the cliff; the other two died after a long time. The surviving Acomans came to the Sky City, where they built the town they live in today.

When Lummis first published the legend, it provoked a heated debate over the validity of oral tradition. Finally, in 1897, an anthropologist named William Libbey, from Princeton, set out to debunk the tale. With a bizarre rig adapted from the Life-Saving Service, Libbey's team managed to shoot a rope across a summit prow on the east side of Katzimo (the side away from Acoma), attach a bosun's chair to it, and, using horses for power, haul the terrified professor to the top.

Libbey made a cursory examination of the summit, noting apparent cairns and possible potsherds, yet convincing himself they were mere "freaks of erosion." He descended, then telegraphed the newspapers that "the Enchanted Mesa was Disenchanted."

Always game for a fray, Lummis recruited a much better archaeologist, Frederick W. Hodge, and set out to debunk the debunker. Two months after Libbey's bizarre visit, a team led by Hodge, which included three Acoma men, found the ancient hand-and-toe trail in a deep concave chute on the west end of Katzimo, facing Acoma. They climbed the trail more than halfway to the top, where they were stumped by a dead-vertical stretch of some forty feet. Returning with a six-section prefab ladder, they surmounted the gap and reached the top.

All across the summit they found abundant signs of ancient visitation: potsherds, flint arrowheads, stone axes, and shell beads. There was no sign of ancient dwellings, but Hodge guessed that stone-and-mud walls would long since have eroded away. Nine months later Lummis repeated Hodge's ascent, finding turquoise beads, agate spalls, and a possible shrine.

Lummis descended, to crow over Libbey's gaffe and to trumpet Acoman veracity. In *Mesa, Cañon, and Pueblo,* he wrote, "The fit scholar never despises an Indian legend as a mere fairy-tale. It is always true, though it may need special side-lights by which to interpret its actual meaning."

There, so far as I could ascertain, matters had rested for nearly a century. I could find no record of anyone, Indian or Anglo, who had reached the top of Katzimo since 1898.

Despite Lummis's assertions, the discoveries of 1897–98 fell far short of proving the old tale. Had the top of Katzimo been some esoteric pilgrimage place for hunters, rather than the Acomans' home village? What about the leaning slab? Why was there no sign of its wreckage beneath the vertiginous chute?

Fired by my fascination with the tale, I arrived at Acoma in October 1994 with a wildly ambitious—one might even say presumptuous—scheme to test the validity of the legend further. I hoped to persuade several Acomans to join me in an attempt to climb Katzimo once more.

Here, a confession is in order. Many years ago, on my first visit to Acoma, I had learned that the whole area around Katzimo was completely off-limits to Anglos. But I had read Lummis, the tale burned in my memory, and I was as yet ignorant of the strength of Pueblo notions of the sacred and the forbidden.

Ignoring the regulation, I had parked my car just off the highway, then walked a complete circle around Katzimo, studying it acutely in my binoculars. It was clear that there was no route to the top that would go without technical climbing of a high standard. Finally, on the west side, I found the ancient hand-and-toe trail up which Hodge had climbed. The lure was irresistible: I scrambled up the lower half of the route, until the forty-foot wall where Hodge had placed his ladder stopped me. To my astonishment, I saw that a six-inch crack split the vertical cliff; inside the crack, tiny facing holds had been gouged. Had the ancients wedged wooden rungs inside the crack to make a desperate staircase?

I turned and headed down. No one had noticed my trespass.

On my most recent visit, I felt ashamed of the selfish profanation

I had performed years before. I did not, however, volunteer an account of it to my hosts. Meanwhile, I took the hour-long tour of Sky City with some fifteen other visitors. Our guide was a blithe, sardonic young woman named Geri Tsethlikai. As I strolled along, I pondered once more the layers of irony and secrecy that separated the Pueblo world from mine.

Of all the Pueblo villages, Acoma remains visually the most startling. A paved road now gives access to the village on top; the old hand-and-toe trail survives as an end-of-tour descent option for the more adventurous visitors. Yet even today, Acoma has no electricity or indoor plumbing. Though Tsethlikai told us as much, some in our group seemed to have trouble fathoming the implications. "What are those?" asked one woman, pointing at a pair of cliff-edge outhouses.

"Those are our ATMs," quipped Tsethlikai. "They only take deposits."

Beneath Tsethlikai's wit, I realized, was a certain sharpness. She had a knack for goofing on the Anglos she guided without most of them realizing it. About casual photography, she had said at the outset, "Some of the older people don't like to have their picture taken. They might be having a bad-hair day."

Later we passed a kiva, off-limits to all women. "I don't know what they do in there," Tsethlikai prevaricated. "Even my brother still won't tell me what they do. So to my idea I think they probably go in there to play poker." Our group chuckled, leaving me to puzzle over the guide's subtle satire of our own notions of the sacred.

Near the end of the tour, we entered the mission, San Estevan del Rey. No photography was allowed, but I was content simply to stare at one of the most perfect Spanish colonial churches in the New World. Built in 1629, the mission still has a dirt floor. The high rafters are huge, skinned ponderosa-pine logs carried on bare shoulders forty miles from Mount Taylor. The adobe side walls sport brightly colored emblems mingling the Pueblo symbols for rainbow and mesa top with the Christian cross. Above the altar hangs a vivid painting on buffalo hide of the fatal stoning of Saint Stephen.

Exquisite though the building was, I knew something of the mission's dark legacy, and so I pressed our guide: "Don't the Acoma people feel a certain bitterness about the church and what it stands for?" I asked.

"Not at all." Tsethlikai had already told the group that although 80 percent of Acoma's people had converted to Catholicism, they all practiced their ancient Indian religion at home.

"Isn't there a conflict between the two?" I had probed.

"Not at all," she had answered. The veil of Pueblo privacy had risen before my impertinent questions.

I thought again about the events of 1598. Late that year, a colonizing army of 129 soldiers under Don Juan de Oñate had camped beneath Acoma. The Spaniards were astounded at the airy village built of stones and mud atop the sheer-sided sandstone mesa, with but a single perilous hand-and-toe trail for access.

An uneasy truce broke into bloodshed. In January 1599, Oñate attacked with the fury of an avenging angel. The Acomans resisted fiercely, but in the end flint-tipped wooden arrows were no match for gunpowder, iron swords, and armor. Oñate took some five hundred villagers captive, then meted out conquistadorial justice.

Every man over the age of twenty-five had his right foot cut off and was sentenced to twenty years' slave labor. All the women above the age of twelve, and all men from twelve to twenty-five, likewise earned two decades of penal servitude. The children were taken from their parents and distributed as servants in Mexico. Two Indians from the distant pueblo of Hopi who had fought with the Acomans had their right hands cut off; they were then sent home as a lesson to other potential rebels.

Many of the men and women thus punished by Oñate helped build, as slaves, San Estevan del Rey. The two beautiful spiraling red-and-white altar posts had been carried by some thirty to forty men each from Mount Taylor without (so Spanish arrogance decreed) being allowed to touch the ground the length of the forty-mile trek.

Why, then, did the mission not still conjure up in the hearts of Acomans Oñate's savagery? "You must remember," said Tsethlikai, lifting the veil ever so slightly, "that during the Pueblo Revolt, we left the church standing."

Her comment gave me pause. In 1680, in a gloriously coordinated effort, the twenty-odd pueblos of Arizona and New Mexico drove the Spanish out of the Southwest, killing the priests and burning to the ground most of the hated churches. Yet San Estevan had been spared. It would take the Spanish thirteen years and much more bloodshed to reconquer the Pueblos.

"The mission was left," said Tsethlikai, "as a memorial to those who died building it." That was as close to an explanation as I was likely to get.

Earlier that day, it had taken only a few minutes with Brian Vallo, the first lieutenant governor of Acoma, to dash my wild plans to climb Enchanted Mesa. Katzimo was off limits not only to Anglos but to Acomans themselves. (I was not the first person that year to request permission for an assault on the sacred mesa. A few months earlier, a Japanese car manufacturer had offered big bucks to the Pueblo in exchange for permission to heli-lift a new auto to the top to film a commercial.)

"So you don't even know anybody who's tried to climb Katzimo?" I persisted. Vallo shook his head. "Nobody goes up there." He paused, then grinned conspiratorially. "When my uncle was just a young guy, about twenty-two, he tried to climb Katzimo. Everybody told him to stay away, that the place was to be left alone. He tried anyway. Fell off and broke his leg."

I found it hard to give up gracefully. "Wouldn't it mean something to Acoma to have the old legend confirmed?"

Vallo smiled, then answered shrewdly: "For the non-Indian, confirmation of that sort is something to get excited about. But for us, we know we have a direct link to those sites. What you want to do is like telling a Catholic that Jesus was crucified at Golgotha."

Midway during our group tour, we had paused at the easternmost point of Sky City and stared across at Katzimo. My yearning was unassuaged. With a bored, mechanical delivery, Tsethlikai recited the legend, telling much the same story that Lummis had recorded.

The tour moved on. I lingered, staring at the graceful, inaccessible butte, longing to come to grips with its mystery. Catching up with Tsethlikai, I nudged her away from the group. "Why is nobody from

Acoma allowed to go up on Katzimo today?" I asked softly.

The guarded look came into her eyes. Who was this Anglo with all his sharp, nosy questions? But she gave me a new inkling. Looking at the somber mesa in the northeast, she murmured, "That is where our ancestors starved." What did she mean? Did her matter-of-fact remark allude somehow to the brutal Spanish conquest? Or was it the echo of some ancient tragedy of which ethnographers remain unaware?

I could do what I wanted, Tsethlikai seemed to be saying, with this strange piece of history. I was on the margin of sacred knowledge, and the Acomans were not about to help me get closer to it.

The Place of One Who Is Standing

RANGER Bruce Mellberg and I walked slowly through the ruins of Betatakin, in the Kayenta region of northeastern Arizona. It was just before noon on a bright day in March 1993. The equinoctial sun swelled through the south-facing dwellings, bouncing soft light into inner crannies. A canyon wren uttered its chromatic descending cry. Tall cumulus clouds sailed out of the west, shape-shifting as they rode the sky. Snowmelt spilled over a waterfall hidden in an aspen grove, plashing the air with a liquid hiss. On the hike in, we had found the earliest flowers of spring: dandelions tight to the ground, tiny violets clumped beneath Gambel oaks.

I had come to Navajo National Monument to see Betatakin and Keet Seel. By 1993, among major Anasazi sites under the custody of the National Park Service and open to the public, these were the only ones I had not visited. By all accounts, they were two of the finest. The proof now lay before my eyes.

The natural cave in which Betatakin lies, a gaping mouth in the ruddy Navajo sandstone fully 452 feet high, 370 feet broad, and 135 feet deep, would loom as a geologic cynosure even if humans had never bothered to adorn it with their houses. Over the centuries, its depth preserved the Anasazi village built inside it as perfectly as any ancient site in the Southwest.

Now my gaze dwelt on details. I admired the daub-and-wattle

wall of a small granary, its reeds and upright sticks caked in mortar. Square knots tied in yucca fiber seven hundred years ago kept the fragile structure intact. On a protruding bench of bedrock, several deep grooves spoke of ancient hunters honing their flint knives. Inside one room, I saw three polished manos (grinding stones) recumbent in their matched metates (grinding basins). From the wall to my right, a baleful rock painting—blank-headed humanoid with raised hand within a disk of white—glared down.

The most striking aspect of Betatakin, however, was the idiosyncratic perfection with which the walls and floors of its one hundred rooms had been tailored to fit the dip and swoop of the cave. For some chambers, this had required gouging grooves in the bedrock on which to foot the forward walls, then filling the cavities behind them with dirt, so that living rooms with level floors might cling to slopes as steep as fifty degrees.

The Anglo discovery of Betatakin had been made in 1909 by a party led by that indefatigable guide and trader John Wetherill, who in turn was guided to the site by a young Navajo named Clatsozen Benully. Hidden in a small side fork of the many-branched Tsegi Canyon, Betatakin had escaped the notice of earlier explorers—including Richard Wetherill, who had passed close in 1895.

Among the 1909 party was a University of Utah student, Neil Judd, whose footsteps I had followed in Moqui Canyon, and whose exemplary excavation of Pueblo Bonito in Chaco Canyon in the 1920s had completed the work begun by Richard Wetherill three decades before. As an archaeologist, Judd had a light hand and a tolerance for ambiguity, qualities rare among the field-workers of his day. In 1917 he came back to Betatakin, and stabilized and repaired the ruin so deftly that it remains today much as he left it. By comparison, the work of later rebuilders at Mesa Verde's Cliff Palace and Spruce Tree House would amount to brutal overkill.

Judd's labors at Betatakin were all the more remarkable in view of his minuscule budget, a field season limited to little more then two months, two feet of snow on the ground when he arrived, and the country's entry into World War I. In March 1917, the young archaeologist arrived in Flagstaff, where he hired five men off the street to serve as field assistants. John Wetherill packed the party in to Betatakin from his trading post at Kayenta, but three times during subsequent weeks Judd had to hike the twenty miles each way to the post and back to reprovision his party.

A few weeks into their work, the team of four was surprised by the arrival of a Navajo policeman from the Indian agency in Tuba City. President Wilson had declared war; the local draft board had taken notice of the only six strangers in the Navajo country; and the policeman had come to serve them their induction papers! Judd's team ignored the summons and continued their work in Arizona.

In the early 1960s, another young scholar with a deft touch, Jeffrey S. Dean, came to Betatakin. (It was Dean who had offered me his skeptical view of Pueblo oral tradition, citing the twin "fault lines" of the fourteenth century and the Spanish *entrada*.) In the 1960s, Dean was becoming a virtuoso of tree-ring dating. By the time he had finished his work at Betatakin, he was able to determine not only the span of time in which the village was built, but the precise sequence, year by year, of additions and remodelings to its architecture. Twenty years later, one of Dean's colleagues could still pronounce Betatakin "the best-dated prehistoric ruin in the world."

What Dean found surprised even the experts. The construction of Betatakin commenced in 1267 and ended in 1286. The inhabitants (Dean guessed the population at about 125 at its peak) may have lingered on for a few more years, doing no more building, but they were gone before 1300. One of the most magnificent of all Anasazi villages, revealing at every hand the craftsmanship of master architects, had been occupied for less than a generation—perhaps for only twenty years.

Now, on my tour of Betatakin, I pondered a forty-foot pole of Douglas fir that leaned against the back wall. A photograph from 1909 shows that the pole stood in exactly the same place when the Wetherill party found the village. The pole provides the only link to a high ledge in the deepest recesses of the cave, along the lip of which runs a low masonry wall. Had this ledge, nicknamed "the gallery," been a hiding place, a desperate last resort for besieged inhabitants? Or did it serve, as Dean concluded, as a storage area safe from even the most acrobatic of rodents? In any event, was the pole a ladder? No steps had been cut in it, and I could not imagine shinnying up the thing. Yet somehow the builders had used the gallery and, when they parted for good, had left the pole in place.

From a stance far inside the cave, I looked out at the trees shining in the bright sun. The tallest of them were Douglas firs, and the tallest of all stood in perpetual gloom, under the vertical north-facing precipice opposite the cave, only four hundred yards away across the tight side canyon. In one of his most beguiling findings, Dean had cored some Douglas firs standing close against that cliff and proved that at least two of the trees still growing there had been alive when Betatakin was built.

Another reason for my visit to Navajo National Monument was to see whether the Park Service could administer Anasazi ruins in a fashion less absurd than the soulless truck-'em-in, truck-'em-out routine that had so dismayed me at Mesa Verde. And at the moment, standing in a back alley of Betatakin, I luxuriated in an experience I had thought it impossible ever to have in a national park or monument.

For Ranger Mellberg and I were the first visitors of the year to Betatakin, and we had the whole place to ourselves. I had spent less than two hours with my companion but had already grown to like him. Tall, in his forties, with a shaggy salt-and-pepper beard and a loose-jointed amble, Mellberg seemed to have escaped the burnout endemic to his job. Here was a ranger who still loved the land he was paid to protect. Now and then, as we walked through the ruin, he had lapsed into the kind of canned spiel he foisted off on tour groups; but then I would interrupt with a question, and we would converse as one Anasazi devotee to another.

Indeed, Mellberg seemed miscast as a ranger, uncomfortable in his uniform. There was too much of the vagabond about him. We had discovered that we shared a passion for the anarchic writings of Edward Abbey. The ex-hippie still peered out of Mellberg's government camouflage, and I was not entirely surprised when he let on that he had sat in the mud at Woodstock in 1969.

Why did we have Betatakin to ourselves that sunny day in

March? The circumstances were too bizarre to have imagined a few months before. At Betatakin, the pressures of visitation have dictated a different solution from the one that has seized Cliff Palace. But in some senses, Navajo National Monument's answer to the eternal problem was even more absurd than Mesa Verde's.

SOME history is in order. Navajo National Monument comprises not only Betatakin and Keet Seel but another splendid Anasazi site, called Inscription House. Distressed at the ravages of pothunters in the Kayenta area, early archaeologists persuaded President William Howard Taft to sign the monument into being on March 20, 1909. This was actually several months before either Betatakin or Inscription House was discovered by Anglos, though certain Indians knew of the ruins.

Taft's proclamation tore a rectangular hole of 160 square miles out of the Navajo Indian Reservation, which itself had been established in 1868. To avoid the inevitable conflict with native pastoralists who had long used the land for grazing, Taft pared back the monument in 1912 to three small tracts: 160-acre plots surrounding Betatakin and Keet Seel, a 40-acre square protecting Inscription House. Along with the unobtrusive colony of ranger quarters, visitor center, and campground, this odd patchwork of Park Service land constitutes the monument today.

For decades Navajo National Monument remained a backwater park that connoisseurs of the Anasazi kept as a happy secret among themselves. As recently as 1952, fewer than a thousand visitors came during the whole year. In 1987, traffic for the first time exceeded fifty thousand. During the six years thereafter, visitation to the monument doubled. The word about Keet Seel and Betatakin was out.

Meanwhile, under the neglectful regimes of Presidents Ronald Reagan and George Bush, the Park Service belt tightened notch by notch. By 1993, through the sheer necessity of stretching inadequate staff and budget across a far-flung domain, the situation at Navajo had reached a dreary state. Inscription House is closed indefinitely—ostensibly because the approach crosses sensitive Navajo land, but mainly because the site, lying forty road miles west of headquarters, would require a separate building and staff to supervise.

In 1993, Betatakin was officially open from early May to the end of September, Keet Seel only between Memorial Day and Labor Day. This despite the fact that summer is the worst season to appreciate these matchless ruins, thanks to the numbing heat and bleaching light. (On our hike in to Betatakin, Mellberg had fondly pointed out a tall trailside pine—the best patch of shade on the whole route and a mandatory oasis for the grueling tours of July and August.)

During the prime months for Southwest hiking—from March through May and from September through early November—the monument shrinks to a vegetative torpor. The ranger who greets each carload of tourists explains again and again that the only trail open is a five-minute walk to the canyon rim, where you can gaze at Betatakin from afar and eat your heart out. Otherwise, you can watch a grainy old film about the Anasazi, tour the small but excellent museum, buy jewelry in the adjoining Navajo gift shop, or park your Winnebago in the soulless campground.

During my own sojourn in March 1993, I had watched one visitor after another react to these gloomy tidings. Most took the news with stolid perplexity, but every once in a while a frustrated tourist simply lost it and started screaming at everybody in sight.

Even in summer, ranger-guided tours of Betatakin (six hours, five miles round-trip) were limited to forty-eight people a day, while a mere twenty was the quota for the two-day hike or horseback ride to distant Keet Seel (sixteen miles round-trip). Often as not, the visitor arrived to find that day's tour slots all booked. About half the would-be pilgrims went away with their hopes of walking through the ruins dashed. In 1992, 126,000 people came to Navajo National Monument. A mere 5 percent visited the ruins that are the park's raison d'être—4,318 to Betatakin, only 1,776 to Keet Seel.

I had telephoned the December before my visit and learned the state of things. My rancorous incredulity provoked the bureaucrat I was talking to to mention the loophole. One ranger among the nine who worked at Navajo—Mellberg—was willing and authorized to guide visits on Wednesdays and Thursdays, his two days a week off.

For standard NPS overtime ($20.55 an hour), I could hire Mellberg to take me on a private tour.

The monument's administrators were not happy with the fact that I planned to write an article about my experience. The superintendent had repeatedly moaned to her colleagues, "We don't need any more publicity. We're maxing out on the crowds that already come." The off-season loophole was not so much an official dispensation as a by-product of Mellberg's enthusiasm, patience, and need for cash. (Another ranger had led off-season tours until pushy clients—especially photographers, who could not abide being told where they were allowed to walk—caused him to throw in the towel.)

By 1995, little had changed. Mellberg was still the only ranger leading off-season tours, but, jealous of his privacy and his free time, he had begun to cut down on his bookings. The prospect seems likely that when Mellberg leaves the monument's service, the ravens and ground squirrels will have Betatakin and Keet Seel to themselves during the six months when the Southwest passes through its vernal and autumnal glory.

I WOULD have to wait a week, until Mellberg's next free Wednesday and Thursday, to visit Keet Seel. In the meantime, I drove south to the village of Kykotsmovi, which stands beneath the Hopi Third Mesa.

Over the years, the borders of the Navajo Reservation (the largest in the country) shifted, until by 1934 it completely surrounded the much smaller Hopi Reservation, initially established in 1882. Between the Hopi and the Navajo stand centuries of antagonism and warfare, and the vexed but ineluctable solution of embedding the former people's reservation within the latter's continues to cause almost daily conflict between the tribes.

As I would come to see during my two weeks in the Kayenta area, the Navajo-Hopi tension could not be separated from the very act of apprehending Keet Seel or Betatakin. The three tiny squares of Park Service land that make up Navajo National Monument are surrounded by grazing lands: Navajos today run cattle up virtually every branch of the huge Tsegi system. To hike to Betatakin or Keet Seel, you must cross Navajo land, and over the years it has taken some delicate negotiations between Park Service personnel and Navajo ranchers to keep the trails open.

The Kayenta Anasazi, however—the builders not only of Keet Seel and Betatakin, but of tens of thousands of other sites on the Navajo Reservation—were the ancestors of the Hopi, who number a mere 4,500 today (versus 220,000 Navajos) and who live in fourteen villages scattered along the southern edges of three arid mesas northeast of Flagstaff.

In Kykotsmovi, I met Leigh Jenkins, the shrewd, articulate, sometimes cranky man who serves as cultural preservation officer for the Hopi people. I wanted to ask him about the Hopi link to Keet Seel and Betatakin.

Jenkins began by railing against the very term "Anasazi"—a Navajo word meaning "ancestral enemies." "The Hopi strongly object to 'Anasazi,'" he told me. "We say *Hisatsinom*—which means 'people of long ago,' or 'ancestral Hopi,' or just 'the Old Ones.'" In like fashion, the Hopi rejected the names of Inscription House, Keet Seel, and Betatakin—the last two being Navajo for "broken pottery" and "ledge house," respectively. The Hopi names are *Tokonavi* ("place of the black rock"), *Talastima* ("place of the corn tassel"), and *Kawestima* (an archaic word of uncertain meaning). The name "Navajo National Monument" was particularly offensive to the Hopi, for the Navajo are Athapaskans, who came from the distant north long after the ancient villages were built.

The term "Kayenta," too, the Hopi find inappropriate. "We call the region *Wunuqa*—'the place of one who is standing,'" Jenkins said, then drew me a map and a diagram of the oddly shaped pinnacle near Marsh Pass to which the term alluded.

Jenkins enumerated the Hopi clans that had strong affiliations with the Wunuqa sites: the Rattlesnake Clan, the Fire Clan, the Flute Clan, and the Sand and Desert subclans. Members of these sodalities regularly visit the prehistoric villages today, worshiping at secret shrines in the region.

I could not resist asking Jenkins the central question of Southwestern archaeology: "Why did the people abandon these villages?"

"It was part of a spiritual quest," Jenkins insisted. "The Hopi came into what we call the Fourth World. We had a spiritual covenant with our guardian deity, Maasaw. The covenant challenged the Hopi to fulfill a spiritual quest. If fulfilled, it would give the Hopi spiritual stewardship of the land. The covenant required us very literally to place our footprints over the Fourth World. This was the cause of the migration of Hopi clans. The fifty thousand Puebloan sites on the Navajo Reservation, the petroglyphs, the shrines—these are the footprints of the Hopi people."

"So you don't give any credit to theories about drought, arroyo cutting, and so on?"

Jenkins smiled slightly. "There are old stories about the clans becoming a little too complacent. The stories say some clans were sternly reminded by natural phenomena that they had to move on. The natural phenomenon was a kind of sign: 'Look, you're getting a bit lazy.' "

So the Hopi could have it both ways, I thought. The abandonment was voluntary, spiritual, part of a quest; yet this explanation could smoothly assimilate any environmental crisis the archaeologists might come up with.

Partly because I knew it would provoke a spirited response, I mentioned Jeffrey Dean's theory about the two fault lines laid across the oral tradition of the Hopi. A key to Dean's argument for the fourteenth-century disruption was the sudden appearance of the Kachina Phenomenon—a religion centered on hundreds of supernatural intercessors, called kachinas, who negotiate with the gods to bring rain, good crops, and health to the people. Today, the kachinas lie at the heart of Pueblo religion: in their dances in the kivas, men put on kachina masks and *become* the supernatural beings. Yet so far archaeologists have found no evidence of the Kachina Phenomenon before about 1325.

Jenkins bristled. "If you look at the rock art," he said dismissively, "you can verify that the kachinas were around. There is no doubt they were around at the time of the migration." He paused. "I don't want to elaborate."

In a like manner, Jenkins scoffed at the fault line of Spanish conquest. "The Spanish," he said, "made a systematic attempt to suppress Hopi religion. But it's not easy to suppress a clan's memory of its ceremonies. We have knowledge of some ceremonies today, even if we don't still perform these ceremonies. I believe our religion was made stronger by the Spanish suppression."

Like most Hopi, Jenkins was sick and tired of condescension from the archaeologists. Earlier I had asked about a research puzzle: the presence of only one kiva at Betatakin, a rectangular one, versus six at Keet Seel and its satellite, Turkey Cave, all of them circular. (All Hopi kivas today are rectangular.)

"With a sly smile I will say to you," answered Jenkins in his arch manner, "that *we* know why a kiva is rectangular or round. But I won't tell you why. It's part of my having fun, to let you guys speculate about it."

"Would you tell an archaeologist?" I asked.

"Not yet."

Finally I asked about the Navajo. Jenkins sighed, "We're so different. We're like oil and water."

His people, Jenkins maintained, had kept the memory of the first contact with the Athapaskans who came from the north. "Our approach to the Navajo was to tell them, 'If you want to be among the Hopi, you have to respect our ways. If not, then leave.'"

Much though he rankled at the nomenclature of Navajo National Monument, Jenkins gave the Park Service some credit. "At least the monument exercises its mandated responsibility of preserving the ancient sites," he said. "For the sites under Navajo jurisdiction, there's no effort at preservation."

ON the following Wednesday I set out with Bruce Mellberg for Keet Seel. We left the visitor center before dawn, wound down the ridge toward Tsegi Point on a trail built in the 1930s, forded the stream in Long Canyon, and entered a broad valley called Dowozhi Biko. In beat-up shoes we waded the cold, ankle-deep stream every hundred yards or so as it meandered across our path.

It was another crystalline day, the sun shaping arches and pinnacles of red sandstone at every bend, a fresh breeze at our backs. From the bushes, juncos and towhees shrilled their territorial mottos. The land we crossed looked hard used, crisscrossed with cattle trails, grazed to stubble.

We branched north at the first tributary, entering narrower Keet Seel Canyon. Soon we were walking in the bed of an arroyo sixty feet deep; the raw mud walls cut off the view, lending a faintly claustrophobic character to the hike.

After six miles, the trail climbed out of the arroyo to avoid a stretch of quicksand. As we wound north along a juniper-covered bench, the canyon regained its beauty. Unlike Betatakin, Keet Seel remains hidden until the very last moment, when it springs into sight. Unprepared, I gasped in astonishment.

The cave that shelters Keet Seel is not so grand as Betatakin's, but the village, with its 160-odd rooms, fills every corner of it. As I could see from a distance, the ruin is even more varied than Betatakin, and every bit as pristine: the most delicate jacal walls—little more than twigs and mortar—stood upright, while the airiest towers thrust intact. The oft-used cliché about Keet Seel seemed apt: the village looks as though it had been built yesterday.

The majestic ruin was discovered in 1895 by Richard and Al Wetherill and Charlie Mason, the same trio who had found Cliff Palace seven years earlier. Just as I had, Richard Wetherill had turned a corner in the meandering canyon to have Keet Seel burst suddenly upon his sight, after he had trudged miles without noticing a hint of Anasazi presence. The men dug in the ruin then, and Richard returned two years later to make a more extensive excavation. The 1895 collection, however, has vanished—the only major assemblage of Wetherill's that is unaccounted for. Because of Keet Seel's importance—it remains the second-largest cliff dwelling ever discovered in the United States after Cliff Palace—archaeologists would love to recover those relics. (Just last year, Fred Blackburn told me that he had a hunch, based on the nationalities of 1895 associates of Wetherill', that the place to look for the collection might be in Germany or England—but he had no idea where to begin.)

Relatively little serious archaeology took place at Keet Seel for the next seventy years, until Jeffrey Dean brought his tree-ring expertise to the site. Here Dean found a more complicated history than Betatakin's. The cave was occupied and abandoned twice (the first time as early as A.D. 950) before the village whose ruins stand today was started, around 1250. In a striking finding, Dean got the same last construction date—1286—as he had come up with at Betatakin. Whatever perturbation had launched the great abandonment, it must have climaxed that year.

Before entering the site, Mellberg and I ate lunch at the ranger cabin (designed in the form of a Navajo hogan) below the ruins. Here, in the summer, a ranger spends eight days at a time, greeting each of the tours and leading them through Keet Seel. The ranger sleeps in his cabin, while the tourists camp out in an oak grove across the canyon.

We were not the first visitors of the year to Keet Seel. The register revealed an entry from the week before. "Kurt A., Claremont, CA," as he coyly signed himself, had made a solo tour on March 15. "Took only pictures, left only footprints," Kurt scribbled—"no offense, I hope." Mellberg sighed in annoyance. The guy had broken the law, but no rangers would descend on Claremont packing side arms. Instead Mellberg would "write it up," adding another crime report to the pile of fussy paperwork whose accumulated brunt may well close Keet Seel to the public for good.

There is in fact already a school of Park Service thought that sees closing the peerless ruins as the only way to save them. Most cliff dwellings in the national parks and monuments have been closed to the public—Antelope House and Mummy House in Canyon de Chelly, Montezuma Castle south of Flagstaff, nearly all the ruins at Mesa Verde. The previous week, just before we had entered Betatakin, Mellberg had warned me that if the ceiling of the natural cave looked friable, he would not be able to allow me inside. Once, as he had led a tour, several tons of sandstone had cut loose, fallen four hundred feet, smashed a couple of granaries, and scared the daylights out of twenty-four tourists. "All it would take is one death," Mellberg had mused, "and they'd close Betatakin up tight."

Now, as we approached Keet Seel, I felt hamstrung by the finicky Park Service rules, even though I had to grant each one its logic. We had eaten lunch at the hogan because food is banned in the ruin, on the grounds that crumbs attract rodents, who burrow in the dirt. Rather than urinate in the weeds, I had to use the chemical toilet. Whole sections of the ruin (and of Betatakin) are off-limits because tourists cannot be trusted to walk softly through them.

I was also distracted at first by the Park Service "improvements" to Keet Seel. An Anasazi toehold trail leads up the fifty-degree slab to the village; my feet itched to follow it, but Mellberg hauled a heavy wooden ladder out of a storage nook, roped it in place, and insisted that I climb it. Elsewhere in the ruin, earlier NPS savants had drilled the graceful Anasazi toe trails into a modern staircase. Mousetraps in the dust, a rescue litter tucked inside an ancient living room jarred my sensibilities. Near the entryway a pair of reconstructed pots sat atop an Anasazi roof; handsome though the vessels were, the self-conscious display struck me as hokey.

Gradually, Keet Seel won me over. Inside a kiva I saw three intact loom anchors, fragile loops of yucca fixed in holes in the floor, used seven hundred years ago to hold a weaver's blanket tight. Within one room, I was entranced to see that scraps of turkey-feather fabric, made originally as clothing, had been recycled to tie the cross-sticks of the roof in place. The famous anomalies of Keet Seel smote me: a ten-foot-high, 180-foot-long retaining wall that made an avenue of tons of fill and dirt, unique in the Southwest; a heavy pole of Douglas fir slung horizontally across the entryway as if to say, in Dean's paraphrase, "Keep out—this place closed."

Inside one room, I saw a delicate inscription on a cross-beam: "J. Wetherill—7/15/09." Twenty-five days after scrawling his signature here, John Wetherill would discover Betatakin.

I had photocopied Dean's report; now as I held the pages, the bewilderment of Keet Seel's jumble of rooms began to cohere. The room clusters took shape, each complex of living room, granaries, storerooms, and kiva defining a family's trials and hopes. I could trace the fledgling Keet Seel of 1271, the larger town of 1275, and Keet Seel in its glory in 1286, the year the Anasazi ceased to build.

Finally I stopped thinking and just stared. The tall, bearded ranger beside me stared, too, for even on his umpteenth visit Mellberg still felt an awe for the place it was his job to care for. It was bliss to hear no voice but the birds' and the wind's, to steep oneself in the silence of the ages. Keet Seel, I realized with vague sorrow, was the finest Anasazi village I had ever seen.

One day in 1963, as he worked at his tree-ring cores, Dean had witnessed a vivid lesson in the Anasazi achievement. Across the canyon from Keet Seel, an ancient toe- and handhold trail leads boldly up a near-vertical wall to the top of Skeleton Mesa, nine hundred feet above. Two cocky college boys arriving one afternoon had noticed the prehistoric ladder. Dean warned them not to try it. One of the two, scoffing, started up the route.

He was about a hundred feet up when he got stuck. Trying to climb back down, the youth slipped. Eighty feet below, he landed on his head in a pile of rocks. He was still alive when Dean got to him. The archaeologist started to run to the park headquarters; on the way he met the day's horseback tour, whose leader rode back out. At dusk a helicopter landed. The young man was still alive, but he died in the hospital in Page, Arizona.

The tale, as Dean had told me it, seemed to underscore the paradox with which the Park Service grapples. Even Anasazi children must have been expert climbers, for from infancy on they lived with the void inches away. It was not our business, I thought now, to tame Keet Seel's peril, to make the monument safe for visitors: the danger lurking about the ancient village was as essential to its character as its finest masoned walls.

MY longer outing with Mellberg gave us a chance to feel each other out. In other circumstances, we might have grown to be friends, for he seemed to me by far the most thoughtful and sympathetic ranger I had ever met. But our time together was edged with a tension.

Mellberg knew that part of my agenda in the Kayenta region was to hike to some ruins in the Tsegi system that were not protected by the national monument. None was nearly as grand in scale as Betatakin or Keet Seel, but I knew that each had its enticements. And I guessed that relatively few Anglos had ever visited any of them.

Mellberg wished that he could stop me. The vulnerability of these ruins, which Navajo authorities did nothing to protect, deeply distressed him. At one point, he went so far as to argue that nobody should be allowed to visit such sites. "Archaeological resources are unrenewable," he said time and again. "There aren't any ruins that are going to grow back."

We sat on the ground below Keet Seel and wrangled politely—for I could see, as a frown creased Mellberg's brow and his voice grew softer, that criticizing another human being didn't come easily to this gentle man.

The dialogue, which waxed and waned during our days together, stirred up some of the sharpest thinking I had ever done about the ethics of visiting backcountry ruins. Indeed, the whole of my two weeks in the Kayenta region provoked a relentless debate inside my head, as I pondered alternately Hopi affiliations to those sites, Navajo taboos against them, Mellberg's strictures, and my own desires.

I complained to Mellberg about the Park Service "improvements" we had just seen in Keet Seel: the wooden ladder, the gouged staircase. He winced in acknowledgment, then said carefully, "The Park Service has this problem of balancing our mandate to preserve the ruins and our mandate to allow the public to enjoy them. Maybe that's an impossible paradox."

I got the ranger to admit that he had visited some of the ruins he wished I couldn't see. "So why you and not me?" I needled.

An uncomfortable grimace replaced the frown. "I guess I'd have to say—" He hesitated, searching for words. "I'd like to think I know how to behave in a fragile ruin. It's sort of a professional thing. Like granting a scholar access to an archive that's not open to just anybody." In someone else's mouth, these words might have sounded arrogant. Coming from Mellberg, they were humble.

I said to myself, but not out loud: *Well, I know how to behave, too.* In any event, Mellberg's most passionate argument wasn't going to stop me. I had applied for and received a backcountry permit from the

Navajo Nation headquarters in Window Rock. As congenial as I found Mellberg's company, I craved the chance to get off into the wilderness alone.

THE ultimate goal of my three-day outing was a ruin near the head of another branch of the Tsegi system, even farther from monument headquarters than Keet Seel. The first night, ten miles in, I pitched my tent on a shelf of sandstone overlooking a canyon junction: there was no sign that anyone else had ever camped here before. I drank iodine-treated water from a trickling side stream and made a small fire of dead juniper branches (stoves only at the Keet Seel campground). Hunched before the glowing embers, I watched Orion sink in the west and listened to the hoot of an owl upvalley.

All day I had followed cattle trails, seeing a few piebald Herefords, startling five or six sleek horses half feral in their liberty. The hiking permit from Window Rock was folded in my shirt pocket, but I knew from past experience that no piece of paper could guarantee me easy passage on the reservation. In the backcountry, Navajos often hassle any Anglo who has the gall to cross their land, permit or no.

To spend hour after hour alone in the wilderness induces a beatific trance, but it also edges the spirit with a kind of paranoia. The fantasy lodged in my head that, if I saw a Navajo rancher approaching in the distance, I might hide in the bushes until he passed.

In terms of the Anasazi legacy, it is tempting to cast the Navajos as the bad guys. One dismal outcome of the struggle between Navajos and Hopis has been a series of acts of vandalism against Anasazi sites. For centuries, the Navajo scrupulously avoided the ancient cliff villages, in part because of an Athapaskan dread of places occupied by the dead. In the last few years, however, there have been reports of Navajo teenagers spray-painting rock-art panels, of kids knocking down the walls of thirteenth-century dwellings. Mellberg had seen Navajo youths urinating on Anasazi petroglyphs.

A year after my Kayenta foray, on a raft trip down the San Juan River, I would see my most shocking—and yet fascinating—example of this vandalism. At a site now called Desecrated Panel, petroglyphs from as early as the Basketmaker II era range for some two hundred yards along a smooth vertical wall facing east. Many of the designs have been savagely gouged with metal picks. Kenny Ross, the founder of the company running my trip, had actually witnessed the desecration in the 1950s and was thus able to comprehend it. It seems that several members of a Navajo family living nearby fell ill with a serious malady. The medicine man brought in to cure them claimed that the "rock writings from the sun people" were the cause. The only way to "break the power" was to destroy the evil designs. The gouging was precise and selective, often obliterating the heart, head, or joints of an anthropomorph while leaving the rest of the figure intact.

From Mellberg's point of view, however, an even darker threat than such vandalism lurked in the Navajo indifference to Anasazi ruins such as the one I had set out to find. Because the Navajo Nation does nothing to protect these sites, they are wide open to the professional pothunter, whose booty, thanks to an international black market, can make a poor man rich overnight. Pothunters tend not to be Indians: the classic type is the Anglo rancher whose prowling springs from a tradition handed down in his family from one generation to the next. (As a kid growing up in Colorado, I had hunted Ute arrowheads with my father on the piñon benches above the Arkansas River, and it was hard even now for me to see anything wrong in that euphoric pastime.) But in recent decades, systematic looting of backcountry sites, sometimes employing heavy machinery, has become a minor industry in the Southwest.

Succumbing to lazy stereotypes, I had formed my own prejudices against the Navajo, only to have them shaken up by a talk with Alan Downer, an eloquent Anglo who is historical preservation officer for the Navajo Nation. Downer began with simple numbers. "Leigh Jenkins says there are fifty thousand Anasazi sites on the reservation?" he asked. "There are fifty thousand in our files, and less than two percent of the reservation is well surveyed. There may be *one million* Anasazi sites on the reservation. They're not all great villages—they range from the kind of site only an archaeologist could love to Keet

Seel. But how would you even start to make a priority list?

"The next thing to look at," Downer went on, "is financial reality. We just don't have the money. And the budget is going to get worse before it gets better. What's more, Native Americans all over the country—not just Navajos—are a little fed up with seeing all these dollars go to archaeology, when there's so few dollars for living Indians."

Downer acknowledged the tragedy of Navajo defacement of ancient rock art. "But we also know of instances in which fundamentalist Christians destroyed petroglyphs as idolatrous images," he added.

"It's a gross oversimplification to say that Navajos tend to steer clear of Anasazi sites because of a superstition about the dead. To Navajos, a place like Keet Seel has sacred significance. What they call the Holy Beings frequent Anasazi sites, which are imbued with a dangerous power. The average Navajo cares deeply about these places and wants them protected—but for different reasons from the Hopis' and different reasons from the archaeologists'."

A reading of Robert S. McPherson's canny *Sacred Land, Sacred View* deepened my understanding of Downer's last point. In Navajo mythology, in the underworld, before creation, the Anasazi lived in harmony with the Navajo. After the Emergence, the Anasazi gave the nomads from the north the inestimable gift of corn. But an estrangement separated the peoples, and the Anasazi went on to displease the Holy Beings. It was for this reason that they were forced to abandon the Colorado Plateau. In the Navajo view, the Anasazi were essentially a people who had gone wrong by transgressing the laws of the gods.

It is true that, on the whole, Navajos avoid Anasazi sites. Having showed John Wetherill the way to Betatakin in 1909, his Navajo guide, Clatsozen Benully, waited in the canyon below the ruin while the Anglos explored it. But the aura of an Anasazi site is more complex than a simple fear of the dead. Some Navajo gods are even believed to reside in Anasazi ruins. Such sites have immense power about them, both for good and for evil. To enter one is, for a Navajo, a grave act, requiring ritual preparation before the act and a purifying ceremony after it.

• • •

AT 10 A.M. on my second day, in a bend of an obscure canyon, I caught my first glimpse of the ruin I was seeking. For a day and a half I had seen no other human being, nor would I see any on my journey back to the road. I scrambled up talus, through thorn bushes, around an overhanging ledge, and found myself at the foot of the ancient village.

It was only a middling ruin, less than a fourth the size of Keet Seel. But to have found it on my own and now to explore it without the aid of rangers or archaeologists turned delight into something deeper. The four hours that I spent at the site passed in a daydream.

Above the village on its right end, the winds had worn a vertical slit clear through the cliff, carving a fifty-foot-high window that would someday become an arch. I might have thought the aperture postdated the abandonment, but an Anasazi toe trail led up to the slit. I fancied that whatever name the ancients had given to this lordly place, it had carried an allusion to the giant needle's eye through which the wind shrilled on stormy afternoons.

Beneath the sandstone wall that backed the mortared rooms, I inched along, dazzled by pictographs: red handprints with mazelike palms, angular white snakes, a herd of bighorn sheep, a grim gray anthropomorph with upraised arms and twin hair knots such as Hopi women wear today. I found a bracelet of linked yucca loops, a mano that perfectly fit my palm, the crisscross crescents of a score of tool-sharpening grooves.

Behind one kiva, the façade of a pair of contiguous granaries bore the finest masonry I had seen in the Kayenta region. Why had this wall been singled out for special care? Five of its stones, bordering the doorways, had been carved with geometric patterns mimicking certain pictographs. In all the Southwest, I had never seen the like.

As I poked through the site, I observed my own code of what Mellberg had called "knowing how to behave." The essence of it was to step lightly and to take or move nothing. Years earlier, on my first jaunts to out-of-the-way ruins, I had pocketed a few pretty potsherds and a couple of arrowheads: rare is the Anasazi archaeologist

1 The pot.

2 The canyon of the pot.

3 The author (left) and Fred Blackburn examine Wetherill inscriptions at Sandal House.

A "hex" pictograph at Jailhouse Ruin in Bullet Canyon.

John Wetherill inscription near Surprise Valley.

6

Keet Seel.

Pictographs in the Tsegi Canyon system.

An Anasazi hand-and-toe trail in Montezuma Creek.

8

A "cubist" bighorn sheep petroglyph, near Bluff.

Intact kiva roof, Cedar Mesa.

Obscure, well-preserved ruin, Cedar Mesa.

Granary with intact door, Cedar Mesa.

Hoodoo, Slickhorn Canyon.

13

14

Moon House.

15

The gloomy, north-facing alcove of a typical Basketmaker II site.

16

Basketmaker cist, mesa top.

17

The great Basketmaker II petroglyph panel at Lower Butler Wash, San Juan River.

18

"Baseball Man," near San Juan River—possibly a Pueblo III "hex" sign superimposed on a Basketmaker anthropomorph.

19

Thirteenth-century potsherds below Organ Rock in the Kayenta Valley.

2

Marie-France Moisi at Desecrated Panel, San Juan River. The petroglyphs were deliberately destroyed in the 1950s by Navajos who were convinced relatives had fallen ill because of the Anasazi rock art.

21

An enigmatic petroglyph on Six-Foot Ruin, looking across at Organ Rock. The two butte tops were Anasazi refuges in the Kayenta Valley after A.D. 1250.

Paiute rock art, by Joseph Lehi, on the Rainbow Bridge trail.

Inside the huge Basketmaker alcove, base camp for the Mystery Canyon trip.

Deep in Mystery Canyon.

Ascending the rope on the first pourover, on the way out of Mystery Canyon.

Grand Gulch from the air.

Big Man Panel in Grand Gulch.

Sharon Roberts leads a pair of llamas in Grand Gulch.

29

Detail of the Great Panel, Grand Gulch.

30

The Basket.

today who will not admit to such foibles in his youth. Later, in Grand Gulch, for the first time I saw a tableau of the kind that is becoming increasingly common in the backcountry: a rock surface covered with sherds that visitors have picked up elsewhere in the site and left on display for future travelers to appreciate.

That first time, I had been beguiled. Now, whenever I saw such a tableau, I felt only vexation. It is not simply the air of smug magnanimity about it, the implicit boast of having found the object and resisted the temptation to take it home. Piling the sherds on a rock destroys their provenience almost as surely as removing them does: robs the future archaeologist, for instance, of the chance to compare styles of pottery to the kinds of rooms they were left in.

Yet my own code allowed me to pick up and examine potsherds before dropping them where I found them. No doubt in the future this practice will be scolded as destructive. The business of prescribing how to visit an Anasazi ruin is a hopeless one, though parks and guidebooks show no reluctance to lay down their codices. What the best archaeologists did in the 1910s and 1920s would shock even the most heavy-footed trespasser today. In those days, everyone walked on walls and fragile roofs. Digging in Tsegi Canyon in 1909, Byron Cummings routinely burned in his campfires the roof beams from which Jeffrey Dean might later have wrung vital data. In 1921 in a canyon east of the Tsegi, that pioneer of careful research, Samuel Guernsey, took a geological hammer to an Anasazi hand-and-toe trail to enlarge the steps so that he could reach a high cave, and felt so little compunction about the act that he blithely included a photograph of his toil in his Peabody Museum paper about the site.

No doubt in some glum future, perhaps not so many years away, authorities will decree that the only responsible way to visit an Anasazi site is not at all. Already such murmurings are on the wind. In December 1994, when three French *spéléologues* found a cave in the Ardèche teeming with 31,000-year-old paintings, the equal of the fabled Lascaux, the Ministry of Culture decided instantly and irrevocably that the Grotte Chauvet would never be opened to the public.

Absorbed in my solitary homage at the obscure ruin far up the

Tsegi, I was awash in a happiness as pure as a traveler can stumble upon. And yet, in the moment of recognizing that happiness, I felt it dim. Perhaps the cloud of Mellberg's doubts drifted across my sun.

Why did it take being alone, I wondered, being free of books and rangers and rules, to deliver me this Anasazi trance? What right had I to have a site like this one to myself? At the worst, could I recognize in my exuberant possessiveness the same crude greed that drove the pothunter, that infantile lust to own something priceless, to clutch it tight and keep it from the others?

In the center of the site stood its finest building, a circular kiva fourteen feet in diameter, its roof not only intact but in perfect condition. It was the best-preserved kiva I had ever seen. Yet even as I knelt beside it, admiring its shafted chimney, the wattle work in the ceiling, the fire pit in the floor, a tremor of outrage crawled up my spine.

Despite the devious scramble to reach the site from the canyon floor, Navajo cows had found a way up. Cow pies lay here and there about the site, and now I saw that several of them had been dropped on the kiva roof. In their bovine stupidity, cows had walked across the kiva and would walk again! It was a miracle the roof had not collapsed. The shock of this discovery seemed to make a mockery of all my maunderings about how to approach fragile sites.

Yet the cloud blocking my sun drifted on. I stood up and surveyed the village, all but lost to human knowledge, and regained my happiness. Not everyone would hike twelve miles to see such a thing, or camp in the cold and dark, assailed by the lunatic hooting of an owl.

The Hopi believe that a pot should never end up in a museum; its proper fate is to go to pieces in the soil. The ache of beauty that had throbbed through my four hours under the needle's eye was all the sharper for the vulnerability of the things I saw. I dropped a last potsherd in the dirt and started the hike out.

5

In Praise of Cedar Mesa

THE same craving that had driven me to Alaska in my twenties in search of unclimbed mountains had sent Richard and John Wetherill hunting all over the Southwest for ruins. To discover a Cliff Palace in the wilderness might be the deed of a lifetime. It was the hope of finding another Cliff Palace in a blank on the map of southern Utah that sent Clyde Kluckhohn and his three young friends to the top of Kaiparowits Plateau in the summer of 1928. As Kluckhohn described it: "that feverish craving for the distant and the unknown . . . the lust for danger and adventure in exploration and discovery."

Though he would become one of America's most distinguished anthropologists, the leading expert of his day on the Navajo, in the mid-1920s Kluckhohn was merely a restless undergraduate at the University of Wisconsin. A summer-long, twenty-five-hundred-mile horseback jaunt all over the Four Corners, culminating in a trip to Rainbow Bridge—no mean feat in those days, when the nearest railroad stop was Flagstaff—only whetted Kluckhohn's appetite. He soon published a high-spirited book about his adventure *(To the Foot of the Rainbow)* and plunged back into the landscape of his craving each summer for the next four years.

On Kluckhohn's first trip, one of John Wetherill's cowpuncher guides laid the bait in an offhand remark, telling the young vagabond about a high, distant mesa he would see to the northwest when he topped a nearby rise. "They say no white man's ever been on it," the cowpuncher averred. "Zane Grey tried to get there this last year, but the river was too high, and he didn't make it."

During the next two summers, the best efforts of Kluckhohn and assorted chums simply to get to the foot of the mesa were thwarted. Their problem was that, approaching from Arizona, they had to cross two great rivers, the San Juan and the Colorado, as well as traverse the roughest country in all the Southwest to reach Wild Horse Mesa, as Grey had dubbed the phantasmal place. (The name "Kaiparowits," in use today, seems to be a Paiute allusion to "One Arm," or John Wesley Powell, who, in leading the first descent of the Colorado River in 1869, glided just east and south of the great plateau.)

Back at Wisconsin, as they lounged in the Union after dinner, two of Kluckhohn's future teammates caught the bug when one of them brought in Neil Judd's recent article in *National Geographic* about his trip through the Clay Hills and down Moqui Canyon. The friend scoffed at Judd's vaunts about "areas which are still practically unknown and unexplored" and "unmapped mesas [that] stretch away mile after barren mile."

"I know the article, and I call it good stuff," Kluckhohn rejoined, like a character out of a dime novel. "Judd, the man who wrote it, and John Wetherill, his guide, are about the only people who know anything at all about that country."

Finally, in July 1928, packing mules and riding horses, guided by a sometimes timorous Navajo, Kluckhohn's team of four succeeded in fording the two rivers, winding through difficult canyons, and climbing thirty-five hundred feet to the top of Wild Horse Mesa. They set up camp and spent two months on the plateau.

It was the discovery of an Anasazi hand-and-toe trail on the ascent that sent visions of new Cliff Palaces dancing through the young men's heads. But it was three days before they found their first potsherd, five before they spotted any pictographs, and seven before they stumbled upon the first rude dwelling. In their prowlings they came upon initials and signatures from Anglo visitors as early as 1918—cowboys, they deduced, chasing cattle from the Utah side. The realization that they were not the first white men to climb the mesa was so dismaying at the time that Kluckhohn admitted that, had they known this beforehand, they might never have launched their expedition.

By the end of their two months' stay, the men had discovered dozens of small ruins, most of them tucked just under the rims of the sprawling mesa. Far from finding a Cliff Palace, however, they had come upon only the most marginal habitations, seldom larger than a room or two each.

As later archaeologists would show, Kaiparowits, whose summit averages seventy-three hundred feet in altitude, lies close to the upper limit of land that can be farmed. The Anasazi occupied it for less than two hundred years, during the Pueblo II and early Pueblo III phases, roughly from A.D. 1000 to 1200. The mesa also stands on the northwestern fringe of the Anasazi domain. In 1964 archaeologist Florence Lister would speculate that only some crisis—population pressure, social upheaval, or drought—had driven a portion of the Kayenta Anasazi to the cold, high plateau. The poor quality of the masonry in the dwellings could be blamed partly on the lumpy, irregular stones that abound on Kaiparowits; but a nearly complete absence of kivas was puzzling. By the twelfth century, Lister imagined, the mesa was home to a band of "third and fourth generation provincials" who had drifted far from the Anasazi mainstream.

Kaiparowits, however, had always been a hunting ground par excellence. Kluckhohn's untrained team recognized as much when they found vast quantities of flint flakes scattered everywhere.

So, in a sense, the great adventure of 1928 was a wild-goose chase. Yet the lyrical book Kluckhohn published in 1933 about Wild Horse Mesa, *Beyond the Rainbow,* makes it clear that those two months of solitude and comradeship atop the remote plateau amounted to an idyll every bit as sweet as Huck Finn found on his raft—"so strange and precious an interlude in ordinary humdrum life," as Kluckhohn wrote. How those four must, the rest of their lives, have gazed back on that summer's escape with the longing of those who have tasted paradise! And how, reading the book sixty years later, one envies them an experience the Southwest can no longer offer—even though in 1928, those young idealists rued that they already lived too late.

Near the end of the book, as he contemplates John Wetherill and Charles Bernheimer's efforts to turn the whole region surrounding the junction of the San Juan and the Colorado into a big national park, Kluckhohn strikes a prescient note:

> It must also be remembered that this is not a cheap scenery; it must be bought with time and sweat. But at Grand Canyon one does get cheap scenery in this sense. One can look down into Grand Canyon without having abandoned a single comfort or luxury. . . .
>
> That is why I wonder if we want to make Wild Horse Mesa into a National Park, after all.

Thank God the park never came to be! Today there are jeep roads up Kaiparowits, but you can still spend weeks on the mesa without seeing anyone else. And the tangled canyons scoring the red rock country where the San Juan joins the Colorado still hold many a secret.

Forty years before Kluckhohn's adventure, what might be called the wildest and most glorious of all wild-goose chases in the Southwest was concocted in the mind of a Norwegian naturalist-explorer on a visit to London. By 1887, Carl Lumholtz, then thirty-six years old, had spent considerable time among the Aborigines of Australia. What had begun as a quest for zoological specimens had led Lumholtz far afield: as he wrote, in the phraseology of his day, "I became so interested in these primitive people that the study of savage and barbaric races has since become my life's work."

Lumholtz had never been to North America, but even by 1887, a year before Cliff Palace was discovered, "the wonderful cliff dwellings in the Southwest of the United States" were common knowledge among European intellectuals of an adventurous bent. There in London, Lumholtz pondered a hypothesis that would drive him to eight years of the most intense exploration. None of the builders of the cliff dwellings could be found living in the United States: they were a "vanished race." But the Spanish in the sixteenth and seventeenth centuries had reported coming upon similar dwellings still inhabited. Perhaps the cliff dwellers had retreated southward and could be found still flourishing in the vast terra incognita of the Sierra Madre of northern Mexico.

From 1890 to 1898, Lumholtz crossed and recrossed this majestic range many times over. He found, of course, not a single living Anasazi. But he made so many other remarkable discoveries that the exploration of the Sierra Madre became the obsession of his life.

For centuries, the high valleys and plateaus of this formidable range had been the secret refuge of the Chiricahua Apache. In 1890, it had been only four years since the final band of "renegades" from that tribe, under the brilliant and hopeless leadership of Geronimo, had made their last stand in the Blue Mountains, as they called the Madre. As he passed through Mexican villages on the fringes of the range, Lumholtz found a populace still terrorized by decades of Apache raiding. The villagers knew nothing of the heart of the range and could not be persuaded to venture into it, for rumors persisted of desperate remnant bands of Chiricahuas still holed up there.

As he wound his way in and out of one remote canyon after another, Lumholtz became closely acquainted with other mountain-dwelling tribes, particularly the Tarahumara, sometime enemies of the Apache. He found many signs left by the Chiricahua and many more tales about these great warriors. And everywhere he went, he found in prodigal abundance the stone walls and potsherds of the ancients. Despite Lumholtz's bravest efforts, the cliff dwellers remained a vanished race; but he showed that they had left their marks all over the Sierra Madre.

Unknown Mexico, Lumholtz's narrative of his epic quest, is one of the true classics of the literature of North American exploration. The book unfolds in 1,075 pages of unhurried, lucid prose (by 1902, Lumholtz wrote well in English) spangled with piquant anecdotes, curious finds, and sage deductions. In the century that has passed since Lumholtz's time, the Sierra Madre has been far less tamed than even the wildest parts of Utah and Arizona. There are still many corners of that rugged fastness that no other *norteameri-*

canos but Lumholtz's party (as opposed to Indians and Mexicans) have ever seen.

The ruined villages, the hundreds of *trincheras,* or stone check dams blocking rivulets, the austere cave dwellings that Lumholtz found all over the Sierra Madre were not, we know now, the work of the Anasazi. In the 1890s, with scholars still ignorant of the chronology of prehistory, all builders of ancient houses made of flat stones and mud, from central Utah south into northern Mexico, were lumped together as cliff dwellers. Indeed, the simple fallacy that ruined Lumholtz's inspired hypothesis was his failure to realize that the stone-village dwellers of the Spanish accounts were today's Pueblo people. This is strange, for on his way to Mexico in 1890, he visited both Hopi and Zuni, two of the Pueblo tribes. By that date, such scholars as Jesse Walter Fewkes and Frank Cushing already knew that the descendants of the Anasazi lived in the Pueblos, not in the Sierra Madre. But an idée fixe is a powerful thing.

Today's archaeologists distinguish between the Anasazi proper, whose southern frontier is a line drawn roughly between Flagstaff and a point fifty miles south of Albuquerque, and such neighboring, contemporary, and superficially kindred peoples as the Hohokam (south-central Arizona) and the Mogollon (southern New Mexico, southeastern Arizona, extending well into the Sierra Madre of Mexico). This is no taxonomy gone mad: fundamental cultural distinctions separate these ancients. The Hohokam, for instance, cremated their dead and built extensive irrigation canals; the Anasazi buried their dead and made no canals.

Most scholars would call the ruins Lumholtz found Mogollon, but what precisely that means is anybody's guess. Even today, very little excavation has ever been done in the Sierra Madre: the logistics of working in the range are fiendish, and Mexican archaeology has always focused on the more spectacular civilizations far to the south. One great ruin, Paquimé, near the town of Casas Grandes in western Chihuahua, has given the name "Casas Grandes Culture" to a whole Sierra Madre manifestation of the Mogollon. But we still know precious little about these people. Some tantalizing recent research suggests that a huge area stretching from Phoenix to Casas

Grandes underwent an abandonment of its own around 1450, as massive as the one that swept the Colorado Plateau in 1300. Here lies the life's work of a future generation of scholars.

In November 1989, photographer Terry Moore and I made a journey into the Sierra Madre. Our goal was not ancient ruins, but traces of the Chiricahua. In particular, armed with an old map, I hoped to find the obscure mesa on top of which General George Crook's troops had attacked Geronimo's band in 1883, turning the tide of the Apache resistance. I doubted that any Anglos had been there since Crook's men departed.

At the time, Terry lived in Sonora. He was working on a book about Baja California and he knew parts of the Sierra Madre, but he had never been into the Apache heartland. For five days we drove Terry's Isuzu Trooper south from the border on dirt roads that got worse and worse as we probed into country very few gringos had ever seen. We passed through the same series of small towns that Lumholtz had visited: San Miguel, Bavispe, Bacerac, Huachinera, Bacadehuachi, Nacori Chico. I had *Unknown Mexico* with me; the towns had changed so little that Lumholtz made an excellent guide. In Bacerac, where we spent the night, the locals rode horses through the streets rather than pickups, and we watched a family make adobe bricks from the mud in their backyard.

Tall, lean, and taciturn, Terry is a cross between an aging hippie and a Viking, with wire-rim glasses, wavy gold locks, and a great red beard tinged with gray. He had mastered a drawling colloquial Spanish (I spoke none) that never failed to charm and surprise the villagers he tried it out on. Everyone stared at us, for few tourists had ever landed in Huachinera.

A self-taught naturalist, Terry would narrate our crawling progress: "Did you see that acorn woodpecker?" "Look, *palo santo.*" "Hey, we're getting into blue palms." If we found a solitary calf by the side of the road, Terry would stop the truck, roll down the window, and address the startled bovine: "What are you doing out here, all by your lonesome?" Kids in the towns would grin and giggle as he saluted them with a hearty *"¡Hola!"*

From Nacori Chico we turned east and plunged into the high

sierra. The only road had been built for logging: it amounted to a gauntlet of ruts, holes, creek fords, and gouging bedrock. For a day and a half we drove almost as slowly as we could have walked. Fussy about his truck, Terry coaxed it over the worst bumps by uttering prolonged, theatrical groans. Even so, we ruined one tire and shortened the lifetimes of the others.

The ordeal of driving failed to numb me to the landscape, which was more beautiful than I had guessed. Though its summits seldom rise more than nine thousand feet above sea level, the Madre unfolds as a maze of jagged crests and gloomy ravines: sometimes we had to climb and lose four thousand feet between hills only a few miles apart. The cactus and mesquite of the poor frontier towns gave way in the mountains to pines and oaks.

As we drove, we began to see what Lumholtz called *trincheras:* every other dry rill was crossed perpendicularly by an ancient stone wall that had once trapped water. Gaining height, we wended our way through a latticework of towering ponderosa pines. Finally we came to the edge of a great plateau, called Mesa Tres Rios, and saw far below us the bends of the blue Bavispe River as it swept among sycamores. With mounting excitement I spotted in the distance the small, steep butte that I suspected was the site of Crook's attack.

We camped that night in a serene grove beside the Bavispe. In the morning, we climbed a grassy hillside dotted with oaks, junipers, and giant agaves. Just below the summit, we scrambled over broken cliffs.

I had prepared myself to look for the fugitive signs of the nomadic Apache: at best, a pile of stones used as a breastwork or lookout post. Instead, a startling sight greeted us the moment we pulled on top.

Stretching before us were the stone walls of a large prehistoric pueblo. During the next hours, as Terry and I walked through the ruin, I measured its size as eighty-five by sixty-five yards. At the time, I was only a dabbler in Anasazi matters: a few years later, I could have calculated that two hundred to three hundred rooms would be a conservative estimate of the pueblo's extent. The walls had been built without mortar, stones shaped and fitted in place.

Scattered across grassy acres of ground, thousands of potsherds gleamed in the sun. There were many different styles, ranging from dull-gray-and-buff to orange to black-striped to corrugated; a particularly pretty type of cream-colored sherd was scored with crisscross incised grooves. We found two polished manos made of a porous black volcanic rock and two broken metates of the same stuff.

Gradually the shape of the vast ruin revealed itself. Today I might be able to compare the masonry and ceramics with those of certain Mogollon sites I had seen in New Mexico. In my relative ignorance in 1989, all I knew was that I had never stumbled upon a prehistoric site one-tenth as grand as this one.

Though the previous night the temperature had dropped below freezing, now a warm sun baked our shoulders as we strolled across the mesa, lost in a trance of detail. Far below, from the Bavispe, came the yipping of coyotes, unusual at midday. Later we startled a pack of javelinas lounging in the shade: they took off snorting and squealing as they careened down the hillside.

At dusk that evening, a few miles from the mesa, we met an old rancher named Augustin Fimbres Vargas. Using his serviceable Spanish, Terry told him about the ruin on the mesa top. Though Fimbres Vargas had spent much of his life on the Bavispe, he had never climbed our mesa. But he was not surprised at our discovery. He pointed to three other mesa tops in the distance, nodded, and said, "Montezuma."

After a long search, Terry and I had also found, farther west on the mesa, a four-foot-high cairn that looked like the kind of Apache breastwork we had been searching for. From the lichen growth on the stones, we could see that the cairn was old, but not as old as the ruins. In the 1880s, no Mexicans had lurked around the upper Bavispe: the only inhabitants were the Chiricahua.

By the end of our jaunt into the Sierra Madre, I could convince myself—though hardly prove to a skeptical scholar—that I had located the battle site where Crook had surprised the Chiricahua. But what haunts my memory six years later is that Mogollon ruin and the certainty that all through the trackless Sierra Madre stand the enigmatic works of those ancients whom Lumholtz had, in a sense, discovered, but who, a century later, glide on like formless clouds through the blank sky of our archaeological ignorance. I want to go back.

BUT it's a long haul to the heart of the Sierra Madre. Over the years, in Utah, Arizona, and New Mexico, on trips as short as five days, I had been able again and again to wander off the beaten track into the landscape of the Old Ones, where, camped in some little-known canyon, I could tease myself once more with the patchwork puzzle the Anasazi had left behind.

Gradually I realized that my affinities had centered on a favorite place. That was Cedar Mesa, in southeastern Utah. By 1995, I had made fourteen separate excursions into its labyrinth.

Cedar Mesa forms an oblong of tableland roughly thirty miles square; it is bordered on the north by State Highways 95 and 276, on the east by the hunchbacked geological thrust called the Comb Ridge, on the south by the San Juan River. The mesa is bisected by a single paved road, Route 261, which follows the gently arched divide that separates the eastward-flowing streams from the southwestward. Slashing diagonally across the heart of Cedar Mesa is Grand Gulch, which twists and turns so sinuously through its course that it covers fifty-six miles between its headwaters, at sixty-eight hundred feet on Grand Flat, and the gorge where it empties into the San Juan, at thirty-seven hundred feet.

Grand Gulch is by far the best known of Cedar Mesa's attractions: despite its growing popularity, it is still probably the best place in all the Southwest to see unrestored Anasazi ruins in something like their pristine state. Yet the mesa hides another seven canyons, none quite so long or beautiful as Grand Gulch, but each worth an extended visit: Slickhorn, Johns, Lime, Road, McLoyd, Owl, and Fish.

Twenty years ago, even Grand Gulch remained something of a secret among Anasazi devotees. By now, the Bureau of Land Management, which supervises the canyons, estimates that fifty thousand visitors a year come to Cedar Mesa; of those, well more than half head for Grand Gulch. Uneasy with such impact, the BLM envisions limiting the number of visitors per year, as the Park Service does at Navajo National Monument, perhaps with a reservation system. At the moment, the whole mesa teeters on the edge of bureaucratic regulation.

And yet, on my fourteen outings, I managed always to bask in solitude and to see things that few others had seen. A rhapsodic impulse tempts me to expound on the quirks and pleasures of each of the canyons. But the memory of two single days in late autumn of 1993, two days as charmed as any I have spent in the wilderness, distills the savor of Cedar Mesa.

The first came during the solo journey recounted in the Prologue of this book, when I found the intact pot perched in its niche on the dead-end ledge. That moment of astonishment could hardly be duplicated in a single trip; months afterward, the shock of the find still prickled in my nerve endings. But the day before the day I discovered the pot had been almost its equal.

I had camped five miles in, choosing my tent site on the shelf eighty feet above the canyon floor by compass, to maximize the hours of sunlight during the short days at the end of October. I woke at six-thirty, with Venus bright in the eastern sky, a rim of pale blue light repealing the night. As I cooked breakfast, the sun, still below the horizon, painted the bands of cloud overhead a vivid salmon. The sun did not rise until seven-forty, when it appeared exactly in the *V* notch to the east-southeast, the only place where the skyline dipped close to the horizon.

The day before, on my way in, I had caught myself now and then as brief jolts of apprehension surged through me—nothing rational, just existential blips of fear that asked, "What are you doing here?" In the first hour I had come across the decomposing carcass of a small coyote, curled in the dead leaves, its skull stretched in a grinning rictus.

It had been too long since I had hiked and camped alone. Indeed, like everyone who lapses into a workaday urban life, I had gotten out of practice at being alone.

On my way to Cedar Mesa, I had stopped in Cortez to visit Fred

Blackburn, the friend who had guided me through Wetherill country the spring before. Of all the canyons on the mesa, the one I was headed for was the only one Blackburn would never visit. "That place is bad juju," he said solemnly. Not only were the Anasazi sites hard to get to, Blackburn went on, but the canyon had a certain danger built into it. Years before, a friend of Blackburn's had hiked in the canyon with his wife. Descending a steep hillside, he had dislodged a boulder that rolled on top of him, pinning his leg. The wife had gone for help. The man was rescued, but his leg had to be amputated.

As I loaded my day pack, I heard the thrumming trill of a hummingbird's wings nearby. I scrambled down the eighty feet to the canyon floor, into the cold shadows, where I filled my water bottle from a pothole glazed with a skin of ice. Looking back, I saw again how invisible my camp was: from nowhere on the canyon floor could a passerby see my tent. The afternoon before, with the vague fears flickering in my brain, with the story of Blackburn's friend like a stone in my pack, I had considered hanging a bright-colored stuff sack from a bush beside the canyon floor: a signal, just in case something went wrong, for the searchers who might eventually come looking for my camp. But I decided not to: that kind of fussy precaution had its own bad juju.

My goal for the day was to hike downcanyon, circle up a side fork that entered on the right, and with luck, find a way to loop back to camp. Half a mile down, I hit a pourover—the lip overhanging forty feet of space, preventing further descent. The pourover forced me onto a ledge on the canyon's right wall. It was a typical Cedar Mesa configuration, and the ledge was always a gamble: in other canyons, I had threaded my way forward for as long as a mile, only to have the ledge blank out, dictating retreat.

But this time, the ledge "went." Soon I came to the side fork. I turned and headed up its smaller canyon, and emerged suddenly in the sun for the first time since it had dawned on my campsite. At once the chill and gloom dispersed; I took off my jacket and treated myself to a candy bar.

As I hiked on up the side fork, I found three or four gray-and-white potsherds in the dirt, giving me hopes of finding an Anasazi site. The wall on my right towered six hundred feet, a vertical precipice seamed with ledges. Dividing the side fork from the main canyon, the wall made a kind of peninsula jutting east into the ocean of canyon space. With morning light raking sideways across it, every detail stood out; but I saw nothing on the ledges that looked Anasazi.

I climbed farther as the side canyon squeezed into a bowl. Once more I let my gaze sweep up the peninsular wall. I froze and said involuntarily, "Oh, my God!"—the first words I had spoken out loud all day.

I had been looking too low. The Anasazi site lay at the very summit of the peninsula, six hundred feet above me. My binoculars confirmed the glimpse: five or six beautifully masoned rooms, tucked under a caprock dome. But how to get there?

For two hours I squandered effort, working out clever traverses among the ledges at the side fork's head. Each time I ran into blank, unclimbable cliff. Impatience made my movements ragged: I was panting and covered with sweat. *This is stupid,* I said to myself. *Think of it as the Anasazi would have.*

That was what it took. Cursing my wasted effort, I descended two hundred feet to the floor of the side canyon, back all the way to the place from which I had first spotted Peninsula House, as I had begun calling the lofty ruin. Then I trudged up the brushy north-facing slope opposite the peninsular wall. Thistles scratched my arms, and big stones rolled underfoot. *Be careful,* I scolded, slowing myself down; *this would be a hell of a place to sprain an ankle or . . .*

I climbed all the way to the canyon rim. Just below the top I came to a deep, low alcove filled with soft dirt. Far inside, in the dim recesses where the rear wall arced low to the ground, I found the vertical slab cists of a Basketmaker II storage site. Tiny pieces of charcoal littered the cists. Sometimes the ancients had also built their pithouses in these low caves, and often they buried their dead in them.

It was a choice I had always found unfathomable. These Basketmaker II caves almost always faced north. Within them, the denizens had often chosen the most cramped inner crannies, places where you had to stoop or even crawl beneath the low ceiling, to carry out their affairs. It was as if, in those hunting-and-gathering days around A.D. 200, with corn still an uncertain gamble, the Anasazi had been troglodytes, a people who shunned the sunlight and the fresh air as they huddled around their smoky fires, hiding their goods and their dead in the gloomiest places they could find.

From the rim, I studied Peninsula House once more with binoculars. It stood at equal height, directly opposite me, less than half a mile away. And now I saw what I had to do to reach it.

I rim-walked for a mile, circling completely around the head of the side canyon. At last the mesa top narrowed toward the peninsula itself. As I got closer, the setting looked more and more spectacular. A curving gangplank of sandstone, with six-hundred-foot cliffs on either side, snaked out toward a pedestal in space. It was tricky to find the right approach, but by 1 P.M. I was walking the gangplank.

Two low rubble walls ran across the fin of stone where it was narrowest: barriers against the uninvited. The dwellings stood at the very end of the peninsula, facing south, just under the bizarre lid of a capstone. It took another scramble to climb up to them.

From a distance, I had recognized Peninsula House as a Pueblo III site. The six rooms—five contiguous, one detached—were larger than usual and superbly built, the masonry trimmed flush and chinked with tiny stone spalls. None of the rooms needed a roof, for the ceiling of the capstone closed them off at a convenient six feet high. Inside several rooms, small sticks protruded from the walls like coat pegs; another had a cunning nook built in like a double shelf.

I had found other dwellings on Cedar Mesa that were the equal of these in craftsmanship, but I had never seen a setting to match that of Peninsula House. A short walk along its ledge led me in a circle around the capstone. In back, a chimney gave access to the top, where I found a mortarless wall built like a fence to hide behind, facing the gangway approach.

The builders had commanded a 360-degree view. And what a view! From the top of the capstone I could look west up the main canyon, southwest up the side fork, or east all the way down to the Comb Ridge. Far to the north I saw the twin buttes called the Bears

Ears, and beyond them, the Abajo Mountains dusted with new snow. Even farther, in the east, I gazed at the high summits of the La Plata Mountains, way off in Colorado.

There are those who argue that Pueblo III sites such as Peninsula House are not necessarily defensive. The walls across the gangway some would see as ceremonial portals. The inaccessibility of the rooms themselves, some argue, has more to do with maximizing crop yield on every square foot of alluvial mesa top (and so building in barren caves and under overhangs) than with a perceived threat.

But at the moment, I could give such theories no credence. If ever a site seemed guarded against the enemy, Peninsula House did. Its sentries had a bold command of every possible approach: not even in the depths of the canyons could warriors have slunk toward the village unseen. The walls across the gangway could have thwarted attack, and the scramble up to the rooms themselves would have been hard to perform with arrows or stones raining down from above.

No doubt, to the ancients, the aesthetic impulse had been utterly subordinate to the pragmatic. They built Peninsula House to be safe, not to look good. But if constant fear had ruled their lives, that fear had nonetheless given birth to beauty. Those six humble rooms, where perhaps no more than fifteen people had taken refuge in the thirteenth century, made up the most lordly Anasazi site I had seen on Cedar Mesa.

That evening back in camp, after dinner, I sat before my fire of juniper sticks and pondered the wonderful day. My edgy apprehension had all but vanished, although the intensity of being alone had not waned. Twice during the day I had been startled. First, as I sat in camp just after sunrise, loading my pack: from behind the cliff above me, thirty feet up, a squadron of tiny swifts had burst with an all but supersonic whoosh. Second, in late afternoon, just before dinner: I had clambered down to the canyon floor to fill my pot with water, and as I hiked back up, I saw in a flash of panic that a stranger stood beside my tent. But it was only my jacket, hung on a juniper bough to air out.

Now, feeling warm and safe, I tried to think why being by myself when I found Peninsula House had made the day deeper than if I had shared it with someone else. To be alone in the wilderness can induce a kind of inanity: a phrase from a banal song (in my case, usually a Christmas carol or a pop tune I haven't heard in forty years) runs through your head like a stuck record. Performing camp chores, you become as fussy and fretful as a neurotic housewife. (I had read some of the literature of solo sailors who had circumnavigated the globe. Their finicky-cabin keeping had clearly helped ward off the terror of the void.)

But silence works a spell that reopens the world. All day I had heard every caw of a raven, every trickle of water in the streambed. I had blocked nothing out. Even my camera had come to seem irrelevant: it was the pattern of stone spalls in the façade of Peninsula House under the glancing sun that proved I was alive. If silence is crucial to communion, as mystics believe, then I had come closer to the ancients than I otherwise could, in those moments at Peninsula House when I managed to stop thinking and just look, listen, and touch. Words would have stood in the way.

ALTHOUGH Grand Gulch had been vigorously dug in the 1890s—not only by Richard Wetherill, but even before him by two Durango ranchers, C. C. Graham and Charles McLoyd—Cedar Mesa would not receive serious archaeological study until 1967, when Bill Lipe launched the first of nine field seasons there. Lipe's teams narrowed their focus down to six quadrats, sampling areas defined to include the full range of Cedar Mesa landscape. The teams did not excavate or even gather artifacts, but surveyed for sites as thoroughly as possible. Against the fruits of those surveys, they rigorously tested a set of a priori hypotheses.

Here was modern field technique at its best, and Lipe's work on Cedar Mesa remains a model of careful research. Looking back in 1995, what seems particularly admirable about the survey was how much information Lipe's teams wrung from the sites without in any way disturbing them.

Yet, in another sense, Lipe's work was old-fashioned. He believed (and still believes) that it takes extensive fieldwork to develop a feel for the people and for the environmental challenges they faced. In an era when it was all too common among professional archaeologists to sneer at Richard Wetherill, Lipe saluted his predecessor. Lipe is that rarity today, an archaeologist who writes well. In a delightful 1980 essay titled "Grand Gulch: Three Days on the Road from Bluff," he claimed that

> Wetherill's Grand Gulch work had a substantial influence on the development of Southwestern archaeology. . . . Also apparent is his empathy with the Anasazi. Not only had he spent years probing their buried secrets, but he, too, had lived most of his days directly on the land. He, too, knew how it felt to see his crops wither and fail, or to slip on a high ledge and catch himself just in time. He had what we would now call a "feel" for the pattern of Anasazi life.

The results of the nine-year survey provided some real surprises. Although it is the cliff dwellings that draw those fifty thousand visitors a year to Cedar Mesa and had drawn Wetherill and others, Lipe found that sites built within canyon alcoves made up a much smaller percentage of the total than anyone had suspected. Far more important in the scheme of things were the hundreds of mesa-top dwellings and storage sites that the teams discovered. (Even today, only the trained eye will detect most of these.)

Even more surprising was a consistent pattern stretching from A.D. 200 to 1300 of successive occupations and abandonments of the whole Cedar Mesa area. Lipe's teams found absolutely no sign of Archaic Anasazi—not a single artifact from before about A.D. 200. Then, for two hundred years, the mesa was covered with inhabitants. Around 400, the people abruptly left and stayed away for more than 250 years. In the late seventh century, the Anasazi came back, but only for a brief span. The mesa was abandoned again from A.D. 750 to almost 1100—a hiatus lasting three and a half centuries. The final phase, from which the cliff dwellings date, covered the two centuries from 1100 to 1300. With the wholesale abandonment of the Colorado Plateau in 1300, Cedar Mesa was depopulated. Except for the rare hunter far from his home, none of the Anasazi or their Puebloan descendants ever returned.

The causes of these fluxions remain a mystery. There is a facile temptation to link them to environmental changes; but so far the paleoclimatological data for the Southwest do not show the vivid swings that might account for—as Lipe and R. G. Matson subtitled a professional paper about Cedar Mesa—such a pattern of "Boom and Bust on the Northern Periphery."

In the two decades since the Cedar Mesa work, however, the pattern of advance and retreat, of mini-abandonments, seems to crop up all over the Anasazi world during all periods. In a real sense, no matter how successful their harvests of corn, squash, and beans, the Anasazi never became truly sedentary. Hunting and gathering remained a central stratagem for them, and migration was in their blood.

In 1994, Rick Bell, then director of public affairs at the Crow Canyon Archaeological Center in Cortez, told me about the visit of a professor of architecture from Pennsylvania. Bell took the man, who was in his sixties, to Sand Canyon, where a ten-year dig at a major Pueblo III site was nearing completion. It was the professor's first encounter with the Anasazi, and he was dumbfounded. "This turns around everything I believed," he told Bell. "I've never before seen a place where people built in stone and then just left."

During his summers on Cedar Mesa, Lipe pondered, in something like the fashion I would later ponder, the question of how best to apprehend the Anasazi. Already, by the 1970s, a new breed of hypertheoretical grad student was appearing who would rather work on paper than in the field. (Last year a Santa Fe contract archaeologist told me about a moment that occurred as she drove her team of school-fresh researchers to a site. One young woman blurted out in shock, "You mean we're going to have to camp out?")

And in the 1970s, despite Grand Gulch's obscurity, Lipe was beginning to see signs of casual pothunting. "Tent camps," he wrote in "Grand Gulch: Three Days on the Road from Bluff," "are part of the 'romance' of Southwestern archaeology.

At its worst, however, the romance of the Southwest bears the seeds of its own destruction. It so often finds expression in no more than shallow curiosity, in a destructive rummaging through the sites in search of some treasure, some tangible relic of the past that can adorn a coffee table, or worse, be discarded after a few days or weeks as would another plastic novelty. And even those who come with respect will be frustrated if too many come at once. The sites are fragile, but even more so are the understandings that are sought. For these, there must be time, and quiet—not crowds, or lectures, or guided tours.

During those nine years on Cedar Mesa, Lipe was often struck by the beauty of certain ruins in the canyons, but even more by the weirdness of many of them. Last year I met Lipe at Crow Canyon, where he still leads fieldwork during his furloughs from a teaching post at Washington State University. We talked about Cedar Mesa. He cited a unique structure on a high ledge in Slickhorn Canyon, which I would visit a few months hence. Lipe had nicknamed the site "Wooden Kiva," for the structure, the likes of which he had seen nowhere else in forty years of canvassing the Southwest, was a true kiva whose walls were made not of the usual mortared sandstone, not even of daub and wattlework, but of deadwood logs bashed into shape, stood on end, and mortared together.

"On Cedar Mesa," Lipe said, "the Anasazi were really going their own way. These people were escaping the confines of normative thought."

IN the year 1250, perhaps several thousand Anasazi men, women, and children lived on Cedar Mesa. Every canyon echoed to their cries; every upland flat was crisscrossed with their trails.

In the mid-1990s, the year-round population of Cedar Mesa is zero. The Kane Gulch ranger station, monitoring post for the Bureau of Land Management, has a staff of two; but during the winter off season (from late October to April) the station is closed. One family works a ranch on a small plot of private land out on Snow Flat, but they, too, depart for the winter.

Ten days after my visit to Peninsula House, I returned to the neighboring canyon. My companion was a French friend, Marie-France Moisi, who had worked for five years for a travel company based in Cambridge, Massachusetts. On her first tour with the company, she had discovered and fallen in love with the Southwest.

Ever since the days of Lumholtz and Nordenskiöld, Europeans have taken a keen interest in the Southwest. Today, that passion, particularly among the French and Germans, verges on a cult. In rarefied magazine articles, the Navajo and the Anasazi are mystified as shamans and visionaries of the desert. The canyonlands gleam with the exotic allure of some impossibly remote Third World Elysium.

A few years ago, I hiked several crowded trails in Arches National Park, near Moab, Utah. Inevitably, the first mile was all jabbering Americans, with toddlers slung in kiddie packs and dogs frisking underfoot. By three miles out, the children and pets were gone, and European tongues claimed half the air. Five miles out, it was all Germans, who had the rapt stare of pilgrims.

A friend of mine was recently browsing in a gift shop at Canyon de Chelly when a French bus tour arrived. One woman bought a poster and tried to ask the Navajo salesclerk for a tube to carry it in. Linguistic confusion ensued. To demonstrate what would happen to her tubeless poster, the Frenchwoman pounded on the counter. Whereupon the tour leader pounced. *"Madame,"* he thundered at the woman, *"vous n'êtes pas dans le Bazar de l'Hôtel de Ville! Vous êtes parmi les Navajos sauvages d'Arizona!"* ("Madame, you are not in the Hôtel de Ville department store! You are among the wild Navajos of Arizona!")

It was November 9, almost too late for Anasazi country. We car-camped on a shelf of bedrock sloping south. In the early darkness we could see the lights of Bluff, tiny stars in the distance, twenty-five miles away. The sunset had washed the west with crimson ("sailor's delight"), and the wind was still. But the temperature plunged to around fifteen degrees Fahrenheit. Marie-France took a rock heated in the campfire, wrapped it in a sack, and stuffed it inside her sleeping bag.

There are some otherwise sensitive souls who remain unmoved by Anasazi ruins. Curiously, Edward Abbey, whose writings more than those of any other author in the last thirty years helped create the mystique of the desert Southwest, never showed much interest in the ruins, and his books reveal only a shallow grasp of Anasazi facts. According to Neil Judd, Teddy Roosevelt, whom John Wetherill guided to Rainbow Bridge in 1913 (only four years after Wetherill made the Anglo discovery of the arch), cared not at all for ruins: as he told his guide, he "lived for the present and the future."

Marie-France, however, had become a devotee. Though she had returned to Paris in 1988 to pursue another career, the Southwest was probably her favorite place on earth, and when she ventured back to the United States, it was to head for the Anasazi canyons. Nor could she abide the mystical glaze with which French travel companies and TV documentaries painted the works of the ancients. It was the specifics of a single potsherd, a single petroglyph, that captured her.

We were off early, navigating by compass to the rim of perhaps the most obscure of all Cedar Mesa's canyons. The sun worked its magic: despite the bitter cold to which we had awakened, by 9 A.M. we stretched in the warmth, feeling the frozen ground thaw to mud under our boots. A tributary ravine led us gently into the canyon. At once, we came upon a row of three rooms and two granaries squashed under a severe boulder. It was the first of seven prehistoric sites we would come upon before dusk—the richest single day I had ever spent in Anasazi country.

The tight, twisting canyon was not easy to descend. Several pourovers forced us onto ledges, and twice we wound our way into cul-de-sacs before retreating and finding the line. As always on Cedar Mesa, as the canyon deepened, it progressed from an intimate to a formal scale: the walls soared steeper and more impossible, and wild hoodoos, bulbous towers and knobs of wind-worn stone, festooned the canyon rims and the tops of isolated pinnacles.

The first six sites, each small, possessed a remarkable variety. Torn between lingering and pushing on, we dwelt on a collapsed kiva here, with intact benches and pilasters, a frieze of Basketmaker pictographs there, guarding a trio of hidden cists. In one of the darkest corners of the canyon floor, just beneath an impassable pourover, we entered a complex Basketmaker II site even gloomier than the one I had found opposite Peninsula House—cists, sharpening grooves, faint triangle-bodied anthropomorphs in red. The north-facing cave hung only twenty feet above the streambed: it was hard to fathom how for fifteen hundred years not one flash flood had risen high enough to scour it clean.

Marie-France's way of appreciating a site was different from mine. I tried to seize the thing whole, analyzing its layout, guessing at room walls, using the smears of campfire smoke to deduce the sequence of building. Mine was at base an intellectual approach. For her, however, the process was tactile and dreamy. She combed the slope below a ruin, bent at the waist, picking up one potsherd after another. "I could do this for hours," she said. "I could pay you to do this." Or she sat before a pictograph panel, patiently sketching it into her notebook instead of guessing what each figure represented.

Around 2 P.M., as we pushed downcanyon, we were forced up on the north wall almost to the rim. I found a devious route that wound through and under giant hoodoos, poised like the pendulous omens of some delirious nightmare. We turned a corner and glimpsed, a hundred feet below us, our seventh site, ensconced in a deep ledge facing southeast.

Another winding scramble brought us down to the site. Its main feature seemed to be a long, windowless façade, punctuated with small peepholes; it stood eight feet high and stretched across some eighty feet of ledge. The ledge itself stood on the "second story." Marie-France climbed the toeholds that led to the small door at the right end of the façade, its only portal. She stuck her head inside, then pivoted and said quietly, "David, you're not going to believe this."

In turn, I poked my head through the low doorway. I had assumed the façade was the front wall of a series of linked rooms—

windowless, as a number of such Cedar Mesa walls seemed to be, for defensive reasons. Now I saw that it was indeed a true façade, a wall that screened the dwellings behind it. A kind of alley, three feet wide, ran the length of the ledge. On the left stood the inner wall of the guardian façade; on the right, eight or ten rooms ranged in a complex configuration back into the ample cavern. Thanks to the façade, the preservation of these inner rooms was immaculate. Along the top of the outer walls of the rooms ran a bold four-inch stripe painted a gleaming white; a string of white dots, like grace notes, paralleled the stripe, just above it, and pairs of dangling triangles, like daggers, hung at regular intervals from the stripe.

Above the tops of the rooms, the natural wall and ceiling of the alcove were painted with equally lucid designs. One band of white mimicked the room-front motif; another looked like a brilliant polychrome zigzag snake. Inside the finest room, the dot-stripe-dagger motif ran the course of the four inner walls, just two feet off the ground, below perfect sitting benches.

I had never seen anything like this ruin, but I recognized in a flash that I had seen photos of it somewhere in a museum display. This was the storied Moon House! I had overheard the cognoscenti in Durango and Moab whispering about the place, but no one seemed willing to tell me how to find it. Marie-France and I had stumbled upon it by accident.

Later, around a bend to the right, I found another set of dwellings a hundred yards away. The front wall of one of the rooms had the same dot-stripe-dagger motif, executed not in paint but in carefully chosen white stone spalls trimmed and laid in a mosaic within the brown mortar. Moon House seemed to resonate with meaning—if only we could read the code. I was reminded of early Spanish accounts of kivas decorated with vivid paintings on the outside as well as inside. None of those painted walls survived into the twentieth century. Moon House was the closest thing to them that I was ever likely to see.

I peered through the peepholes (if such they be: archaeologists do not agree on their function). Each seemed to align with a critical spot on the approach to Moon House from below. To my mind, here again, it was fear that had dictated the architecture, necessitating the outer wall that had, as if by chance, so perfectly preserved the inner sanctum. Though not the grandest, Moon House was perhaps the most striking Anasazi ruin I had ever seen.

Just inside the doorway, BLM rangers, who monitor the site, had left a tin can holding a few sheets of paper that served as an informal register. The entries were spaced weeks apart. Each one strove clumsily to express its own sense of wonder. One fellow had written, "So much for the notion of los Indios as savages."

Later I learned that just a few years before, Robert Lister, one of the grand old men of Anasazi archaeology, then well into his eighties, had died of a heart attack at Moon House. Was there a better place to end one's days?

The sun was low in the west. With the sharpest regret, we turned to climb the opposite slope out of the canyon. It would be dark before we regained camp.

Frost's wistful words ran through my head: "Yet knowing how way leads on to way, / I doubted if I should ever come back." But of course, I promised myself fiercely, I would come back!

From the far rim we turned for a last look at Moon House. The slanting sun caught only a corner of the eighty-foot façade. Above the site, the hoodoos loomed, ambiguously guarding and threatening the ruin. The sense of lost significance pulsed in the air, but when I strained my ears to listen, I heard only wind softly tossing the junipers.

6

The Trail to Awatovi

ONE day in Grand Gulch in October 1994, I sat on a natural bench at the mouth of the tributary canyon. At my back, stretching across many yards of smooth sandstone wall, ranged the Quail Panel, one of the finest displays of pictographs on Cedar Mesa. The paintings date from the Basketmaker II era, probably between A.D. 200 and 400. The panel is named for a striking white bird, drawn in profile, with one glaring, round eye painted red-and-green. The complex panorama also includes anthropomorphs with crescent heads, two green humanoids (green being one of the rarest colors of Anasazi art), two yellow anthropomorphs with red bird heads, three jumping stick-figure humans in profile, and a fierce red visage with teeth bared that looks like a mountain lion—or a mask of a mountain lion.

As I studied the panel, I was reminded of a remark I'd heard over coffee a few months earlier. At Crow Canyon, archaeologist Steve Lekson, speaking of Anasazi rock art in general, had said, "It makes up an amazing set of data. But we'll never decode it."

At the moment, however, with my back to the panel, I was peering through my binoculars at quite another ancient work. The four-hundred-foot cliff that formed the opposite wall of the side canyon was dead vertical. Two hundred fifty feet up it, where an alcove swelled into a gaping mouth in the cliff, I could see the upper reaches of sturdy masoned walls. The oddest feature about the site was a pair of vertical wooden poles wedged in place, stretching from the floor of the alcove to the ceiling.

There was no way to climb to the habitation site. And 150 feet of precipice loomed above it, equally steep. I could imagine that it might just be possible to throw a rope from a sloping ramp near the canyon rim to a narrow ledge fifty feet left of the alcove, then rappel down the rope and traverse into the site. I wondered whether any Anglos had visited the perilous dwellings. And I wondered how the Anasazi had gotten there.

Pieces of cord, woven from yucca fiber, dog hair, and even human hair, have been found in the Anasazi sites, but they are generally too flimsy and too short to serve as ropes. The cordage was more commonly used to make snares and nets. It does not seem likely, in fact, that ropes were a crucial piece of gear for the ancient climbers. From the mute testimony of their least accessible sites, one suspects that Anasazi technique amounted to some virtuosic combination of traversing on ledges, using poles as ladders to get from one ledge to another, and carving hand-and-toe trails in otherwise featureless walls. As far as I know, no twentieth-century visitor has ever found an Anasazi rope tied in place in the fashion that a modern climber might use to reach a difficult site. (The fearless Wetherills used their hemp lariats to enter cliff dwellings, sometimes lowering one brother off an overhang to a point in midair from which he could swing into the site. And subsequent visitors have occasionally found the Wetherill ropes in place.)

Staring through my binoculars, I itched to try the approach—although just that year the BLM had prohibited the use of climbing gear to reach sites in Grand Gulch. The next day, as I hiked up the side canyon, for miles I saw no way to climb the four hundred feet to the narrow fin of mesa top from which such an approach could be attempted. The site with the vertical poles was one of the hardest places to get to in which I had ever seen Anasazi ruins.

What could possibly be going on there, I mused, except the most desperate defensive gambit? What else could persuade a family or a clan to build in such a dangerous and inconvenient eyrie?

The notion that the cliff dwellings are defensive is indeed the obvious explanation, or, as archaeologists like to say, the most parsimonious one. It was proposed as early as 1877 by some of the leading experts of the day. Why did later theorists ever diverge from it?

The question has a complicated answer. Much of the early thinking about the cliff dwellings was governed by the assumption that the Anasazi had retreated to the alcoves in the face of invasion by an alien people. (Both in the popular mind and in the theorizing of professionals all over the world before the 1960s, invasions were very much in vogue. Richard Wetherill, it will be recalled, thought the Basketmakers whom he unearthed five feet down were a different "race" from the Pueblo people who succeeded them and who, he thought, had driven or wiped the Basketmakers out. That Basketmakers and Pueblos were all one Anasazi people was not firmly established until the 1940s. Today, among archaeologists "invasion" is almost a dirty word.)

To the early scholars, the obvious candidates for enemy invaders were nomadic tribes such as the Navajo, Ute, and Paiute. As a more sophisticated anthropology began to show that there was no trace of these Athapaskans or Shoshoneans in the Southwest before about A.D. 1400, the invasion theory went out the window—and with it, much of the desire to see thirteenth-century dwellings as defensive. It is surprising just how reluctant the experts were to postulate internecine warfare as an alternative to invasion.

A second argument against the defensive explanation came from archaeologists who pointed out the scarcity of burned or decimated villages, of massacred populaces, among the ruins. If the whole Anasazi domain had been gripped in the thirteenth century with the threat of warfare, surely there should be more evidence that carnage and looting actually took place. Yet so many of the cliff dwellings looked as Cliff Palace had to Richard Wetherill and Charlie Mason in 1888—as if the inhabitants had walked away the previous month.

Perhaps even more forceful than either of these counterarguments, however, was a deep and little-examined belief about the Pueblo people. They have long figured in the minds of scholars and public alike as *peaceful* Indians par excellence.

As I traveled around the Southwest talking to Anasazi experts, I tried to dig to the source of this stereotype. Steve Lekson pointed me to Ruth Benedict's 1934 book, *Patterns of Culture.* One of the most popular and influential anthropological works ever written, Benedict's treatise borrowed Nietzsche's distinction (in speaking of Greek tragedy) between the Dionysian and the Apollonian. The essence of the Dionysian is excess, the effort to break through boundaries and annihilate limits. The Apollonian, in contrast, is all about moderation, restraint, the middle of the road.

Benedict applied the distinction to cultures. Having spent several summers among the Zuni, she concluded that while "the American Indians as a whole, and including those of Mexico, were passionately Dionysian," the Puebloans were uniquely Apollonian. In Benedict's view, all other North American Indians sought transcendence through violence, torture, drugs, alcohol, frenzied rituals, and vision quests. "In the pueblos, [however], there is no courting of excess in any form, no tolerance of violence, no indulgence in the exercise of authority, or delight in any situation in which the individual stands alone."

That this typing of cultures might be wildly overstated or even downright bunk was not a popular view. Benedict had the imprimatur of her mentor, that formidable guru of ethnography Franz Boas, and she wrote brilliantly and persuasively.

At the Museum of Northern Arizona in Flagstaff, David Wilcox pushed the stereotype of the peaceful Puebloans back before Benedict. In the 1920s, the Fred Harvey Company first brought tourism to the Southwest in a big way. Selling the Indian encounter as a safe, rewarding experience was crucial to the company's success. Harvey's Indian Detours—several-day automobile jaunts into Pueblo country—promised "buried cities that flourished when Britons crouched in caves." The Harvey hotels sold Indian arts and crafts, and at the Grand Canyon, the company built Hopi House, a glorified gift shop modeled after the houses of Oraibi, where tourists could watch living Hopis make pots and jewelry.

Even before Fred Harvey, as early as the late nineteenth century, Wilcox pointed out, the Puebloans were commonly referred to as "the Quaker Indians." In Wilcox's view, the Puebloans themselves realized early that it might be to their own advantage, under the American government, to portray themselves as peaceful Indians, in contrast to the "aggressive," "warlike" Navajos, Apaches, or Utes. A certain political savvy underlay this effort. Works of otherwise responsible ethnography will tell you today that the Hopi name for themselves is *Hopitu-Shinumu,* translated as "little people of peace." But the linguist Ekkehart Malotki, who learned Hopi in order to translate the people's legends directly from the narratives of elders speaking their own tongue, takes issue with the rendering.

Malotki's immediate quarrel was with Frank Waters, whose 1963 *Book of the Hopi* became a best-seller and a hippie cult classic. Translating *Hopi* as "people of peace," Waters, in Malotki's view, "unjustifiably characterizes the Hopis as elitist pacifists."

According to the linguist, a better translation of *Hopi* would be "good" or "well behaved," or even "civilized," in the sense that the people thereby distinguish themselves from their nomadic neighbors. Malotki is eloquent on the mischief done by the mistranslation:

> The fantasy that *hopi* means "peaceful" is both erroneous and misleading. Not only has it created "the unreal Hopi," it has also contributed to the widely held view that the Hopi constitute an edenic society living in tranquility and harmony on the high plateau. . . . This falsehood about them has led people from around the world to expect something of them that is impossible.

The stereotype of the peaceful Puebloans projects backward, half unconsciously, to create a kindred view of the Anasazi—and not only in the popular mind, but among scholars. (A similar fantasy about the Classic Maya, cherished by most of the leading experts, posited them as peaceful philosopher-priests obsessed with pondering the nature of time. It took the archaeology and epigraphy of the last twenty years, as Maya glyphs finally yielded to decipherment, to overturn this picture and do justice to the warfare and brutality that drenched Maya society.)

Thus, in a 1982 *National Geographic* article titled "The Anasazi: Riddles in the Ruins," the paintings illustrating daily life at Chaco Canyon and Bandelier breathe a spirit of harmony, peace, and orderliness. Women sit trading turquoise pendants; workers cheerfully mason a second-story wall; complacent farmers dig harrows to plant their corn. Inside a kiva, an elder tells a tale, while his audience (including a weaver at work on his loom) sits rapt and silent. In the bustle of the courtyard, even the dogs and turkeys look happy and well fed. This fantasy cannot be blamed on the artist or even on the editors, for many Anasazi scholars were consulted in the creation of these tableaux.

Today one of the liveliest debates in Anasazi studies might be characterized as the attempt to answer a single question: "What happened in 1250?" Virtually all the experts agree that the thirteenth century, and particularly its latter half, was a hard time for the ancients. As one of the deans of Anasazi scholarship, Charlie Steen, wrote in 1981:

> The 13th century must have been a miserable time on the San Juan. The entire century, according to the tree ring record, was a dry one with a drought climax during the last quarter of the period. In addition, the development of large pueblos with no sanitation led to much disease. A third major contribution to the miseries of the century was the extensive arroyo cutting which prevailed over the northern part of the Southwest during the time.

The debate takes off with the effort to divine just what part that misery played in the movement into cliff dwellings, and with the further conundrum of whether cliff dwellings are per se defensive.

Consider first the case against the defensive explanation. It has never been put more cogently than by Linda Cordell, a leading Anasazi scholar who works at the University of Colorado's Henderson Museum in Boulder. In a 1976 paper titled "Anasazi Nucleation for Defense: Reasons to Doubt an Obvious Solution," Cordell makes the following arguments:

- The intense autonomy of Pueblo villages in historic times argues against any notion of organized warfare among the Anasazi. If there was aggression, it was mere raiding for food.
- Cliff dwellings are of no use in preventing raiders from pillaging mesa-top fields.
- Cliff dwellings are exceptionally vulnerable to attack by ambush.
- In historic accounts of Pueblo attacks on other Pueblo villages, the favored method is to feign friendship, surreptitiously plant tinder, then set fire to the village. In such a circumstance, "about the last place anyone would want to be is in a rock shelter with limited space and escape routes."
- In the Spanish Reconquest of 1692, sieges were highly effective against cliff-top villages such as Acoma. Had the Anasazi known sieges in the past, they ought to have developed a response to them that they could have used to thwart the Spanish.
- In battles with the Spanish, Puebloans consistently fled to the mountains rather than defend their homes.

Finally, Cordell argues that the move into cliff dwellings in the thirteenth century could have had other motives than defense. With the wild game all but depleted, the Anasazi came to depend more than ever on their crops. Every square foot of cultivable soil was precious: caves offered building sites at no expense of arable soil. If the Anasazi, pushed to the limit, planted on both mesa top and canyon bottom, cliff dwellings, halfway between the two, minimized the time spent walking to fields and the labor of hauling home grain. And if, in the desperation of the diminished yields of the thirteenth century, the Anasazi pulled out all their agricultural stops—check dams, terraces, hand-watering—they had little time left over to build their villages. A house protected by an overhang can be more carelessly and quickly erected than one that must withstand the rains and winds out in the open.

Cordell's is a compelling argument, and no expert on the other side of the fence has yet been able to dissolve her objections. But within the last five years, there is an unmistakable trend in Southwestern research to grant raiding and even warfare a larger role in Anasazi life than they had previously been seen to play.

During three days in October 1994, I got a vivid hands-on demonstration of another answer to "What happened in 1250?"—an answer diametrically opposed to Cordell's. My tutors were Jonathan Haas, of Chicago's Field Museum, and his wife, Winifred Creamer, who teaches at Northern Illinois University. To make their point, Haas and Creamer led me up a nine-hundred-foot flatiron—a tilted slab of red sandstone—above the Kayenta Valley in northeastern Arizona.

As we approached the base of the great rock, nicknamed Happy Valley, Creamer pointed out potsherds strewn here and there, naming the styles: "Sosi black-on-white, Dogozhi black-and-white, Flagstaff black-on-white. All three are typical of the early thirteenth century. Remember those patterns." Thanks to the work of Jeffrey Dean and others, Kayenta ceramic styles have been dated with greater accuracy than the styles of perhaps any other part of the Anasazi domain. A sherd can date a ruin within twenty years.

We started our ascent, scrambling up soft earth, then spidering flat-footed on the tilted stone. At one point the only way to continue was to traverse left in shallow toeholds carved by the ancients. As we climbed higher, new scatterings of potsherds appeared underfoot. Even to my eye, these were clearly different from the ones we had found at the base. Creamer picked up a sherd with heavy black parallelograms and a cross-hatched pattern of black lines on a white slip. "Kayenta black-on-white," she said. "You only get it after 1250." She bent and picked up a pair of colored sherds, one black-on-red with white lines, the other red-on-orange. "Keet Seel polychrome," said Creamer, "and Tusayan polychrome. Both also only after 1250."

As we gained height, the barren valley stretching east of us took on coherence and shape. Buttes and pinnacles stood out, vividly limned by the afternoon sun. "Look how close we are to the road," Haas commented, pointing at a few autos trundling along U.S. 160, only a mile away. "Starting with Byron Cummings in 1908, archaeologists have prowled all over this country for more than eighty years. Yet none of them ever thought to look on top of Happy Valley, until we discovered the site in 1984. In their minds, it was a completely unlikely place for the ancients to build."

Breathless and exhilarated, I reached the summit of the flatiron to discover a sandy clearing dotted with small junipers. All about me stood the crumbling walls of back-to-back room blocks. Thousands of potsherds, including jar handles, rims, and pipes, lay scattered in the sand, along with flint and obsidian flakes.

We lingered for two hours, poking through the ruins, marveling at the severe exposure on all sides of the flatiron's summit. Then we sat on the highest knob in the orange glow of approaching sunset, while Haas ran through the argument. "We estimated some hundred and fifty rooms here. Yet it *is* an improbable place to build. Except for the occasional Navajo sheepherder, I'd be willing to bet that only about five parties have climbed up here since 1300. And three of those parties we've led.

"Look how far you have to go to get water," Haas continued, pointing at the creek bed far below, beside the highway. "And where do you plant your corn? Not up here. And look here, on the overhanging backside. Do you see those hand- and toeholds? Those are two emergency escape routes." Haas addressed his absent opponent: "I don't care what Linda Cordell says. Tell me this isn't a defensive site!"

From our lofty perch, Haas pointed out other butte-top sites in the distance, all inhabited after 1250. "There's Table Top Ruin. There's Tachini Point, in the foreground. Rabbit Ears Ruin is off to the left. You see that they're all linked by line of sight."

Through three field seasons in the mid-1980s, Haas and Creamer explored the contiguous Kayenta, Long House, and Klethla Valleys, through which Highway 160 runs today. During the two days after our climb of Happy Valley, they guided me to a half-dozen other major sites, all located atop difficult mesas defended by sheer cliffs: Organ Rock, Wildcat Canyon Ruin, Long House, Fireside, Tower

House, and Ruin 8. There we found pueblos with as many as four hundred rooms—but no water, and no fields anywhere nearby. All had been built after 1250.

And gradually over the three days, the complex network of lines of sight among these villages became clear in my mind. In one place, the Anasazi had apparently carved a *V* notch out of an intervening ridge to ensure line of sight between Fireside and Tower House. Here, if Haas and Creamer were right, was the answer to attack by siege that the Anasazi had indeed developed: the besieged village could signal its allies to come to its aid. By the time of the Spanish *entrada,* for one reason or another, they had lost this art.

On the last afternoon, we drove ten miles west down the highway and came to the Klethla Valley. Those ten miles, I learned, had been dotted with villages right up to 1250. After that date, not a soul lived there—the gap became what Haas and Creamer call a no-man's-land. In the broad basin of the Klethla Valley, driving back roads, my guides showed me half a dozen more buttes and towers, atop which sites had been built after 1250. The Klethla sites made up another defensive network, also linked by line of sight. And Klethla and Kayenta, Haas and Creamer suspect, were enemies.

Late that day, as we sat, once again in the warm glow before sunset, atop Hoodoo Heaven, an eerie, isolated spike of sandstone, Haas and Creamer clinched their argument. "The trigger was environmental stress," said Creamer. "We know that, after 1150, the growing season shortened, there were periodic droughts, and erosion cut into the arable land. It got harder and harder to live here, and it got really bad around 1250. A possibly expanding population had to compete for fewer resources. The people retreated into the high, defensive sites, formed alliances based on the line-of-sight networks, and raided their enemies."

"Why don't you find more evidence of violence in the burials?" I asked, echoing a criticism of Haas and Creamer's theory that I had heard. So far, only two skeletons dug up in the Kayenta area have shown signs of violent death.

"Warfare doesn't necessarily mean pitched battles," answered Haas. "They're going after each other's stores of corn, not trying to kill each other en masse. You don't raid fields—you go after those granaries full of ground cornmeal. That's far more valuable. And of course, we haven't yet found more than a tiny fraction of the burials."

"How well can you generalize from your Kayenta work?" I asked.

"It's happening all over the Southwest at 1250," said Haas. "The retreat into cliff dwellings and butte-top sites. Environmental stress. Defensive structures such as watchtowers. There's plenty of evidence of violent death, all over. And then comes the abandonment."

"FOR most of this century," Bill Lipe had told me over dinner in Cortez, "archaeologists focused on environmental causes for the abandonment: drought, famine, arroyo cutting, and the like. Or they talked about war with the nomads. They saw the abandonment only in terms of a push.

"But we're coming to see that it takes a pull as well as a push. Something immensely attractive or compelling must have been going on to the south and east, and up on the Colorado Plateau they got wind of it. More and more, we're coming to believe that the pull was the Kachina Phenomenon."

We know the phenomenon chiefly through its present form, where it still anchors the social and religious life of the Puebloans. Today's kachinas, numbering in the hundreds, are reincarnated ancestors who act as messengers between the people and their gods. Benevolent beings, they bring rain, health, and fertility. At most of the Pueblos, the kachinas are believed to spend half the year in residence, the other half living in distant lakes or mountains. At Hopi, for instance, the kachinas are present from December through July; the rest of the year, they live on the tops of the San Francisco Peaks, north of Flagstaff.

Each kachina has a name, a distinctive costume, and a face represented by a sacred mask that is kept in hiding most of the year. (Kachina dolls, representing the supernatural beings, have become tourist knickknacks, but the masks and costumes are sacred objects, never shown to Anglos.) During the kachina dances, Pueblo men not only wear the masks and act out the roles of the various kachinas; they believe that they actually *become* those kachinas. It is utterly tabu to reveal to children that the dancers are their fathers and uncles.

Where did the Kachina Phenomenon come from, and when? By scrutinizing rock art, pottery designs, and the handful of fragile kiva murals excavated over the years, experts have found images of masked dancers dating back to about 1325—and these images first appear well to the south and east of the Colorado Plateau. Thus it looks as though the Kachina Phenomenon must be the powerful pull in the abandonment. By tying together diverse clans and kinship groups in an intricate round of rites and dances lasting throughout the year, the new faith integrated Puebloan society as never before.

The Spaniards, with their Catholic zeal to convert, did everything they could to suppress the "idolatry" of the kachinas. All they succeeded in doing was to drive the religion underground. But so disruptive was Spanish repression that, in the words of rock-art expert Polly Schaafsma, "what we know today of the kachinas is essentially a 'relic population' of a once grander phenomenon."

A few weeks after my outing with Haas and Creamer, I camped in Grand Gulch with Bruce Bradley, from the Crow Canyon Archaeological Center. One evening after dinner, Bradley treated me to his own twist on what happened in 1250—and on the role of the Kachina Phenomenon in bringing it about. The insights had come to him near the end of his work at one of the last full-scale excavations in the Southwest, a ten-year dig at Sand Canyon Pueblo, near Cortez. "It's just one hypothesis among many," Bradley began disarmingly, "but here goes.

"Around 1250, you see an incredible change. Everybody's moving into the canyons, building cliff dwellings. At Sand Canyon, seventy-five percent of the community lived within a defensive wall that surrounded the pueblo. All through southeastern Utah, northeastern Arizona, southwestern Colorado, the same thing's happening.

"Suddenly, at 1250, the trade ware goes to zero. Before that, you had plenty of far-traded pottery, turquoise, shells, jewelry. Suddenly, nothing. And right at 1250, the ceramics revert from Mesa Verde–style pitchers—tall, conical vessels with rounded bulblike bases—to the kinds of mugs made at Chaco two hundred years earlier. Picture your average office coffee mug with a handle." Bradley drew designs in the dirt to illustrate.

"And you start getting *D*-shaped towers. They may be echoes, symbols of the greatest *D*-shaped building of all—Pueblo Bonito. I think that what's happening all over the Colorado Plateau is a reactionary, neo-Chacoan revival. They're harking back more than one hundred years to the glory days of Chaco.

"Maybe it's caused by environmental stress—they're realizing that the old ways of living don't work. And maybe it's a reaction against some new liberal thinking down south, which may be the first glimmerings of the Kachina Phenomenon. In any event, the revivalists become hyperdefensive. They build cliff dwellings and walled towns as refuges against a perceived threat. It's a classic thing for reactionary movements to do. They fortify against the assault that never comes."

Bradley scratched a scruffy beard. "Now here's where I'm really stretching. I think the whole Chacoan revival was driven by a single charismatic figure, a Christ type, if you will. And I think we may have found him at Sand Canyon. In one kiva, we discovered a man of about forty-five or fifty, with his skull bashed in. And he had six toes.

"Now Neil Judd found a six-toed guy in the ruins of Pueblo Bonito, back in the 1920s. There are six-toed petroglyphs on the rock wall directly behind Bonito. And even today, among the Pueblos, polydactyly—having an extra toe or finger—is regarded as a special gift.

"In any event, the Chacoan revival lasts only fifteen or twenty years, before it falls apart. Then the great drought of 1276 to 1299 hits. They kill their leaders—all through Sand Canyon we found bodies showing signs of violent death. They burn their kivas, perhaps to exorcise the trauma of the violence. Then they abandon the Colorado Plateau. They go join the folks down south. They give in to the new liberal thinking.

"The Kachina Phenomenon, by integrating clans and kinship groups, allows socialism to flourish. It's worked in the Pueblos for seven hundred years. It still works. Down there, the Anasazi found an answer about how to live together. They didn't find one up here. Surprise, surprise—up here they're all gone."

EARLIER that month, I had made a brief trip into the Gallina region, a broad valley extending north from Cuba, New Mexico. The area remains a cultural backwater well off the tourist track: poor villages, largely Hispanic, are scattered along the trickling headwaters of Capulin Creek. My guide was U.S. Forest Service archaeologist Bill Wyatt.

Archaeology in the Gallina area began relatively late. In 1937, Frank Hibben dug the Cerritos site, finding burned rooms and towers and eighteen bushels of burned corn. Two of the towers contained human skeletons: one still had three arrows embedded in its chest, another two arrows in the hip, yet another a severe wound above one eye. Hibben also found the skeleton of a female still holding a bow and some arrows.

From Hibben's time to the present day, no part of the Anasazi domain has produced as much evidence of prehistoric violence as Gallina. More than half the excavated sites contain the remains of murdered men, women, and children. And though the valley lies far to the east and south of the Colorado Plateau, it too ceased to be occupied around 1300.

As I toured the valley with Wyatt, I realized that I had come across no stranger ruins anywhere in the Southwest. The normal height for Anasazi walls is about five feet. In Gallina, they average nine, and the walls are thicker than could possibly be required just to hold up the roofs. Each living site is guarded by a tall circular structure that may have been a lookout tower. In gloomy, cul-de-sac side canyons, small villages huddle on cramped ledges. "This whole place just breathes paranoia," Wyatt said at one point. And later: "You get the feeling these were the bad guys. It's as if the others said, 'OK, you can live in this area, but we don't want you showing up anywhere else.'"

From Gallina I drove south to Jemez Pueblo, where I met William Whatley, a long-haired maverick who for nine years has worked at the Pueblo, the last four as official Jemez tribal archaeologist. Like

Bruce Bradley, Whatley had learned how to listen and not to ask rude questions. By fiercely championing Jemez claims for land and sacred objects, Whatley slowly gained the trust of the people.

Earlier ethnographers had concluded that the Jemez were the descendants of the Gallina Anasazi. Whatley flatly contradicted this assertion. As we sat on the porch of the visitor center, he told me the parts of the Jemez migration epic that he was allowed to share. "They have no Gallina stories," he said. "You've seen those sites? They don't look anything like Jemez dwellings. These people aren't descended from Gallina.

"Over the years, the elders have given me pieces of the migration story. The whole thing takes twelve hours to tell. But the gist is this. The people came from the Four Corners area, somewhere near Sand Canyon. As they migrated south and east, they left markers. I've actually found some of these on the ground, just from the elders' descriptions—markers that no living Jemez have ever seen.

"On their way here, an advance party of Jemez came through the Gallina area. At first they were treated hospitably by the people living there; then the Gallina turned around and killed the Jemez. The Gallina people didn't realize that the large main body of Jemez was coming right behind. That main body eliminated all of Gallina, maybe in only a few days."

I mused on the Jemez oral tradition, which, before Whatley, no Anglo had been privileged to learn. I realized that it explained a lot. It accounted for the end of Gallina in 1300 and for the extensive evidence there of violent death. And it might be one more piece of the complex puzzle of the abandonment.

When the Jemez people first unmistakably show up after their migration, it is on the southern edges of three high mesas that overlook their present pueblo, at the beginning of the fourteenth century. On a crisp October day, Whatley guided me, via a long four-wheel-drive approach and a short hike, to Kwanstiyukwa, "place of the twin [ponderosa] pines." The site is a high one, at 7,650 feet, and it remains remote: very few Anglos have visited it.

"According to Jemez oral history," Whatley said as we walked the grassy clearing, "this was the first major city the people built after the migration. We've tree-ring dated it as early as 1410, but the pottery goes all the way back to 1325." For hours we strode across the ruin, whose surface swooped and undulated as we crisscrossed the buried walls of some two thousand to three thousand rooms. Lying on Forest Service land, Kwanstiyukwa has never been excavated—nor will it ever be, if the Jemez people have their way. Here and there the tops of stone walls protruded above the yellow grasses. From the top of a high mound within the ruin, I could make out the grid of rooms sprawling about me, a crosshatched pattern of faint ridges scoring the ground. I could also discern the flat depressions of seven big plazas, a reservoir, and an underground great kiva. The ruin's height—twenty-one feet at maximum—suggests that some of the room blocks had towered four and maybe five stories high. Buildings of four stories' height would not again be erected in the United States until the 1870s.

All told, Kwanstiyukwa covers an area of 160,000 square feet. "It's so big," Whatley said, "we need two-way radios to survey it." Not even at the height of Chaco's glory had the Anasazi built a village so large. Yet towns of more than one thousand rooms become the norm in the fourteenth century—directly as a result, archaeologists think, of the socially integrating effect of the Kachina Phenomenon.

The site of Kwanstiyukwa seemed blissful, with lordly views south all the way to Albuquerque, east to the summits of the Jemez Mountains, dusted with new snow. Wind tossed the tall ponderosas around us, carrying the scent of pine sap. Cones thudded softly on the ground, and tangles of brown needles drifted like sand dunes.

On our drive out from Kwanstiyukwa, Whatley spotted a black bear in the distance, running from the sound of our engine. "The Jemez people still come up here on the mesa all the time to maintain their shrines," he told me. "They believe that the ancestral sites are guarded by bears, mountain lions, and eagles."

That night I camped alone on the mesa. With sunset, the wind died. I built a small campfire out of ponderosa twigs and watched Cygnus and Lyra wheel overhead. The temperature plunged below freezing. In the night I was awakened by the nearby yips and howls of half a dozen coyotes.

Dreamy and warm, I contemplated the power of Pueblo animism. I wished that I could convince myself that the coyotes too were guarding the ancestral mesa. But in my agnosticism, the mournful howls spoke only of territory and rank. The ground on which I camped was a far more alien place for me than for the Jemez.

ON the day I had watched Bruce Bradley teach flint knapping at Jemez, I asked Whatley about certain well-guarded secrets of the pueblo. In the 1950s, an ethnographer named Florence Hawley Ellis had closely studied the Jemez. Her monograph *A Reconstruction of the Basic Jemez Pattern of Social Organization* insisted that the Eagle and Arrow Societies, whose duties adumbrated a war cult, stood at the center of Jemez social life. Formerly, claimed Ellis, the Opi, or Scalp, Society had been equally important, and at one time a man had to take a scalp (usually that of a Navajo) to become a member; but Ellis thought the Opi Society had gone extinct. Her report offered many details about the purging of witches and the practice of human sacrifice in former times.

All this was extremely touchy ground for Whatley. Like other young Anglo archaeologists who become deeply interested in a Pueblo people, Whatley had to balance his scientific objectivity against a passionate advocacy for the tribe with which he worked. Furthermore, much of what Ellis and other earlier ethnographers had dug out of their informants was sacred or secret lore, not for outsiders to know.

Now Whatley, laughing at the irony, told me, "The Jemez people tell me that Ellis got it sixty percent right, forty percent wrong. But they won't say which sixty percent is right!"

Later, as I sat talking quietly with a Jemez elder on the porch of the visitor center, to my astonishment he admitted to me that the Opi Society still flourished. "The Opi take care of everything for us," the man said cryptically.

Then I pushed too hard, as Whatley and Bradley never would. "Do they still keep scalps?" I asked.

"I don't think so," the elder said, edging away from my impertinence.

The prohibition against sharing tribal lore with the outside world does not apply only to Anglos. In 1982, a university-trained Jemez man, Joe Sando, published *Nee Hemish,* a history of his pueblo. In the book, Sando deals only cursorily with myths and traditions, and he attempts to reconcile the Jemez view with archaeology—denying, for instance, on quasi-scientific grounds that humans came to the New World across the Bering land bridge. Nonetheless, Sando was severely ostracized by his fellow Jemez when his book came out.

Despite this secretiveness, ethnographers over the years have uncovered plenty of evidence that warfare and violence played a central role in Pueblo life. Especially in the early days, when informants were less guarded, the scholars learned of dark doings in the past. Thus a governor of Zuni, speaking Spanish, told John Gregory Bourke in 1881:

> In the days of long ago (*en el tiempo de cuanto hay*) all the Pueblos, Moquis [Hopis], Zuni, Acoma, Laguna, Jemez, and others had the religion of human sacrifice (*el oficio de matar los hombres*) at the time of the Feast of Fire, when the days are shortest. The victim had his throat cut and his breast opened, and his heart taken out by one of the Cochinos (priests); this was their "oficio" (religion), their method of asking good fortune (*pedir la suerte*).

Whatley was inclined to dismiss Florence Hawley Ellis's work at Jemez in part because she was a woman. As such, he argued, she would have had mainly Jemez women for informants, to whom most of the mythic lore was not imparted.

It is in fact quite striking that several of the anthropologists most responsible for revealing the role of warfare and violence among the Pueblos have been women. They include, along with Ellis, Matilda Coxe Stevenson at Zuni and Zia from the 1880s on and Elsie Clews Parsons at a number of Pueblos from 1916 to 1939. It may be that, despite being locked out of the circle of elders telling tales, these scholars had an advantage in being women. For gossip is as rife in Pueblo society as among any other people, and women who have not been entrusted with guarding a secret might be more willing to tell what they know—and in the Pueblos, they know a lot—to an outsider.

Parsons's 1924 study of the Zuni Scalp Ceremonial, parts of which she was allowed to witness three years earlier, makes harrowing reading. According to her, the importance of scalps for the Zuni lies in the control that enemy dead have over rainmaking: the ceremony is in essence a rain dance. During the twelve-day ritual, a female scalp kicker kicks the scalp across the ground into the village; scalp washers, on the way to the river, imitate wild animals and bite the scalp; finally the scalp is hoisted atop a tall pole around which the whole village dances.

Ellis's 1951 study, "Patterns of Aggression and the War Cult in Southwestern Pueblos," is a concise but comprehensive survey of the role of violence across the Pueblo world. She saw a fundamental tension at the heart of the Pueblo psyche: a deep, conservative belief that to stand out in any way from one's peers is wrong, in conflict with an innate competitive instinct. Thus even when a man buys a new truck, he may be bitterly resented by his neighbors for "leaving the Indian way." Ellis claimed, "It is admitted that even recently an unusually beautiful woman or successful hunter might be killed—quietly and *accidentally*—or someone's exceptionally fine horse be found dead or his big house despoiled."

In the politically correct 1990s, these disturbing old reports are often brushed under the table. Yet since the Puebloans of today are the direct descendants of the Anasazi, the work of Ellis, Parsons, and others may cast an oblique light on what happened in 1250.

"ARE we uncovering the dark side of Anasazi life?" I asked Bill Lipe over dinner. The pat phrase had been bandied about in newspaper and magazine accounts of some of the new research.

"I wouldn't call it the dark side," he answered. "Call it the human side. We're simply bringing the Anasazi into the human kingdom. They did marvelous things, but they were also capable of violence and evil."

No Southwestern research in the last few years has been more controversial than Christy Turner's discoveries about prehistoric cannibalism. In October 1994, I visited Turner in his office at Arizona State University at Tempe to see the evidence for myself.

For more than two decades, Turner has reexamined skeletons and bones exhumed from digs that took place years earlier. Focusing at first merely on sites where the remains showed signs of violent death, Turner was bemused to discover consistent markings that he could account for only as the result of cannibalism.

Recognizing the explosive nature of his finds, Turner became his own toughest critic. He developed a set of six rigorous criteria; if any of the six is absent, he will not conclude that cannibalism took place.

Reaching among his shelves, Turner now brought out several boxes full of bones dug at Burnt Mesa in northwestern New Mexico in 1969. The skeletal remains of eleven murdered persons dated from around A.D. 950. Taking a long, broken leg bone, he said, "This is a fibula. It's a tough bone, hard and dense—the hardest of all to break. No natural process is likely to produce this kind of fracture. They must have broken it open to get at the marrow.

"Now look at the cut marks." I peered close and saw thin parallel grooves running across the bone, unmistakably the kind of marks a flint knife would make. "That's a second criterion."

Turner replaced the fibula and handed me a diminutive skull. I sucked my breath in as I held the skull. Glued back together, it had been viciously fractured; even the tooth sockets were smashed. "This was a child between six and eight years old," said Turner, "probably a girl. You see cut marks here"—he indicated parallel grooves on the forehead—"probably from scalping. Also anvil abrasions." I looked even closer and saw tiny scrape marks different from the cutting grooves.

"What are they?"

"You place a bone on a stone, an 'anvil,'" Turner said, demonstrating with his fist, "then smash it with another stone to break it open. The bone slides off the anvil, leaving these scrape marks. That's a third criterion."

Turner went on to demonstrate his other criteria: burning of the bones, the pulverizing of the vertebrae to get at marrow, and the oddest of all, called "pot polishing."

"You need a microscope to see pot polishing," said Turner. I stared through the lens at the end of a broken tibia. "See the sheen on the outer corners of the tip?" Turner asked. I nodded. "That's the polish caused by bones bouncing around in a pot as they're being stewed."

"The clincher," added Turner, "is that the process is exactly the same as the Anasazi used to butcher and cook antelope and prairie dog, two of their staple foods. What other possible explanation could there be?"

In twenty-five years of work, Turner has amassed some three dozen separate instances of Anasazi cannibalism, comprising more than three hundred victims. "No one," he says, "who has ever seen the physical evidence has doubted our conclusions." Yet so volatile is the issue of cannibalism that Turner has come under vehement attack by other archaeologists and by Indians. Posters announcing his lectures have been torn down, and at the 1988 Pecos Conference, a symposium on cannibalism was canceled after protests by Native American groups—the first time in the sixty-one-year history of the annual gathering that any presentation had been censored.

I had heard archaeologists attack Turner's work with a passion that seemed to transcend scientific judgment. Kurt Dongoske, an Anglo who serves as archaeologist for the Hopi Tribe, had told me, "Turner's using cannibalism as a sensational way to promote his own work. This is deeply offensive to all Pueblo peoples. As far as I'm concerned, you can't prove cannibalism until you actually find human remains in a human coprolite [prehistoric excrement]."

If one accepts Turner's findings, however, the crucial question is what purpose the cannibalism served. At first Turner assumed he was finding evidence of survival cannibalism, such as occurred, for example, at Donner Pass in 1847 or after the Andean plane crash in 1972. One day in 1993, however, Turner and David Wilcox plotted the three dozen cannibalism sites on a large map. "Suddenly," Turner recalled, "we had a kind of 'Eureka!' Nearly every site lay close to a

Chaco outlier. And the dates were right—between 900 and 1200."

Before A.D. 900, the Anasazi had always been a fiercely individualistic, egalitarian people. Their villages remained small, each autonomous from its neighbors. Suddenly, around 920, in a shallow canyon in western New Mexico, a whole new way of life sprang into being. For the first time, Anasazi villages affiliated in a vast network stretching 250 miles from north to south. Scattered for eight miles along Chaco Wash, fourteen Great Houses, symmetrical, planned towns with a uniform architectural style, centered the network. The greatest of all, and the true hub of the Chaco universe, was Pueblo Bonito. More than seventy villages all over the Southwest, called outliers, were tied into the Chacoan system, mirroring the structure of the Great Houses and sharing their culture. The complexity of the network itself, scholars believe, required the Anasazi for the first time to abandon their egalitarian ways in favor of a hierarchical society. Neil Judd's discovery at Chaco of several burials teeming with precious grave goods suggests that these dead might have been powerful rulers.

At the peak of its glory, near the end of the eleventh century, Chaco commanded an even farther-flung trade in exotic goods: macaw feathers from Mexico, seashells from the Sea of Cortez, turquoise from eastern New Mexico. The Mexican links may prove that Chaco was in contact with the Toltecs, who ranged from central Mexico to Yucatán and Guatemala, and who at the time were the most advanced civilization in North America.

The strangest aspect of the Chaco culture, discovered only in the last twenty-five years, is an interlocking system of roadways, now known to exceed a total of four hundred miles in length, radiating outward from Chaco Canyon as far as southeastern Utah and southwestern Colorado. The roads are often thirty feet wide and stretch for miles in dead-straight lines, ignoring natural contours. They pose a great puzzle: why should people who had no vehicles, no beasts of burden, need highways? Some experts think the roads bore laborers who carried heavy roof beams, felled and trimmed with stone axes, on their shoulders—two hundred thousand of them, all told—from at least forty miles away to build the Great Houses. Others see the roads as routes for ceremonial pilgrimages to Chaco. A few, including David Wilcox, argue that Anasazi armies marched up and down the highways.

By the year 1200—and perhaps as early as 1125—Chaco had collapsed. The causes of the fall of so spectacular a culture remain mysterious.

Until recently, archaeologists saw Chaco as an orderly, peaceful civilization dominated by astronomer-priests, tradesmen, and governors. But Turner and Wilcox's "Eureka!" may overturn that picture. Their theory is that ritual cannibalism played a pivotal role in Chaco's domination of its allies. In a fashion perhaps comparable to the gory Aztec rites witnessed by Cortés, Chaco rulers may have intimidated potentially rebellious chiefs by forcing them to look on as they sacrificed and cannibalized chosen victims. Terror may have been the glue that held the Chaco culture together.

The most disturbing of all Turner's discoveries has to do with the pueblo of Awatovi. One of the first Hopi villages to bear the brunt of the Spanish impact, in the year 1700 Awatovi saw a tide of conversions to Catholicism—as many as hundreds of souls a day—thanks to the zealous work of Franciscan priests installed in the mission church.

The Hopis' own oral tradition tells that Ta'polo, the chief of Awatovi, grew so upset with the transformation of his village that he plotted in secret with the men of Walpi and Oraibi to wipe out his own town, offering himself as a sacrifice in the massacre. One morning in late autumn 1700, the warriors attacked when all the Awatovi men were inside their kivas; the attackers pulled up the ladders, set fire to the kivas, and burned the men alive. The whole village was razed.

The tradition says further that a band of surviving men, women, and children was marched toward First Mesa, when a dispute broke out between Walpi and Oraibi men over the disposition of the captives. Out of spite, the victors killed many of the prisoners and left their carcasses on the ground.

Guided by Kurt Dongoske, I walked across the site of Awatovi.

The leveling of almost three centuries ago had failed to obliterate the erstwhile grandeur of a village that, at some five thousand rooms, had been as large as any in the Indian Southwest. Across acres of cactus and sagebrush lay strewn millions of brown-and-pale-yellow Sikyatki polychrome potsherds. The grid of crumbled walls still proclaimed a well-knit civic order. From the edge of Antelope Mesa, we gazed south at the Hopi Buttes.

With us was a young Hopi man, Patrick Joshevama, who had never before been to Awatovi. As we poked around the ruin, he seemed lost in private thoughts. Finally he spoke softly: "This is where they accepted Catholicism, and they were destroyed for it. I think it serves as a good lesson for us to stick to our own ways."

In 1970, Christy Turner examined the remains of some thirty murdered Puebloans dug five years before at Polacca Wash, below First Mesa. To his surprise, the criteria for cannibalism fit. A radiocarbon date placed the remains within a range close to A.D. 1700. "I'm ninety to ninety-five percent sure that the massacre at Polacca Wash represents the captives from Awatovi," Turner told me. "And there's no doubt they were cannibalized."

Later I spoke to Leigh Jenkins, the Hopi cultural preservation officer. He did not directly dispute Turner's cannibalism claim. "My main point of contention," he said, "is, how does Turner know it was Puebloans cannibalizing Puebloans? Could it have been some other people doing this?"

At the mention of Awatovi, however, Jenkins had grown somber. "It's still very sensitive," he said. "We have people living today who are the descendants of clans that destroyed others at Awatovi, and descendants of clans that suffered there. Most Hopis will never publicly voice their feelings about Awatovi. There's too much pain, too much to answer for. It's too tough to swallow. Many of the elders think that we Hopi should just forget about what happened there."

Is it possible that oral traditions still current at Hopi might confirm the findings of Polacca Wash? It is not for Anglos to know, though Turner thinks it conceivable.

In the version recorded by Ekkehart Malotki and translated and published in 1993, the captives below First Mesa have their arms and legs cut off; some men's penises and testicles are severed; some women's breasts cut off. And Malotki's informant goes into great detail about what had gone so wrong at Awatovi by 1700 as to justify the town's decimation.

It is not simply a question of Catholic conversions. All kinds of witchcraft were rampant at Awatovi, and the large pueblo was riven by clan feuds. Gradually the Hopi order broke down, until the village became a lawless place. Theft and rape were daily occurrences. "People seemed to be blind to what they were doing," said Malotki's elder. "They got worse and worse. For example, if children encountered an old person relieving himself, they would smear excrement all over him." Two years passed without rain—and in the pueblos, drought is caused by witchcraft. Finally, Ta'polo, the chief who enlisted the Oraibi and Walpi men to destroy his village, was motivated by a dark rage after catching his wife committing adultery. In a grandiose fury, he decided that "life was out of joint," that the whole pueblo had gone bad and must suffer purgation by massacre.

One of the first white men to hear the legend of Awatovi from Hopi informants was Jesse Walter Fewkes, in 1892. At the time, he was less than two hundred years from the event—not long, in Hopi memory. Near First Mesa, the ethnographer was shown the sites of Mas'-ki (Death House) and Mas-teo'-mo (Death Mound), where the captives were tortured and killed. In a paper published the next year, he recorded the story. In this version, the prisoners below First Mesa "were again tortured and dismembered and left to die on the sand-hills."

But Fewkes was told several different versions of the legend by different elders, and Christy Turner argues persuasively that the version he published (which is dire enough) was the least offensive of the ones he heard. In a suggestive endnote, Fewkes hints at the substance of the other versions:

> In some variants of the legend gruesome tales of the cruelties to which the women were submitted at Mas'-ki are told. Most horrible

mutilations were made of the persons of those wretched ones who would not go with the captors, and, if the stories are correct, the final butchery at Mas-teo'-mo must have been horrible.

Was that final butchery cannibalism? Was Mas-teo'-mo Polacca Wash?

7

The Outdoor Museum

AFTER years of traipsing through the canyonlands, I had developed my own Anasazi habits—my notion of where to pitch the tent, the sequence in which I appraised the rooms in a ruin, the way I looked at a pictograph panel (trying to seize the ocher subtleties with averted vision, a trick my astronomer father had taught me), the habit of spitting on a potsherd to wash off the dirt and bring out the color. When I ventured into the backcountry with friends less conversant with the Anasazi, I tended to impose my style on them—not always to their gratitude.

On my 1993 trip into Grand Gulch with Fred Blackburn, when we had traced the footsteps of Richard Wetherill, I realized that I had fallen into the grips of an Anasazi buff even more fixed in his ways and dogmatic about his procedures than I. Only a broad streak of self-deprecating humor saved him from his obsessiveness. But by the end of our jaunt, as he puzzled over Wetherill's penciled note in Sandal House, I knew that Fred had become a friend. I wanted to head out with him again, and I recognized that he had much more to teach me.

So in the fall of 1994 we went back to Grand Gulch for eight days. Joining us were Bruce Bradley, flint knapper extraordinaire, and photographer Ira Block, on assignment for *National Geographic.* In terms of our talents and experiences, we were a motley bunch who managed to hit it off well. As a professional archaeologist, Bruce knew far more about the Anasazi than the rest of us, but he had never been in Grand Gulch. Though he would blush to make the claim himself, as an ex–BLM ranger in Grand Gulch, Fred knew the canyon better than perhaps anyone alive. I alone had any training as a climber. And Ira, born in Brooklyn and happily ensconced in Manhattan, was a true city boy: despite having once flown to the North Pole on assignment for *Geographic,* he had never camped out in the wilderness for anything like eight straight days. But his eye taught us all how to see anew what we thought we had always seen.

On the 1993 trip, as we lingered in the shade at Perfect Kiva ruin, waiting out the worst of the June heat, Fred had shown me a piece of his characteristic mischief. Back in the late 1970s, the BLM had stabilized and partially reconstructed Perfect Kiva, one of the finest ruins in the Gulch but, thanks to its accessibility, one of the most vulnerable. Behind the kiva stands a handsome dwelling with a neatly trimmed front wall. Rebuilding that wall, Blackburn had masoned in place some thin pieces of tabular sandstone in classic Pueblo III style, the gaps chinked with even smaller stone spalls. But if you cocked your head and looked at a certain several square inches of the wall, you could see that the chinking spelled out a diminutive "FB" turned sideways. The work was done so deftly that it in no way violated Anasazi technique, and I am sure that no one has ever detected it without Fred's pointing it out.

The jeu d'esprit was pure Blackburn: at once a private joke, an anarchic snub at the government agency with which he was already growing disenchanted, and an inscription of his own in the spirit of the charcoal signatures left by Wetherill and his cronies, the finding of which would come to be one of the passions of his life.

Yet when Fred showed me his chink-stone joke, it was with a mixture of boyish pride and mature embarrassment. By 1993, Blackburn would not have left his initials anywhere in the Anasazi country. Now, in October 1994, as we traveled leisurely up Grand Gulch, I came to understand some of the pivotal turns Fred had made in his long and thoughtful journey to his own Anasazi style.

Growing up in a mining family in Telluride, Colorado, Fred absorbed the values of his family and neighbors. Among the joys of the outdoor life were fishing, horse-packing, and hunting. To this day, Fred horse-packs as part of his living as a guide, and each November he and Bruce Bradley still go up into the San Juan Mountains to get their elk for the winter.

Among his boyhood chums growing up near the Four Corners, another great sport was arrowhead hunting. Fred had never gone after pots, but men he still counts as friends continue to pothunt, both legally (on private land) and illegally (on public).

It is tempting to characterize all pothunters as rapacious vandals, ripping apart ruins to nab treasure they can sell on the black market. The worst of the breed (and alas, they are not few) fit this profile exactly. Some have been known to use backhoes and bulldozers to clear away the dwellings, digging straight for the precious pots; the most ambitious have hired armed bodyguards to discourage rangers and sheriffs who might interfere with their fun.

But in Springerville, Arizona, in 1991, I met a seventy-five-year-old rancher who had pothunted all his life—only on private land, he insisted. The man invited me into his home to show me his trophy case full of pots and spear points and arrowheads. He had given some of these away, but never sold a single artifact. I liked the fellow: he seemed the epitome of a type we think Western movies invented, the honest, laconic homesteader who loves the land and knows every inch of it. It was perhaps no coincidence that one of the man's good friends was John Wayne, who had bought a ranch in Springerville.

In the ease of his company, I was almost seduced by the old man's rationale. "Why should this stuff be left in the ground to disintegrate?" he said quietly. "This is the history of our country, of our Indians. I don't see why it should be buried away. It's interesting to people all over the world." The man planned eventually to donate his pots to a local museum.

It was this climate Blackburn had grown up in. In his first year as a BLM ranger in Grand Gulch, in 1974, as he patrolled the backcountry, he still snagged the odd arrowhead and took it home. Many another park ranger did the same in those years.

"One day," Fred told me as we stopped to eat lunch in Grand Gulch, "another ranger called me on it. She said, 'You know, that just isn't right.' And it hit me real hard.

"That year I turned everything I had collected in to the Edge of the Cedars Museum in Blanding. And that was the year I was most tempted to pick up arrowheads. I kept finding them everywhere. It was like quitting goddamn cigarette smoking."

I flashed back on a startling moment from the year before, which now made sense. On the way into Whiskers Draw with Fred and Winston Hurst, approaching Wetherill's lost Cave 7, the site of the Basketmaker discovery, Fred had spotted a pretty arrowhead in the sand. He had picked it up, passed it to me to admire; I fondled it and handed it to Hurst. Then Fred dropped it back in the sand. I thought he was going to leave it there, as he had found it, but suddenly he kicked loose sand on top of it, and then, as if that were not camouflage enough, ground the sole of his boot almost viciously on the spot. The deed was a catharsis of his past.

By 1994, Fred had come a long way in his thinking. He had, in fact, designed his own modus operandi in the backcountry Southwest, which he called the outdoor museum. My first glimpse of its workings had come on that 1993 trip, when, in an unremarkable bend of Grand Gulch, Fred had reached inside a cubbyhole at the base of a sandstone boulder and pulled out the rusted tin cans that just might have been Wetherill's. Fred had discovered the cans lying in the open eight years earlier. From inside one can, I retrieved a brittle piece of notebook paper that bore the message Fred had penned at the time:

> This can may have belonged to Richard Wetherill. The solder at the bottom dictates to the late 1890s. Please leave as an important piece of the Outdoor Museum of Grand Gulch.
>
> *Fred Blackburn*
> *May 6, 1985*

Now, in 1994, we hiked up a side canyon that forked north midway along the fifty-six-mile serpent of Grand Gulch. A few miles upstream, we paused beneath a shallow overhang facing south. It was not an obvious Anasazi site: I might have walked past it without checking it out. No ruins were visible.

In 1979, however—the last year he worked as a BLM ranger in the Gulch—Fred had led a group of hikers into this side canyon. On previous trips, his keen eye had recognized the site as a Basketmaker burial ground. Most of Fred's clients in those days seemed to be of the right sort, well-educated Anasazi devotees with a respect for the past. They were not the good old boys with whom he had grown up, who saw only treasure for the taking in a prehistoric site.

The 1979 group had poked about the overhang for an hour or two, behaving with the decorum Fred expected. Just before the group left, Fred got on his hands and knees to peer inside a dark slit beneath a huge boulder lying in front of the site. His eyes adjusted to the shadows, and his heart started pounding.

Gently he pulled from its ancient cache a wooden staff about five feet tall, crooked at the head like a walking cane, made of a single piece of wood, superbly whittled and smoothed. It was one of the rarest of all Anasazi artifacts. The group, along with Fred, was mesmerized. When at last they had finished admiring the staff, Fred replaced it in its dark cranny, exactly where he had found it.

"This one woman in the group," Fred told me now as we sat next to the boulder, "made it her goal in life to remove the staff." His voice had that tired note of outrage I had come to recognize. "She contacted the Utah state archaeologist. He came in and removed it. It's now at the Edge of the Cedars, in Blanding. And the woman never even told me she did it or asked me to cooperate."

By 1979, fed up with the BLM, Fred had made up his own mind about how to deal with an artifact found in a remote place: it was to leave it in situ. Here was the germ of the outdoor museum. "It's not the artifact," Fred likes to say, "it's the geography." The wooden cane left under the boulder had so much more power there—more value, even—than under glass in some display case. In the great museums, Fred had seen too many storerooms full of dusty pots and baskets, vaguely catalogued, if at all, the proveniences often lost through shoddy record-keeping.

Now Fred tossed out some ideas about the cane. In an adjoining side canyon, less than a mile away, he had found a pair of similar staffs pictured in an Anasazi rock-art panel. What was the relationship of the cane in its hiding place to the rock-art site around a few corners? Of the cane to the burials only a few yards away?

"At Pueblo Bonito, they found three hundred canes, some with feathers attached," Fred drawled on. "At Hopi today, similar canes symbolize the four stages of life. And you see them in rock-art processional panels.

"So the cane we found here may have to do with some high-status burial. And it's old—at least as old as Basketmaker II. It might even be Archaic. Some people think the canes have to do with *pochteca* trade." I had read about the *pochteca:* long-distance traders and spies who hailed from Aztec Mexico. Though we know them only from an era well after the A.D. 1300 abandonment, they serve as a powerful model for hypothesized earlier traders who may have brought Mesoamerican ideas to the American Southwest, particularly at Chaco Canyon. What Fred was suggesting was that the cane might hint at *pochteca* trade going way, way back.

Fifteen years afterward, the deceit of the woman who had gone behind Fred's back to engineer the cane's removal still rankled. The deed had provoked another turning point in his thinking. You could not trust just anyone you guided into the wilderness with the secrets of the outdoor museum. Over the years, Fred's invention evolved into an expanding club of insiders pledged to certain ideals. In 1993, I had been in effect a novitiate trying out for membership. As we had retraced Wetherill, Fred had been giving me the once-over. Was I the sort who could be trusted, or was I a mere dilettante—or worse, a saboteur? As a writer, I loomed as a particularly dangerous type.

In his role of curator and chairman of the board of the outdoor museum, Fred could be maddening. One of his tests for apprentices was all too reminiscent of the drill of some sadistic kindergarten teacher. In 1993, he had led photographer Terry Moore and me to an obscure ledge, then sat down on a rock and said, "OK, find it. It's within a hundred yards of here." He wouldn't even tell us what *it* was. As Terry and I stumbled around, looking for rock-art panels, peering behind lumps of stone, our mentor cackled smugly. "Christ, Fred," I groused, "you really get off on this."

But after twenty minutes I found *it:* a small, nearly intact gray pot cached almost at the end of the ledge. Fred had propped stones on the near side of it to make it harder to find by accident, but he had not moved the pot. Terry and I had graduated from kindergarten to first grade. A year later, I guided a friend of my own to the pot (omitting the Easter egg hunt). When I told Fred I had done so, I worried that he might think I was spreading the secret too blithely. Instead he gave a little cluck of approval, impressed, apparently, that I had found the pot from memory—for the ledge looked like any of a hundred others in the side canyon.

It would be facile to regard the outdoor museum as more elitist than any curated exhibit: a small band of explorers guarding their private lore as jealously as Renaissance sailing captains playing Venice against Genoa. But as I came to see, there was little vanity in Blackburn's mission. Despite the charade on the ledge, what mattered to Fred was not the exclusivity of his esoteric knowledge. It was that the artifact stay united with the landscape and that the modern visitor do his homework to find and appreciate both. A museum handed you wonders for a $5 ticket and told you what to think in a fifty-word caption: no wonder it was so easy for the mind to wander, the magic to evaporate. The outdoor musem was the work of days and weeks, and the rewards could be comparable.

Two years before, on my own, I had traveled nearly every foot of the stretch of Grand Gulch that Fred now led the other three of us through. At least half of what he showed me I had completely missed in 1992. A single moment on our seventh day demonstrated the profundity of Fred's knowledge of the Gulch. The willows through which we pushed along our corridor of trail looked much as they had all morning. We caught only glimpses of the surrounding walls. All at once, Fred veered off the path to the left. We bashed through the brush, came to a pair of low ledges scattered with crumbling stones. Fred hunted for ten minutes before he found what he was looking for.

It stood at chest level, on a mundane patch of sandstone wall. I beheld a pair of tiny pictographs in red paint: one depicted a turkey, the other a bighorn sheep. Only three inches long, the sheep was a masterpiece—as perfectly drawn as any Anasazi pictograph I had ever seen. The figure, in profile, captured the grace of a bighorn browsing at cliff top with a simplicity Picasso might have envied.

Fred called the site the Miniature Panel. That had been Pete Steele's name for it. Already long in tooth in the 1970s, Steele had been a rancher and one of the first guides ever in Grand Gulch. As a novice ranger in 1974, Fred had been taught the Gulch by Steele. By 1994, the old man had moved out of the region, leaving the store of his knowledge in the heads of Blackburn and a handful of other protégés.

If, as the BLM estimates, about thirty thousand people entered Grand Gulch in 1994, it is reasonable to guess that perhaps eight thousand of them walked within a hundred yards of the Miniature Panel. I doubt that a dozen of them saw that matchless pictograph.

During each evening in the Gulch, the four of us launched into an impromptu colloquy about what we had seen during the day. One of our liveliest debates had to do with loopholes (as I called them, pushing for a loaded analogy with European castles)—those tiny, well-aimed tubular apertures in the windowless outer walls of certain cliff dwellings. Grand Gulch abounds in such façades. One in particular, at a site called Long House, bore eleven loopholes canted at different angles in a massive, sixty-foot-long wall. Visiting the place in 1992, I had naively imagined ancients shooting arrows through the holes, like Arthurian knights. Now, two years later at the same site, Bruce Bradley, the flint expert who had made many Anasazi-style projectiles with his own hands, ridiculed my notion: eyeing a hole, he laughed and said, "You sure as hell couldn't shoot an arrow through that!"

All right, I conceded that evening, so they were peepholes, not loopholes. I still believed they had to do with some enemy. But both Fred and Bruce—despite the latter's theory of a hyperdefensive neo-Chacoan movement springing up around 1250—wanted to see the holes as observation posts. At Long House, they argued, a flat platform beneath the ruin might have served as a dance plaza. Behind the sixty-foot wall, dignitaries or priests could have watched some rite without being seen themselves. Fred went so far as to picture the tubes as viewing points for a procession moving up or down the canyon, along the lines of the Shalako Ceremony, the central ritual of Zuni culture today.

One thing we agreed upon: the tubes or holes had nothing to do with astronomical alignments, the likes of which have been demonstrated at Chaco Canyon, Chimney Rock, Hovenweep, and other major Anasazi sites. The reason was simple: nearly all the holes pointed down, not up toward the sky.

Two days later, off on a jaunt by myself, I came to yet another ruin with loopholes in the front façade. There I made a fascinating discovery—or perhaps, as happens so often in archaeology, I mistook coincidence for meaning. The ruin was unmistakably Pueblo III. But four large boulders sitting in front of the site were covered with Basketmaker petroglyphs, depicting anthropomorphs, snakes, atlatls, birds, bird tracks, bighorn sheep, and spirals that might signify springs, sun disks, or migration maps (or, of course, something else entirely).

Four of the loopholes in the Pueblo III façade stared directly at certain Basketmaker petroglyphs.

Was I detecting some mute trace of ancestor worship, some ritualistic link between the thirteenth-century villagers and those dimly known forebears who had occupied the alcove a thousand years before? All over the Anasazi domain, you find Basketmaker sites reused in Pueblo II and III. Often the reworking looks brutal—the large slabs that built Basketmaker pithouses and cists simply ripped from the ground and used as raw stone for the new, masoned buildings. There is no doubt that the original looters in the Southwest were the Anasazi themselves.

Sometimes a gentler renovation seems at work, as upright slabs remain in place to form the lower walls of Pueblo structures. The look is incongruous, as if a half-timbered Elizabethan house in England gave way, a few feet above the ground, to Georgian brick. On rock-art panels, often Pueblo II and III figures are gouged or painted directly atop Basketmaker anthropomorphs. But is this desecration? Among Australian Aborigines, some of whose rock-art traditions extend into the twentieth century, we know that painting new figures directly over old ones was a way of reanimating their power.

Our loophole debate came to no consensus. Yet on my solo outing, as I squinted through a tube in the dwelling wall at a great triangle-bodied anthropomorph on the boulder before it, my puzzlement gave way to exhilaration. The most basic and humble features of Anasazi sites baffle even the experts. Rather than cause for dismay, here lay the challenge of the unknown.

I was reminded of a moment two months before, when I had walked through a site near Cortez with Steve Lekson. On a bedrock slab beside a small dwelling I spotted five deep vertical incisions running parallel to one another, still dusty with abraded sandstone. "Nice sharpening grooves," I said. Every Anasazi textbook describes these slits as the legacy of generations of hunters filing their axe and knife blades to keen edges. I assumed the matter was self-evident, like the use of metates and manos to grind corn.

But Lekson said, "Maybe they're sharpening grooves. Maybe not."

I was startled. "Why not?"

"Why do you need five of them, when one would do?"

"What else could they be?"

"I haven't got the slightest idea," said Lekson.

In seven hundred years, the processes of everyday life could pass from the banal to the mysterious.

During our days and nights in Grand Gulch, Ira Block kept up the rapt vigilance of a wary acolyte. The other three of us admired his pluck as he scrambled along ledges fifty feet above the void, lenses and camera bodies and light meters dangling about his torso. "This is an amazing place," he would grant, looking around, "but, you know, *weird*." Yet with his city boy's curiosity he relished every aspect of the pilgrimage we were dragging him on, even as he scarfed down the bland noodle-and-cheese glops I cooked for dinner. Ira had smuggled along a bottle of his favorite spiced tequila, which he had discovered in some Mexican backwater, and his postprandial toasts capped our blissful days.

Only at odd moments did the photographer betray an anxiety that may have lurked constantly beneath his skin. In the morning, he would crawl out of his one-man tent, stand up, rub his eyes, shiver in the dawn chill, stare around him, and ask Fred: "Now, this way is downcanyon, right?" Fred would nod. "And that's just a side canyon over there?" It was hard not to laugh as Ira pointed more or less randomly. "And today we're heading upcanyon, huh?"

Though I had bought and packaged all our food, at regular intervals we caught Ira slipping a Power Bar out of his pack and nibbling furtively on it. "Where'd you get all those Power Bars, Ira?" Fred finally asked.

"Madeleine gave them to me." Madeleine was his wife, as confirmed a Manhattanite as Ira.

"Didn't she trust me to buy the food?" I needled.

"That wasn't it," answered Ira earnestly. "She said to take these along, you know, just in case you guys abandon me or something."

On one of our best days, we climbed a rincon, a great square plug of rock three hundred feet high that had been formed by the stream cutting through a cliff to isolate an oxbow. The plug sat stranded, as it were, between the dry meandering loop of the ancient river channel and the sandy wash where the stream now flowed. Fred had been atop the rincon once or twice before. His research revealed that the first Anglo visitors had been those Durango ranchers McLoyd and Graham, who in 1891 had beaten even Richard Wetherill to the Gulch.

Fred had tracked down C. C. Graham's grandson in Houston and obtained from him a photocopy of the laconic diary the rancher had kept. From this document, he was able to pinpoint the very afternoon—February 2, 1891—that the two men had ascended Arrow Point, as they called the plug.

Today, as for the Anasazi, there is only one route up the rincon, and that none too easy. We managed it by climbing to the top of a piñon pine and stepping delicately across space to surmount one overhang, then using that hoary alpinist's technique the shoulder stand (I climbed on top of Bruce's and Fred's shoulders) to breach a second.

The summit of the island, some thirty acres in extent, was covered with vestiges of the Anasazi. Several rows of crude dwellings crouched under ledges; a scattering of late Mesa Verde–style pottery sat on the benches; and we found one splendid petroglyph panel inside a clean rock crevice—bighorn sheep, abstract designs, and a flute player lying on his back.

But the glory of the place was flint: tens (maybe hundreds) of thousands of flakes, ranging in color from white to creamy tan to ruddy brown to gray-blue to black, lay strewn across the bedrock. From a distance, each dazzle of flakes catching the sunlight announced a shallow sandy depression where the trickling runoff of the ages had concentrated slivers of stone.

Bruce was in ecstasy. For half an hour at a time, he would crawl across the bedrock on hands and knees, picking up flakes, muttering to himself, sometimes bursting into cries of wonderment. Many an Anasazi archaeologist can recognize potsherd styles and assign them to the different phases of prehistory; it takes a true lithic expert to do the same for flakes knapped loose from lumps of flint and chert and obsidian. Bruce knew his stuff, and to his astonishment, he found fragments testifying to every epoch from Basketmaker II through Pueblo III. (This despite Bill Lipe's conclusion that there were periods as long as 350 years when Cedar Mesa had been abandoned.) To my eye, the flakes all looked more or less alike, but out of the bewildering mélange Bruce kept seizing partial points—mere corners or tips of half-finished blades that had broken in the making. His proudest find was a piece of an eccentric; in twenty years, he had seen only two or three others. This was a crescent of thin flint, shaped, apparently for artistic or religious purposes, into a delicate pattern that looked like a parrot's claw.

As rich as the rincon top seemed to us that day, Fred knew how much richer it had been 103 years earlier. From Arrow Point, McLoyd and Graham had retrieved 120 whole projectile points, ranging from the long, slender blades the Basketmakers had lashed to their atlatl darts to the tiny but deadly arrowheads Pueblo III hunters had fashioned. All of these had found their way to the Field Museum in Chicago. To study the collection today would tell us things about Grand Gulch that we may otherwise never deduce. But in his archival probes, Fred and his Wetherill project cronies had learned that all but two of the projectile points had been bartered in the early 1900s by a Field Museum representative to a trader who set up shop across the street. The incomparable collection is dispersed forever, lost in the attics and shoe boxes of the great-grandchildren of Edwardians seized with a moment of curio fever.

That evening's colloquy was all about the rincon. The obvious puzzle was why so difficult a place to get to had been for more than a millennium a locus of flint working so intense that it suggested a shrine. Did the very act of knapping a point require the artisan's removal to some sublimely isolated site? Or did the site's remoteness hint instead at defense? Had the ancient craftsmen working furiously on that pedestal in the sky been warriors first and hunters second?

Bruce pointed out that, generally speaking, points get steadily smaller through the Anasazi epochs. Experts suspect that a time-honored practice was to take a damaged point, or even a large discarded flake, from an earlier age and rework it into a smaller point in the current style. "Yet we also know," Bruce added, "that the Pueblo II and III people didn't always rework older points. Sometimes they kept them and put them in their medicine bags.

"And modern Pueblo people today still have a great need for Anasazi points. An old arrowhead always represents a very special gift."

We camped that night beneath a cottonwood tree at the northeast corner of the rincon. As my mind slid toward sleep, a kaleidoscope of flakes tumbled past my eyelids, their colors and shapes a blur; but the sharp, scalloped feel of each stone chip I had held and rubbed still tingled in my fingertips.

BY the end of our trip in Grand Gulch, Fred had decided that Ira and I had shown enough of the right stuff to be admitted in good standing to the outdoor museum. He had overcome his qualms about the havoc I might wreak as a writer; indeed, he hoped I would write about the museum, or at least about the quandary that had given birth to it. Too many of even the most conscientious back-country hikers had never analyzed the consequences of the manner in which they approached a prehistoric site.

In the last few years of hiking in the Southwest, I had seen two symptoms of that obliviousness spread like fads across the Anasazi domain. One was the tendency of travelers who worked out a devious route down some canyon or along some ruin-hung ledge to build small cairns as guideposts for pilgrims to come. The other was the gathering of potsherds and laying them out on display on some prominent rock face. Both practices stemmed from a magnanimous impulse: the urge to share with future strangers something wonderful that one had discovered. Yet in that very motive, both practices smacked of the mechanistic paternalism that had built the asphalt trails at Mesa Verde, that had filled those storerooms in the great museums with pots and baskets that no one looked at anymore. Fred had taught me to kick down the cairns, to sweep clean from the rock faces the mosaics of pretty sherds. A tenet of the outdoor museum was that the best discoveries were made on one's own.

A skeptic might jeer that in showing Ira and me the Miniature Panel, Fred was indulging in much the same paternalism as the cairn builders. But there was a qualitative difference: Fred's guiding us to an arcane site was an act of friendship, trust, dialogue. It partook, in a sense, of the intimate; in an odd way, it mirrored the oral tradition of the Pueblos—for Pete Steele had handed down his knowledge to Fred, an acolyte ready to receive secret lore, and Fred to us, and we . . . The cairn builders' helpful handiwork was no more intimate than a highway crew's.

So, at the very end of October, Fred guided Ira and me to eight or nine Anasazi sites in another canyon on the Colorado Plateau, where at last the doors of the outdoor museum opened wide. A condition of our visit was that in print I identify the place no more specifically than I have above—and that Ira photograph it in a fashion that would not give away its location. The almost paranoid vigilance with which Fred strived to suppress any document that could be turned into a road map had inquisitional overtones. In Grand Gulch, when he had caught me inking a tiny *X* on the USGS map as we sat in a ruin he had taken me to, Fred muttered, "That's a no-no."

"How come? I won't show it to anybody."

"Keep it up here." Fred pointed to his head.

Joining us on the second trip was Vaughn Hadenfeldt, a wilderness guide like Fred, a good climber, Fred's buddy for twenty years, and a charter member of the outdoor museum. Over the next several days, I found Vaughn entirely likable—a modest, soft-spoken, brainy outdoorsman, the phlegmatic foil to Fred's choleric idealist.

Hiking west across a blank mesa toward the secret canyon, we struck the wrong promontory rim (another of Fred's atavisms is his refusal to use a compass). We were a mile or so too far south. But the error was serendipitous: beneath an isolated hoodoo we found a cliff dwelling that neither Fred nor Vaughn had seen before. The roofs of the granaries were all intact, and in the mud mortaring the stones on one tall dwelling wall, we saw not only rows of dimpled indentations where corncobs had been used like rollers to smooth the surface, but also—five feet above the ground!—the unmistakable impression of a footprint.

Both pictographs and petroglyphs decorated the nearby walls and boulders, and though the dwelling was clearly Pueblo III, the rock art looked Basketmaker. Three figures in particular beguiled me: anthropomorphs with a distinctly penguin look. They had fish-shaped bodies, round heads sunk into their torsos, horizontal slits for eyes, and silly, sticklike, truncated arms held out to the sides like penguin flippers. I suspected the paintings were variants on Basketmaker III humanoids. According to Polly Schaafsma, after about A.D. 500 the severe, magnificent tapering-bodied anthropomorphs of Basketmaker II grow smaller, "cuter," squatter, and more triangular. But I had never seen anything quite like these penguinoids. Again I thought of Bill Lipe's phrase for the Anasazi here in the northwestern hinterland: "escaping the confines of normative thought."

We got our bearings and rim-walked north. All at once Fred stopped and exclaimed, "Look at this!" A smear of blood ran along the bedrock across our path. With my eye on distant features, I had walked over it without even noticing. Now we traced the streak as it ran down a natural watercourse into a shallow groove. We came across bits of hair and hide, more blood, then, near a bedrock pothole filled with water, a dark pile of entrails from which a putrid odor wafted. To Fred and Vaughn, both veteran hunters, the scene was self-evident. "It's a deer kill," said Fred. "Mountain lion got him when he came here to drink. Killed him, then dragged him up the rock to hide somewhere." So fresh were the blood and entrails, the kill must have happened within the past day or two.

In thirty-five years of hiking in the West, I had never seen a mountain lion in the wild. Fred and Vaughn had seen only a few themselves. Nor had I ever hunted, and though the idea of pushing deep into the high country to shoot a blameless elk dismayed me, I had nothing but admiration for the tracking skills of hunters like Fred. In Grand Gulch one day, he and Bruce Bradley had stopped to examine some deer tracks in the dirt. I recognized deer prints when I saw them; but from the particular configuration we hovered over, Bruce and Fred could tell that within the past twenty-four hours a baby deer had suckled its mother here. They could even point out where the baby had dug its hooves in to get a better purchase.

We meandered north along the rim, skirting branches of the intricate canyon. A major tributary ran athwart our path ahead, offering a good route into the depths. But instead of steering for that, Fred and Vaughn led us toward an obscure archipelago of hoodoos and swirling domes. At last we dipped to a low saddle and climbed back onto a rimrock island—nothing so isolated and majestic as the rincon in Grand Gulch, but perhaps equally well defended.

We spent the whole day on the island, where I saw many things the likes of which I had never before encountered. The first was a Basketmaker cist—five upright slabs protruding from the ground, forming a pentagon that defined a storage area. I had seen other such cists, but this was by far the most perfect I had come across. Inside it on the sand lay a smooth white mano.

Around a couple of corners, we found something much more remarkable. It was the remains of a Basketmaker pithouse, the semisubterranean living chamber that long preceded the aboveground rooms the Pueblo Anasazi started building after A.D. 750. Well-preserved pithouses have been excavated from beneath the soil, but to find one still exposed to the air is rare indeed. Its architecture echoed that of the cist: the lower course of walls (all that remained) was built of big stone slabs wedged upright into the earth, not of small, dressed stones laid horizontal and chinked with mud.

From their hiding places, our guides pulled five manos and two big metates. One of the latter had a hole punched through the center. Fred argued that it was thus a "killed" metate, deliberately rendered useless as a way of retiring the object, perhaps for some spiritual reason, or to bury it with its maker. The argument comes by analogy with Mimbres pottery found in southwestern New Mexico. To our modern sensibility the most beautiful prehistoric pots ever made in the Southwest (they fetch by far the highest prices on the black market), these Mogollon vessels abound in stylized renderings of humans, animals, birds, fish, insects, and chimeras that allude to myths we shall never glimpse. (Figuration in ancient Southwestern ceramics is the great exception: virtually all Anasazi designs are abstract.) Mimbres pots are nearly always found buried with the dead, and virtually every one has a kill hole punched in the bottom.

The whole island was littered with flint flakes, but we found not a single potsherd or remnant of corn. "What's amazing about this place," said Fred, "is that, as far as I can tell, it's absolutely pure Basketmaker II. It may go back into the Archaic, but it doesn't even reach up to Basketmaker III. And the later people of Pueblo II and III didn't touch the place. They didn't live here, and they didn't vandalize it for slabs and metates and dart points to use for themselves. And the modern pothunters haven't hit the place yet."

From beneath a ledge backing a shelf particularly rich in flakes, Vaughn pulled a Ziploc bag. Ira and I gasped as he shook onto the ground a jumble of perfect and slightly damaged projectile points, thirty-eight all told. "Every one of these," said Vaughn, "we found right here, fanned out on the shelf within a few yards. And before we picked them up, we made a sketch map of the exact location of each one, to preserve the proveniences."

I read the note Fred had left inside the Ziploc bag six years before:

> Nov. 4, 1988. We found these points and left them here as part of the Outdoor Museum. Please consider and follow this ethic. Thanks,
>
> *Fred Blackburn et al.*

Prowling along other benches, I found a well-made dart point half buried in sand. Atop a slickrock dome, Fred found two that he hadn't seen before. One appeared to be a dart point reworked to make a drill.

At last we sat and contemplated our surroundings. Despite the lateness of the season, at the end of October, the westering sun was warm on our backs. In the silence, the only sound was juncos clicking from the junipers. "A place like this, you hate to leave even a footprint," said Fred.

"I can't say this for many places I've been," he went on, "but when I walked out to this island a few years ago, I think I was the first person to come here since the last Basketmaker left. Fifteen hundred years, minimum." It was not a boast: the possibility seemed vibrant with the grace of happenstance. "The research questions that could come out of this place . . ." Fred paused. "It just scares the hell out of you."

For twenty years after Wetherill's discovery of the Basketmakers, they languished in a scholarly limbo. Many of the leading archaeologists of the early twentieth century came to regard them as semi-apocryphal, even spurious. Then, in 1914, digging in the Kayenta region, Alfred V. Kidder unearthed four bottle-shaped cists filled with ancient skeletons (one cist contained nineteen dead), covered with disintegrating baskets, with not a single potsherd in evidence. The following year, Kidder's closest partner, Samuel Guernsey, worked other sites nearby. He found sixty caves, many skeletons, and rich troves of grave goods ranging from tightly woven baskets to rabbit-fur blankets to atlatls to cords made of human hair. The Basketmakers had been rehabilitated.

At the first Pecos Conference, in 1927, Kidder and his colleagues proposed the scheme of phases of Anasazi culture that is still in use today (see Appendix: Anasazi Chronology). Because the preceramic remains that Wetherill, Kidder, and Guernsey had dug up seemed to adumbrate a remarkably sophisticated culture, the experts dubbed it Basketmaker II, postulating a more primitive, hypothetical Basketmaker I phase out of which it must have evolved. All this took place before A. E. Douglass's breakthrough discovery of tree-ring dating, so the absolute chronology of the Anasazi presence in the Southwest was utterly in doubt.

Over the decades, sifting the sands of scores of ambitious digs, archaeologists found nothing that cohered as a Basketmaker I culture. What preceded Basketmaker II seemed to be pure hunter-gatherers who, like most nomads, left only the most fugitive traces of their passage across the landscape. Today we call that phase Archaic, lumping together, at a very minimum, five thousand years of human presence in what would become the Anasazi domain. Archaic thus swallows Basketmaker I without a trace.

Meanwhile, Wetherill's assumption that the Basketmakers were a different people from the Puebloans lingered on. J. O. Brew, writing in 1946, pointed out that the notion of a Pueblo invasion around A.D. 700 was still generally accepted. A cardinal sticking point in the archaeological record was the apparent difference in skull shape between Basketmakers and Puebloans. Even though many cradle boards had been dug up at Anasazi sites, it was a long while before the experts reached the simple conclusion that the hard cradle board of the later Pueblo people (Basketmaker cradles had "pillows") artificially flattened the crania of infants, producing the apparent difference in skull types. It took Brew's seminal work in the 1940s on Alkali Ridge, a long Utah mesa just east of Blanding covered with small sites, many of which dated from the crucial transition around A.D. 750, to demonstrate for good that Basketmaker culture developed continuously into Pueblo culture.

Nonetheless, for four decades after Brew, the enigmatic Basketmakers lingered on in limbo, neglected by scholars who concentrated on the "sexier" phenomena of Chaco Canyon, late Pueblo III and the abandonment, and the dramatic appearance of huge aggregated pueblos in the fourteenth century.

Only in recent years has the research spotlight begun to turn back on the Basketmakers. The transition from Archaic to Basketmaker II is defined by the first deliberate cultivation of corn. This seemingly profound watershed, with its potential to transform nomads into farmers, looks fuzzier and more ambiguous in the Southwest than it was once thought to be. A few years ago, the starting point for Basketmaker II would have been placed no earlier than 100 B.C. Now many experts would push the demarcation line all the way back to 1200 B.C.

Dates so far in the past tend to blur in the imagination into a monochromatic haze. But if the new estimates are right, they mean that the Basketmaker II era, far from encompassing a relatively uniform culture of a few centuries' duration, lasted seventeen hundred years, or longer than the entire span from Basketmaker III through the present-day Pueblos. During those centuries, all kinds of spectacular developments must have taken place, of which we remain archaeologically in the dark. Fred was right: on the Basketmaker II island he had found, the research potential could scare the hell out of you.

Where did corn come from? Nearly all scholars agree that it diffused slowly northward from Mexico. Squash, the second Anasazi staple, may have been cultivated soon after corn; but beans, the third basic crop, were not mastered until Basketmaker III times, after A.D. 500. The search for the first corn in Anasazi country animates researchers today.

Yet the old paradigm—taught us in grade school textbooks, with their bucolic images of the Mesopotamian Fertile Crescent—that agriculture irreversibly transformed human civilization, making possible cities, kingships, written language, art, and the march of progress, no longer works. It works particularly feebly in explaining the Anasazi.

University of Utah archaeologist Jesse D. Jennings, summing up in 1966 the eight years of desperate and heroic survey work along Glen Canyon and its tributaries as the waters of Lake Powell rose, concluded that even in the thirteenth century the Anasazi could not have survived on corn, squash, and beans alone. They still gathered as many as four hundred different native plants for use as food and medicine. "The entire floral complex essentially made up a large garden," Jennings wrote.

In 1981, the iconoclastic Charlie Steen argued similarly that even by the thirteenth century the San Juan Anasazi had never achieved true agricultural status. Venturing out on a limb, Sheen guessed that in the misery of that era's drought and disease, some bands may have given up farming altogether and reverted to hunting and gathering. Steen is not the only scholar to suggest that such a reversal can take place among human societies. Recent research on Indian tribes near the headwaters of the Amazon suggests that after centuries of an agrarian way of life, some may have gone back to hunter-gatherer nomadism in the sixteenth century, under the pressure of Spanish and Portuguese conquest.

The onset of Basketmaker II, we now suspect, stretches far back before the birth of Christ. What marks the epoch's end, the transition to Basketmaker III? Still dogged by the notion of separate peoples, the 1927 Pecos classifiers saw the great dividing line as the moment when Pueblo I took over from Basketmaker III—which we now date at around A.D. 750. But Bill Lipe, in a 1990 paper, pointed out that the real watershed in Anasazi development came between Basketmaker II and Basketmaker III, around A.D. 450–500.

In those crucial years, the Anasazi invented pottery or learned it from neighbors to the south. They still made baskets, but because they no longer needed to cook or carry water with them, the weaving grew cruder and more slapdash. They discovered how to grow beans. The pithouses in which they lived became deeper and more substantial, and they built the first great kivas, perhaps as places in which to hold intervillage ceremonies. They invented the bow and arrow, and gave up the atlatl. In contrast, the transition from Basketmaker III to Pueblo I is far less revolutionary—a matter mostly of the first surface room block dwellings and the first decorated pottery. Yet old taxonomies survive new understandings: nobody suggests today that we rename Basketmaker III, calling it—what? Proto–Pueblo I?

As deep a question as what led to the discovery of corn and at least as far from a satisfactory answer, is what caused this great cultural revolution around A.D. 500. During our flint-knapping day at Jemez Pueblo, I had watched Bill Whatley and Bruce Bradley wield atlatls they had fashioned after Basketmaker II models. With a heave of the arm, they easily flung their homemade hafted darts fifty or sixty yards through the air before they struck deep and deadly in the earth, like well-thrown javelins. Bruce had calculated the physics of some of his experimental atlatls and found that he could sling a dart into a target with one hundred times the force of the most vigorously thrust spear. A good Anasazi hunter could have hurled a dart clean through the torso of a deer or bighorn sheep.

"So what's the advantage of the bow and arrow over the atlatl?" I asked Bruce.

He looked thoughtful. "I've wondered that myself," he answered. "My hunch is that, first, a bow and arrow is more accurate. And second, you can use it in the woods, as you stalk game, hiding behind rocks, shooting between trees. It's real hard to throw an atlatl in the woods."

Yet the more I pondered what I knew of the Anasazi, the less clearly I saw their course through the centuries as progress. To our modern eye, the finest rock art of all is Basketmaker II petroglyphs. Nine hundred years of less-and-less-impressive work succeed the stunning and provocative panels—are they shamanic visions, as some think?—that crowd such cliffs as Lower Butler Wash on the San Juan.

What of human nature? Did the turn toward violence and warfare that scholars are finding in such abundance after 1250 spring from a late and bitter factionalism? Or was it always intrinsic in the Anasazi psyche?

We know very little about violence in Basketmaker II times, but Christy Turner and Winston Hurst's painstaking reconstruction of what happened at Cave 7 in Whiskers Draw gives a vivid look at one event. In that shallow alcove in the middle of nowhere, sometime before A.D. 500, more than ninety men, women, and children were either massacred in an all-out attack or ritually executed. It was not enough simply to kill these unfortunates: some were scalped, and some may have been tortured before death. Who they were and why they met this grisly end, we have no idea.

I HAD described Fred's outdoor museum to Steve Lekson. The professional's response to the amateur's crusade was genial but dismissive. "I think it's romantic," Lekson offered. "It's one way of enjoying Anasazi sites. Most people are entranced by those ruins. But it's not archaeology."

Later, in a letter, Lekson amplified his critique. As he wrote me:

> Fred's Outdoor Museum is a gallery of his own brilliant design—a Zen garden of earthly delights—which will personally affect a few people but advance scientific knowledge not at all. I like the concept, I'd like a tour, but I can't see changing BLM policies or closing traditional museums because Fred will enrich the lives of a thousand people. That's a tiny audience, for one thing, and it's not archaeology.

But in his own day, Richard Wetherill, that other passionate, self-taught amateur, had been similarly dismissed by professionals such as Edgar Hewett and Jesse Nusbaum. A hundred years later, Wetherill's stock stood higher than either Hewett's or Nusbaum's. Impressed by Blackburn's fervor and integrity, at ease in his campfire company, I had begun to wonder whether his quirky ideas about backcountry sites might eventually win the day.

For archaeology is almost inevitably destructive, and the most scrupulous techniques of one generation tend to be viewed as folly by the next. For four days in November 1993, I had driven a dirt road up Montezuma Creek in southeastern Utah, car-camping and hiking short distances to Anasazi ruins. The canyon had been extensively studied during the 1960s by teams from Brigham Young University, whose reports I used to guide me to the sites.

The journey was strangely disappointing. Some of the modest ruins startled and pleased me; the camping, even in cattle country, was serene; I passed only a handful of other vehicles during my four days and saw no one else out hiking. But the sites had a barren, denuded feel about them. They seemed as picked over as the most sterile ruins under the aegis of the National Park Service. Scarcely a single potsherd or corncob lay in the dirt before the ancient habitations.

It was not a question of visitors' taking home their keepsakes: Montezuma Creek lies well off the tourist gauntlet. Rather, the BYU research plan called for the gathering of every single artifact found on the ground. Hundreds of thousands of potsherds had been picked up, stashed in plastic bags that were marked by site, and carted to the lab in Provo. This was the high-tech science of the day. Statistical analyses of, say, the number of Mesa Verde black-on-white sherds compared with Tusayan polychrome sherds within a given ruin might yield demographic insights into the sway of Kayenta versus Mesa Verde influences in Montezuma Creek.

But I wondered what had become of those plastic bags, what fruits had been plucked from the analyses. And I wondered whether it had ever occurred to the BYU archaeologists that in picking clean the sites to answer one research question, they might have robbed future scholars of the chance to answer other questions that no one could even formulate in the 1960s.

At dinner in Blanding one night with Winston Hurst, I aired these qualms. He put down his fork, and a pained look came over his face. "It's worse than you could ever think," he said. "The sherds were unmarked but kept in marked bags. One year some brain-dead grad student went into the lab, poured the sherds all out on the table, and sorted them out by ceramic styles. He destroyed all the proveniences in one fell swoop."

The day after our sojourn on the island, Fred and Vaughn guided us into the canyon proper, via an eastern tributary. We hiked from sunup till after dark and saw so many odd and unexpected sights that my memory teems with a surfeit of images and emotions. Among the highlights of the day was a kiva with the two poles of the ladder that reached to the entryway in the intact roof still in place. Gathered at the foot of the poles were the ladder's original rungs, once lashed to the poles by sinew or fiber. I had never seen the like.

Fred had been visiting the canyon for eighteen years, and on every trip he made new discoveries even as he checked the old ones to make sure his outdoor museum had not been vandalized. I doubt that ever again in a single day will I see anything like that abundance and variety of Anasazi artifacts in situ.

At successive sites, Vaughn and Fred pulled from their caches—sometimes in crevices, sometimes simply covered with flat rocks—all kinds of beguiling objects. We saw a pair of pristine Basketmaker II sandals, woven from apocynum (a plant in the dogbane family), with yucca thongs for the toes: traces of orange, purple, and creamy yellow paint still tinted their patterns. We handled a bizarre "spoon" crafted from the horn of a bighorn sheep, used possibly as a digging shovel for burials. We held a bundle of flat, shaped pieces of wood as light as balsa: parts of a weaver's loom, Fred thought. We looked at a doughnut ring woven from yucca, the only Anasazi pot rest Fred had ever found. We puzzled over several slender wooden arrows that Vaughn had found only three weeks before; instead of bearing flint heads, the arrow shafts themselves had been whittled to a point and fire-hardened. "Pueblo III," said Vaughn. "For killing small game—squirrels and such—because there weren't any big game left."

At one site, Fred made a new discovery: a small wooden awl honed to a needle-sharp point. After we had all scrutinized it, he found an out-of-the-way ledge on which to stow it.

"But will you remember where it is?" I teased.

"Doesn't matter," said Fred.

"It's still here," added Vaughn.

Ira was in photographic bliss, murmuring with pleasure as he arranged his compositions. Yet the artifacts were subtle, resisting the greedy scrutiny of his lenses.

At each site Fred had left one of his notes, no two of which were ever quite the same:

> We found these sandals here and left them in the Outdoor Museum. Around 50 people have now viewed these. They are still here and part of a larger picture.
>
> *Fred Blackburn*
> *10-9-81*

Near the end of the day, Fred played kindergarten teacher once more and set Ira and me loose on a shelf fifty feet above the creek bed, looking for a relic he had saved for last. Once again, he sat ex cathedra on his rock, chortling as our blind search grew alternately warm and cold; Vaughn restricted his mirth to a smile. It took half an hour this time, and we succeeded only because I thought a piling of stones on the side of an isolated boulder looked unnatural. Peering through an aperture, I saw a slick gray surface inside.

We took apart the stonework, which Fred had built to hide the object inside. It was a huge gray-blue olla, an oblate water jug with a narrow mouth. Cached under the partial shelter of the boulder's overhanging side, it had weathered over the years, leaving erosion holes that precisely matched the wind-worn contours of the boulder itself. The olla was painted in Sosi black-on-white style, which dated it to around A.D. 1200 and indicated a Kayenta influence.

Behind the jar lay a tale that, better than any other anecdote, captured the change of heart that had led Fred to his outdoor museum. The vessel had been discovered in the late 1970s not by Fred but by a Dutchman and his girlfriend, who, picknicking on this unlikely shelf, had glanced over and suddenly seen the olla in its niche. Only a few months before, one of Bill Lipe's survey teams had found a similar giant water jug in Pine Canyon, a north tributary of Grand Gulch. They had dutifully reported the find to the BLM, which brought in a helicopter to remove the treasure.

Though unfamiliar with the Anasazi country, the Dutch couple had responded with an instinctive reverence. They marveled at and drew the olla but declined even to touch it. Since the canyon lay on BLM land, they later reported the find to the ranger at Kane Gulch—who happened to be Fred Blackburn. The Hollanders returned with Fred to the site.

Fred's job required that he report the olla to his BLM superiors in Monticello, which he did. But there he drew the line. When the bigwigs announced their intention of removing the olla, Fred refused to disclose its location. Now, as we sat before the fragile vessel with its eloquent wind hole, still resting where some ancient had carefully laid it eight hundred years before, he told me proudly, "They got the one in Pine Canyon. They didn't get this one.

"Two weeks later," Fred went on, "the Dutch guy died in a car crash in Arches National Park. But he had written his son about the excitement of his discovery—one of the high points of his life.

"That's how a lot of this stuff got started. It wasn't just my idea—the Dutch guy and his girlfriend wanted the olla left in place. After he died, I viewed keeping it here as my responsibility to him."

Before we left, we stacked the stones back in place, hiding the olla from all but the most perspicacious sleuth, allowing the vessel the chance to stay where it belonged for another century or more.

As moving as the olla was, Fred and Vaughn had led us to an even more powerful site only an hour before. At an obscure bend of the canyon, tight beneath an overhanging three-hundred-foot wall, we had crawled under a leaning breakdown slab—a gargantuan piece of the wall itself that had peeled loose many thousands of years ago. In the dim, wedge-shaped enclosure, a matting of earth and grasses stretched flat for twenty yards. I might have mistaken the ground for natural, but in his Grand Gulch prowlings Fred had learned the signature for a Basketmaker II burial site. Such was this, the largest he had ever seen.

"I have no idea how big it is," he told me in a whisper as we hunkered under the slab, "or how many people are buried here, or what's buried with them. So far the goddamned pothunters haven't figured out the signature, but I'm afraid it's only a matter of time. I found this site in 1976, and I've checked it almost every year since. So far, nobody's messed with it. You two are among the very few who have ever seen it."

Thanks to the Native American Graves Protection and Repatriation Act (NAGPRA), passed in 1990, even the BLM is now powerless to touch a burial site without full consultation with all Indian tribes that might claim affinity. And who could know, even among the living Pueblos, what links these Basketmaker dead had with anyone breathing the Southwestern air today?

"I think there's some kind of link between these people and that bighorn-sheep digging spoon we found nearby, and the bighorn rock art. It may be hunting, or it may be magic. But the whole thing's a mystery."

Vaughn added, "I have a real urge to excavate here. Not to take anything, but to find out what these guys were all about. But of course, I'd never touch the site."

"If you're going to write," Fred said to me, still whispering, "write about this. Write about the dilemma of sites like this one."

His fingers rummaged in the dirt at the edge of the burial platform. "The pack rats keep digging up the grass." Fred raised an object for my inspection. It was a bleached bone, a single digit of a human finger. "I come back year after year, and I have to keep covering up this guy." Fred tucked the bone under the matting. I took a last look, and we scuttled back out into the sunlight.

8

Beyond the Anasazi

I SAT in a basement carrel of Tozzer, the anthropology library at Harvard, flipping idly through a bound periodical from the early 1960s. Here was one of my favorite ways of wasting time; but that day, my mind was somewhere else as I yawned past "Pleistocene Cinder Domes" and "Notes on Arizona Plants."

All at once a title caught my eye. The short article, by Christy Turner, later to be known for his theories about Anasazi cannibalism, was called "Mystery Canyon." The laconic text detailed a probe Turner and several friends had made in September 1959. In dry academese, Turner wrote about roping down sandstone slots, only to be boxed in by overhanging pourovers and plunge pools. The photos showed formidable ancient hand-and-toe trails. Too modest to make the claim in so many words, the archaeologist hinted that very few people had entered Mystery Canyon since the last Anasazi had packed up and left in the thirteenth century.

That 1959 jaunt had been launched as part of the far-flung survey of Glen Canyon and its tributaries during the years before the waters of Lake Powell inundated hundreds of square miles of the Anasazi domain. Reading between the lines, however, I could discern that Mystery Canyon itself had proved such a tough nut to crack that it had become an end in itself. A two- or three-year competition by various parties—composed not only of archaeologists but also of desert rats motivated by the lust for pure adventure—seemed to have focused on the well-defended chasm in the sandstone. One pair had used a helicopter to land on the rim near the north end of the canyon, then rappelled into its depths. But plunge pools and pourovers stopped them cold as well, restricting their forays up- and downcanyon to a few hundred yards.

I carried the journal to the photocopier, then went home and called an old friend, Jon Krakauer. We had planned a trip in the canyon country for that spring, with no clear objective in mind. Jon had not yet succumbed to the Anasazi passion, but I knew that any place that proved really hard to get to would appeal to him.

I was seized with the romance of Mystery Canyon myself. It seemed that, with luck, we might stumble into an adventure of our own straight out of the pages of Victorian or Edwardian fiction. In the sagas of Jules Verne and H. G. Wells and Arthur Conan Doyle, the scholar-adventurer burned his candle to a nub as he pored over quaint and curious volumes of forgotten lore. A map drawn in faded ink, a cryptic document in Latin fell into his fingers. From such glimmerings, a glorious excursion into terra incognita unfurled, as the scholar's team wound through an Icelandic volcano down to the center of the earth or traversed a lost Venezuelan plateau teeming with dinosaurs.

As soon as Jon got the article in the mail, he called me back. "We've got to go there," he blurted out. "The place sounds wild." In Jon's vocabulary, "wild" was the ultimate enthusiasm. "We should try to push the whole canyon, all the way to Lake Powell. Maybe nobody's done it."

Jon ordered us each a set of USGS maps. On the seven-and-one-half-minute quadrangles, the jumble of brown contour lines grew particularly frenzied around Mystery Canyon, as if some dipsomaniac cartographer had had a bad case of the shakes when he got down to drawing them. The charts abounded with those eloquent ambiguities where four or five lines run together, announcing OVERHANGING WALL.

Eleven years my junior, Jon had been my student at Hampshire College, an experimental school in western Massachusetts, where from 1970 through 1979 I had taught literature and mountaineering. Many good climbers had passed through Hampshire during those years; among them, Jon was the best. He had become a close friend, the only student I went climbing with outside the curricular orbit.

By 1994, I had given up serious mountaineering, though Jon still pursued the passion. In the meantime, he too had become a writer, with adventure of all kinds as his usual beat. We had managed to share some of these outings: circling Iceland in search of sites from the medieval sagas, packing with llamas into Wyoming's Wind River Range, and the like.

Mystery Canyon promised another such adventure, one refreshingly new to us both. Canyoneering, as it is called, is a sport in its infancy, just starting to be avidly practiced in the labyrinthine Southwest. Essentially it amounts to fusing the skills of rock climbing with those of technical river descents to explore tight canyons in the wilderness. I had done no canyoneering before, Jon only a little. But as with any young sport, the leading practitioners are still more or less improvising as they go. We thought that with a little ambition, we might make a contribution of our own. For me, the hook was still the Anasazi, traces of whose presence Christy Turner's team had found in the most unlikely places, deep in the headwaters of Mystery Canyon. For Jon, it was the appeal of forcing a passage through a demanding landscape where, just possibly, no one else, not even the Anasazi, had ever been.

Mystery Canyon snakes through the chaos of slickrock spread across the Navajo Reservation between Lake Powell and Navajo Mountain. Sometime before 1948, long before Lake Powell was even a mote in the eye of the Bureau of Reclamation, the canyon was named by that cranky pioneer Colorado River rafting guide Norm Nevills, after he tried and failed to find a way into its hidden maze. From the river, Nevills confronted a nearly blank cliff at the canyon's outlet; a hand-and-toe trail had been carved up it with a quartzite pounder by some Anasazi virtuoso more than seven hundred years before.

The steps seemed altogether too scary to Nevills, so he wielded a metal tool to gouge and enlarge them. (Modern ecotravelers cringe at such desecration, but many an Anasazi archaeologist—Samuel Guernsey, for one—did the same in the early decades of the twentieth century.) Even with chiseled help, Nevills gave up low on the toe trail. The canyon would remain a mystery.

Today's rafting guides say that if Nevills gave up, it must have been quite a staircase, for the man was famed for his daring as a cowboy climber. By now, the hand-and-toe trail Nevills blanched at scaling has vanished beneath the lake. Yet though Powell's waters have crept miles up Mystery Canyon, another blank cliff still prohibits access from its outlet in the lake. In the 1960s, the U.S. Board of Geographic Names gave Mystery Canyon a new, less soulful official title, but Jon and I agreed to stick with Nevills's name.

By the spring of 1994, I had yet to meet Christy Turner: it would be six months before I visited his office at Arizona State University to examine his evidence for Anasazi cannibalism. I knew his reputation, however, as one of the leading scholars in the field and had admired the analysis of the Cave 7 massacre he had published with Winston Hurst. Now I telephoned him to talk about Mystery Canyon. In 1959, he had been a relative youngster, and despite the restraint of his journal article, the thrill of discovery leaked from his prose.

Turner knew of no one who had explored the canyon after the '59 excursion. He confirmed, moreover, that his team had entered only a mile or so of the canyon at its headwaters, leaving a long stretch downstream untouched. Reminiscing over the phone about the trip, the archaeologist waxed nostalgic. He remembered well the pourover that had thwarted his team's probe downstream. "We weren't real climbers, but we had ropes," Turner told me. "We probably could have gotten down the pourover, but I'm not sure we could have gotten back up."

The '59 party would never have found their way into Mystery Canyon without the expertise of their Paiute guides, Dan Lehi and Toby Owl. By 1959, it had been a quarter century since Lehi himself had been into Mystery Canyon. Eventually, however, the canny Paiutes not only got the archaeology team into the heart of the canyon but engineered a wild horse-packing route to its shadowy depths. Thirty-five years later, Jon and I would find their horses' droppings, desiccated and preserved like artifacts under the desert sun.

Turner put me in touch with Frank Masland, who had personally bankrolled the 1959 foray as well as several other pioneering reconnaissances in the Anasazi country. Masland had made a small fortune from an automobile upholstery business and, though untrained as an archaeologist, was happy to serve as patron and companion to the likes of Turner. By 1994, Masland was ninety-three years old, living in Pennsylvania, and hard of hearing. But he warmed to my curiosity and mailed me a fifty-page unpublished manuscript he had written about those long-ago adventures.

The homespun prose of his memoir wove a lyrical spell. Again and again, deep in the wilderness, Masland had paused to breathe the ether of discovery:

> One experiences a strange and full reward when he enters the unknown. When he stands where no one stood before, builds his fire where fire has never been, makes his bed where no one has lain before, then all nature is his and his alone.

And:

> It was a certainty no one had been where we camped that night for at least eight hundred years. Quite possibly, no foot had trod that sand, no eye beheld that beauty so long reserved for us. . . . There was nothing to our world but the four walls close by on every side, a fading patch of blue a thousand feet above, the song of the waterfall, our fire and the redbud tree. This was the whole world and we were the first men.

I had set aside two full months in the spring of 1994 for the Southwest. In early April, before Jon could join me, I made a five-day reconnaissance north of Navajo Mountain. Despite all my Anasazi wanderings, here was a region unknown to me. The previous winter, Jeffrey Dean, that master of Kayenta tree-ring analysis, had told me he thought the slickrock plateau north of Navajo Mountain the most beautiful place in the Southwest. Yet except for parties hiking the Rainbow Bridge Trail, few Anglos venture into this territory. To hike anywhere on the Navajo Reservation, you need a permit from the tribal office in Window Rock. That low hurdle, and a vague discomfort about traveling through Indian country, and the fact that, in automotive terms, Navajo Mountain is on the road to nowhere have conspired to leave this wilderness blissfully undervisited.

One should acknowledge also the sheer ruggedness of the terrain. For five days I wandered up and down Cha and Bald Rock and Nasja Canyons. Off the Rainbow Bridge Trail, the only paths are those worn by livestock and wild game. From high vantage points, I gazed across miles and miles of sandstone witchery: soaring domes lapping toward the horizon like ocean waves; deep parabolic alcoves yawning out of vertical cliffs; fins and arches and knobby towers. It was impossible to head in a straight line anywhere: instead, I wound in and out of gorges and tributary rills, stymied by sudden pourovers or ledges that blanked to nothing.

Yet across this chaotic landscape, I found Anasazi sites nearly everywhere. Bald Rock Canyon posed a particular puzzle. The walls of this handsome valley abound in clean orange cliffs in which the winds and seeps of the eons have carved deep alcoves. Just as many of these natural caves face south as north, but it was only in the latter that I found human signs. The whole valley seems devoid of Pueblo I, II, or III presence; yet dozens of cramped Basketmaker sites protrude from drifted sand inside shelters where the sun never shines.

I made my way into Surprise Valley, a sheltered basin full of piñons and junipers that forms a serene oasis in the midst of all the stone savagery. In 1913, Zane Grey was guided here by John Wetherill, only four years after the Indian trader had led the first party of Anglos ever to see Rainbow Bridge. Nasja Begay, for whom Nasja Canyon may be named, was his Paiute guide.

Grey fell in love with Surprise Valley. In his 1915 novel, *The Rainbow Trail* (sequel to *Riders of the Purple Sage*), he locates in this remote basin a secret city where the Mormon settlers of southern Utah have hidden the second wives the U.S. government forbids them to have. In this clandestine Eden, the heartsick protagonist, John Shefford, finds and reclaims his lost love.

All through my five-day wandering, I kept coming upon Paiute rock carvings portraying splendidly saddled horses and solemn men with headdresses and braids. The finest were the work of Joseph Lehi—doubtless some kin to Dan Lehi, who had guided the '59 party in Mystery Canyon. My favorite panel portrayed a big-nosed, hard-bitten man in profile dangling a cigarette from his lips. Was this Joseph Lehi's self-portrait?

I had entered this country all but ignorant of the Paiute presence, assuming that because I was on the Navajo Reservation, the land must always have been Navajo territory. Later I did my homework, uncovering a gloomy chronicle.

For centuries, the terrain north of Navajo Mountain had been the homeland of the San Juan Paiutes. The band, however, was so marginal to Anglo awareness that not until 1989 was the tribe officially recognized by the government. Today it numbers only about 190, living in two communities, Atatsiv near Tuba City, and Kaivyaxaru in Paiute Canyon—some fifteen miles east of where I was hiking.

Thus the San Juan Paiutes are forced even today to live on the Navajo Reservation. Relations between the two tribes have long been uneasy: in the old days, some Navajos kept Paiutes as slaves, yet the Navajos lived in fear of Paiute ambushes north of Navajo Mountain. Nonetheless, in 1864, when Kit Carson rounded up the Navajos to deport them to a concentration camp at Bosque Redondo, on the eastern New Mexico plains, a band led by Chief Hoskininni hid out here amid the slickrock canyons and was never captured.

From their Kayenta trading post, John and Louisa Wetherill had gotten to know Hoskininni in his old age. Because of her remarkable fluency in Navajo, the old chief had been seized with the conviction that, despite her white skin, Louisa was a lost granddaughter of his, miraculously returned to his ken.

On this remote part of the reservation, Hoskininni was the greatest of Navajo heroes. For years he had kept a retinue of thirty-two Ute women taken as slaves years before, who herded the old man's sheep. These, on his deathbed in 1909, he bequeathed to Louisa Wetherill. When she tried to give the women their freedom, they refused to leave, begging instead to be put to work. Louisa built them a hogan of their own, fed them for years, and gave them work to do when they asked for it.

In 1907, in a relatively enlightened act, the government had established a Paiute reservation along what was called the Paiute Strip—the land north of the Arizona–Utah border and south of the San Juan River. The reservation lasted only until 1922, when Albert B. Fall, President Warren Harding's crooked secretary of the interior (who would soon go to prison for his role in the Teapot Dome scandal), aided an oil-exploration crony by ordering the Bureau of Indian Affairs to declare the reservation uninhabited and revert it to the public domain. Eleven years later, the Navajos petitioned to have the Strip added to their own reservation.

Despite these vicissitudes, the San Juan Paiutes have kept their culture intact. The Paiute rock art I kept stumbling upon seemed a declaration of that integrity. I was beguiled by a defiant 1986 inscription I found along the Rainbow Bridge trail:

CLYDE WHISKERS
PAIUTE INDIAN

On the fourth day of my reconnaissance I made my way into an obscure basin beneath arching sandstone walls. By now I thought I had discovered the trick to penetrating the Mystery Canyon labyrinth: indeed, you could see it in the contour lines on the map. The only weakness in the jumbled landscape around Mystery Canyon lies in a series of parallel grooves, or creases, in the rock, almost like geologic faults, all aligned northeast–southwest. These joints, as Jon and I would call them, create chimneys, gullies, and seams in the sandstone. The '59 party had followed a broad joint to traverse one subsidiary canyon, circled on ridge tops around the head of another, and finally entered Mystery by means of a second joint.

Rather than follow their roundabout route, Jon and I wanted to find a way in near the very head of Mystery, then descend the canyon as far as we could go. As I stood at one corner of my obscure basin, I was only one-third of a mile as the crow flies from the head of Mystery. It might as well have been twenty: for six hours, I searched in vain for a way out of the basin.

My predecessors had left traces. On several rock panels covered with desert varnish (a black patina formed by water dripping over the ages), the Anasazi had carved haunting petroglyphs: lizard-men, their arms outstretched and rigid; abstract designs that might have been maps. Twice I found John Wetherill's neatly etched signature, dated 1918 and 1922.

But I could not find a way out of the basin. Every joint I scrutinized blanked out in flared overhanging chimneys dripping moss. Ready to give up, I started for camp. The afternoon sun glanced sideways on a headwall of smooth stone. All at once I noticed a feature I had walked right past in the flat light of noon. An Anasazi hand-and-toe trail rose from behind a juniper, traversed forty feet right, then rose again to a shelf. I started up the steep ancient ladder, but in soggy hiking boots I chickened out. What lay above the shelf, I could not say: but here was a clue for Jon and me.

He joined me in mid-May, having driven his four-wheel-drive vehicle all the way from Seattle. Jon looked fit: his black curly hair and beard the usual unkempt tangle, the perpetually startled look in his piercing eyes, his movements a jerky choreography of pragmatic haste. As a teenager, John had been a good ski racer until, on one memorable day, he broke both legs in a single spill. His father, at the lodge at the base of the mountain, thousands of feet below, heard his screams of pain over the hubbub of the crowd. Ever since, Jon has walked with a slightly bowlegged stride on legs shorter than normal—which in no way hinders his climbing or the daring ski tours he continues to perform.

Having both spent our brazen years in the Alaska ranges, Jon and I had each developed an outdoor style based on manic efficiency. We tended to put our boots on, change the headlamp batteries, and sort climbing gear while we stirred the Cream of Wheat. "Seize the minute" is the alpinist's motto: for life itself is a vanishing window of opportunity.

I prided myself on a fairly high-caliber impatience, but Jon had turned hyper into an art form. As he hiked along, he squeezed off motor-drive snapshots with his camera without breaking stride, gulped down his water bottle like an alcoholic dreading rehab. One's expedition habits leak into everyday life. Often, after I ate in a restaurant with Jon, while I was still paying the bill, he would be outside heading down the sidewalk.

By May 17, we were ready to head for Mystery Canyon. To haul our sizable stash of gear into the distant basin I had reconnoitered, we hired a young Navajo horse-packer named Eric Atene. Eric wielded a prickly wit that seemed to spring from an ambivalence about Anglo hikers: they gave him business, but they invaded his wilderness. At one point on the march in he told me to slap one of his horses on the rump to coax the beast down a bank of round stones. "Harder!" he yelled—but my blows were useless. Eric had to dismount and do the job himself. "Indian pony," he smiled, as the horse leapt forward, rolling stones. "No papers, no registration. He knows his master."

As we pushed deeper into the maze, Eric kept saying, "I know this country like the back of my hand." But it was clear that Mystery Canyon lay beyond his grasp. As we turned into the basin I had discovered, he muttered, "How do you guys know about this place?"

For base camp we chose a shady shelf above a stream fed by a pellucid spring. Eric dumped our two hundred pounds of gear; he would return in six days. The camp lay beneath a gigantic cave facing north, a classic Basketmaker II site.

In the presence of these "ancient enemies," Eric grew somber, voicing his own take on the complicated relationship between the Navajo and the Old Ones. "Those Anasazi people—we don't know how they lived," he soliloquized. "But they left signs. Those guys were holy, like us.

"We can't go up there," he went on, indicating the cave. He held his hands apart. "If I go over there"—he touched fingertips—"I break the bond." Eric glanced up. "They had their power; we have our power. There's unseen spirits over there. Only a medicine man can go into those places, and he has to prepare himself."

After Eric left, with no Navajo qualms to dissuade us, Jon and I prowled at will through the spacious cave. There were pieces of upright slabs indicating cists, and soot on the ceiling from ancient campfires. I found the sandy beds at the back of the alcove, beneath which perhaps the dead still lay. And I saw but did not touch a curious recent structure (to describe it in print would be an offense to the Hopi) that might have been a religious shrine. From villages ninety miles to the south, certain Hopi clans still make yearly visits to ruins near Navajo Mountain, building shrines and leaving offerings for the long-dead.

In the morning Jon and I headed straight for the hand-and-toe trail I had found in April. With climbing shoes on my feet and Jon's manic confidence to nudge me on, I soloed up the ancient steps. On the rightward traverse, I admired the skill of the builder, who had somehow crouched on each foothold as he sculpted the next, chipping at ankle level with his handheld pounder.

Above the shelf, a new set of steps, invisible from the ground, wove a route up a steep inside corner. All at once we had gained a saddle overlooking the head of the subsidiary canyon just east of Mystery. It was a warm day, with high cirrus drifting over from the southwest, cresting the shoulder of Navajo Mountain. We felt as alone in our labyrinth as we might have on some remote glacier in Alaska.

Squeezing through a *V* notch, wading two cold pools, we made our way into the subsidiary canyon and descended it for half a mile. The map had given us hopes of bursting across to Mystery Canyon by means of one particularly sharp-walled joint. Heading toward it, we crossed an alluvial bench. The prickly pears were in riotous bloom, waxy blossoms of magenta, cherry red, or pale yellow, depending on the subspecies. In the dirt I found worked flakes of chert and flint in half a dozen different hues, without a hint of pottery. Basketmakers, again: perhaps it was they, more than fifteen hundred years ago, who had linked our base-camp cave with the hidden canyons to the north by the daring hand-and-toe trail.

As our spirits soared, we followed our chosen joint southwest through an easy pass. Soon we could see the far cliffs of Mystery Canyon. Just below the pass, I discovered a faint inscription scratched on the right-hand wall: "1921 AW." *Al Wetherill,* I thought at first: John and Richard's brother, who claimed to have seen Cliff Palace from afar the year before Richard and Charlie Mason had stumbled upon it. But Al, the melancholic among the five brothers, had left the Southwest by 1921. Could AW have been Angel Whiskers, once headman of the San Juan Paiutes, perhaps Clyde Whiskers's great-uncle?

When Robert J. Franklin and Pamela Bunte worked among the band in the early 1980s—the only ethnographers ever to study the San Juan Paiutes in depth—Angel Whiskers was still alive, a revered elder. In 1921, the Paiutes had been under siege. The worldwide influenza epidemic of 1918 had taken a terrible toll among them: one of the dead was Nasja Begay, the young man who had guided John Wetherill to Rainbow Bridge.

And by 1921, the more numerous Navajos were starting to encroach on the Paiute homeland. Had a young Angel Whiskers, pausing on the remote pass just as Jon and I would seventy-three years later, scratched his initials to declare to the world and the Navajos that this was still Paiute land?

Paiutes are unrelated to Navajos. The latter are an Athapaskan people who, like their cousins the Apaches, traveled over the centuries from subarctic Canada, reaching the Southwest by a long migration from the north and east. The Paiutes, on the other hand, are a Numic people, related by language and culture to the Utes and Shoshone. Archaeologists are fairly sure that Numic tribes were in place in the Great Basin of Nevada as early as A.D. 1100. Very few Anasazi scholars believe that pressure from Numic nomads contributed to the A.D. 1300 abandonment, although one respected expert, J. Richard Ambler, argues precisely that. After spending several field seasons among the San Juan Paiutes, Bunte and Franklin concurred with Ambler, seeing Angel Whiskers's forefathers as overlapping the Anasazi for two hundred years and, perhaps bolstered by

Ute allies, expanding into the Colorado Plateau as the Anasazi were driven from it. Bunte and Franklin's evidence is somewhat flimsy, based primarily on the persistence of Hopi–Paiute hostilities, first picked up in the historical record in the eighteenth century.

Only firm archaeological evidence of Paiutes in the Four Corners before A.D. 1300 might solve this question. But that will be hard to come by. In Surprise Valley, during my reconnaissance, I had found a very old tent ring in the grass. I knew that it was either Paiute or Navajo, and I knew that not even an expert could tell one from the other by looking at it, or date it unless he found carbon from a campfire—of which I saw none on the surface.

There is, however, one great conundrum in Puebloan culture that casts a glancing light on this complicated question. If the twenty-odd Pueblos in New Mexico and Arizona today are truly peopled by the descendants of the Anasazi, we should not expect the extraordinary linguistic diversity among them that in fact we find. In particular, the Hopi tongue spoken today in Oraibi, Walpi, Kykotsmovi, and the other villages on the three mesas is a Uto-Aztecan language, more closely related to Shoshone, Ute, and Paiute than to other Puebloan languages. Where does this bizarre linguistic affiliation come from, if not contact and intermarriage harking far back into the past?

Among those twenty Pueblos, there are four major language groups: Tanoan, Keresan, Uto-Aztecan, and Zuni. The last may be, like Basque, related to no other language in the world. Nor is the Keresan group, spoken at Acoma, Laguna, Zia, Santa Ana, San Felipe, Santo Domingo, and Cochiti, related to any other known language. Two Pueblos almost next door to each other, Zia and Jemez, speak completely different languages, while two Pueblos 125 miles apart, Taos and Isleta, are mutually intelligible.

Since about A.D. 1700, the town of Hano on Hopi First Mesa has been inhabited by Tewa Indians from the Rio Grande, who may have fled their home village to be welcomed by the Hopi to serve as mercenaries and bodyguards against both the Spanish and the nomadic tribes. (Even today, most Hopi policemen come from Hano.) Three hundred years later, the residents of Hano still speak the

Tanoan language of their ancestors from the Rio Grande. They are also fluent in the Hopi tongue spoken in all the other villages on the three mesas. Only a hundred yards from Hano stands the village of Sichomovi. Despite this proximity, nobody in Sichomovi can speak more than a few words of the Tanoan tongue.

I had raised the question of this linguistic diversity with Steve Lekson. "It's one of the most intractable problems in all of Southwestern prehistory," he said. It used to be argued that such diversity, as in New Guinea, with its more than seven hundred different languages, was proof of fierce intertribal hostility and warfare over a very long time, as each people attacked its neighbors, kept to its own ways, and (in New Guinea) walled itself off from the outside by using the deep valleys and precipitous ridges of the landscape as natural boundaries. But this argument is increasingly viewed as reductionist; and in the Southwest—along the Rio Grande, especially—no topographic barriers would serve to keep the peoples so separate.

The linguistic diversity of the Pueblos may in fact reflect a far more complex interaction with outsiders—not only Numic peoples in the West but even Plains Indians to the east (the Tanoan language group has strong affinities with Kiowa)—than has been previously recognized. Over the centuries since the abandonment, each village may have constantly lost dissenting splinter groups and taken in and assimilated refugees from all over the map. Glottochronology, a promising science that tries to link language change with the migration, dispersion, and intermixing of peoples, is still in a theoretical infancy that can produce very few hard conclusions. But if ever a field lay open for its fruitful application, it is the paradoxical journey through which the Anasazi before 1300 became the Puebloans of today.

AS we paused on the pass, musing on "1921 AW," Jon and I could see that the joint we were traversing seemed in danger of ending in a precipice. At the last moment, however, it disclosed a steep gully that led all the way to the floor of Mystery Canyon. Later we deduced that this was the only reasonable route in to the upper canyon; we could even imagine Dan Lehi and Toby Owl crafting a crazy zigzag horse trail down the gully.

By the end of the day, happily fatigued, we had made two trips back and forth from base camp to wrestle the bulk of our gear into Mystery. Our new camp was perched on a rippling shelf of red bedrock next to a tiny stream. Besides food and shelter, we had 350 feet of rope, a rack of hardware (cams and nuts and carabiners to protect our climbing rope work), and a five-pound, one-person pack raft that inflated like an air mattress.

Mystery Canyon seemed a paradise. By day the canyon wrens sang their plaintive descending anthems; in the evening, mourning doves called from the dusk. Junipers gave us shade, and tall grasses, never grazed, billowed like pale curtains in the breeze. The canyon had an intimate scale, yet the swooping walls, the stark towers, the sewn-shut seams of overhanging joints reverberated with the impossible.

Jon was in his element, his frenzied impetuosity honed to a razor's edge. I wanted to hang out in Mystery Canyon and get to know the place. Jon desired only to strap on his gear and head downstream for the unknown. In the end, we compromised, spending three days in the upper canyon, wandering into every nook of its wrinkled fastness—but only after the big push.

May 19 dawned clear, windy, and warm. We set off early, hiking downstream into a gorge that narrowed between three-hundred-foot walls. For half a mile, we followed a set of coyote tracks veering in the sand. The canyon wound and snaked, shutting off the morning sunlight. About a mile below camp, it ended abruptly in the forty-foot pourover that had stopped the '59 party.

We stood only about three miles as the crow flies from the waters of Lake Powell. The squiggles on the map promised a canyon passage at least twice as long.

I wedged myself between the walls, inched near the lip, and peered into the dim void. At the bottom of the pourover loomed a black pool of indeterminate depth, eighty feet across. The smooth rock walls overhung on all sides of it.

"This is wild," said Jon for the first of several dozen times that day. He uncoiled one of our ropes and searched for a boulder to tie it to. I began blowing up the dinky yellow boat that, in days previous, I had silently humored Jon for being so grandiose as to think we might need.

Bug-eyed with anticipation, Jon got on rappel, the raft dangling from his waist harness, then plunged off the pourover. I heard clanking, then rubbery sounds, then splashing, then "Wild!" After half an hour Jon hove into sight, cranking the toy boat toward shore with our toy paddles.

I got on rappel myself and went over the edge. Halfway down, in the stygian gloom, I had to wrap the rappel rope around one leg to lock it off so I could free my hands to haul the boat, which was tied to the rope, back to a position underneath me. My malaise was laced with the visceral awareness that, despite would-be tutors offering their services over the years, I had never learned to swim. Jon didn't help: at the crucial moment, he yelled, "Be careful! Make sure you land in the raft!"

On the far shore, we exulted. After deflating and packing up the boat, we walked for half a mile on dry bedrock, as the canyon twisted upon itself, its walls often five feet apart or less, but never too tight for passage. Then we came to our second obstacle, a long, complex narrows full of chimneys and pools. I shinnied down a body-width slot into waist-deep water. Once again we had to string a rope, for to wriggle unaided back up the claustrophobic fissure with wet feet might prove beyond our powers.

The narrows went on and on, broadening here into a pothole pool, slitting down there to a crevice, ten feet above which we bridged, hands on one wall, feet on the other. At last we came to a kind of moat—a six-foot-wide channel, water well over head deep, that bent around a far corner. We blew up the boat again and never deflated it the rest of the day, dragging it behind us through chimneys and hauling it up pourovers. Now we rode it the length of our moat, pulling ourselves along with palms slapped against the sandstone walls.

Every boat ride required a rope left in place, for otherwise the second person had no way to haul the raft back, and the boat could not carry both of us and our packs in one load. It quickly became clear to me that the yellow toy I had scorned was our most valuable piece of gear. The sky was a perfect blue, but gusts of wind shrieked through our gorge, threatening to seize the boat like a kite and waft it up onto some shelf or wedge it in some chimney from which we might not be able to retrieve it. Without the raft, I doubted whether a wretched nonswimmer such as I could have gotten out of the canyon.

Back in April, wearied by temperatures already in the eighties, I had worried that Mystery Canyon would dry up entirely by mid-May. Instead, we had more water than we knew how to handle. We now waded chest deep in the perpetual shadows; we would have flirted with hypothermia earlier in the season.

The complex narrows made us wonder whether we had found a place where no one had ever been, for it would have been fiendishly difficult to come up the canyon from Lake Powell: there was no way in from the sides, and even the Anasazi, so far as we could tell, had left no traces here.

Jon and I paused for a five-minute lunch taken standing up. The possibility of descending the whole of Mystery to Lake Powell began to awaken yearnings in us.

The canyon turned and folded, plunged and lay level, slotted down and opened into veritable amphitheaters. In places it was broad enough for whole gardens to grow: a gnarled piñon standing guard over clumps of red penstemon, sego lilies, evening primrose; yucca and Indian rice grass bursting from the crusted soil; the wayward tracks of lizards in the sand.

In oases such as these, I wondered again about the Anasazi. That we had found no petroglyphs, no hand-and-toe trails in this inner slot did not prove that some bold Anasazi scout had never found his way into our chasm.

Near our camp, at the head of Mystery—itself, as we had found, a very hard place to get to—Christy Turner's team had found several

Anasazi sites. What could have been the appeal of that narrow hollow? Only a few more acres of alluvium to grow one's corn and beans?

Even if they had never penetrated the difficult midcanyon through which Jon and I now forged our way, surely the Anasazi had gazed into it from the rim above. What had the place signified for them? Was it for them only a useless badlands, a place where no corn could grow and the stream could trap you? Or had it the power of some glimpsed otherworld?

Certain Western canyons that Anglos had enshrined as national parks, picnicking in them with thoughtless delight, had been, in Fred Blackburn's pithy phrase, bad juju to Indians in historic times. Zion is the best example: for the Paiutes and Shoshone, Zion was a place of terror, to be avoided at all costs. They never lived in the canyon, and shunned it even for hunting. Whether the Anasazi had their own kindred landscapes of dread, we may never know.

Despite the occasional flowering oasis, Mystery Canyon never relented. Chimney succeeded pool, chock-stone boulder after slickrock chute. . . . We grew tired, then more tired. And our supply of rope was dwindling.

Early in the afternoon, we came to the second pourover. Once again we set up a rappel, landed in the boat, paddled for shore. Grit in my boots had worn my feet raw. I had wet sand in my ears and teeth. The chimneying had scraped my arms and legs. But suddenly the canyon grew easy, mere hiking. We spurted on, taking turns carrying the boat over our heads like some trophy animal. "It may just go all the way!" Jon crowed.

We turned the corner and beheld a new slot. I wedged myself in chimney position to gaze into its depths. It was a bad one, flaring and squeezing in scalloped hollows down to a green obscurity. Jon chimneyed even closer to the hole.

"That's it," I said. "We have to turn around."

"No!" Jon wailed.

In a surprisingly rational discourse, we analyzed our options. We had only forty feet of rope left. That might get us down the scalloped slot, but the green glimmer meant a deep pool, stretching as far as we could see. We would have to boat it, with no rope left to haul back and forth.

It was getting late. Stupidly, we had left our headlamps in camp. The first clouds of the day were darkening the sky. Within the previous week, afternoon thunderstorms had drenched the land. Mystery Canyon was no place to ride out a flash flood.

Reluctantly Jon agreed. He took a final look down the slot, then spat toward the green glimmer—not in contempt, but as if to reach out for one last contact with the unknown.

Climbing back out of Mystery Canyon seemed endless and tedious. We retrieved every rope, so as to leave no sign of our passage: the snarls of wet nylon weighed like lead in our packs. Even with help from the ropes, it was brutal bashing up the chimneys we had slithered down, and I gouged my knuckles raw coming up the two pourovers. The boat snagged and lodged behind us like an anchor we dared not cut loose.

At last we heaved over the last lip and collapsed in the luxury of our relief. Half an hour's walk through the late shadows took us back to camp.

We had failed to reach Lake Powell, we later calculated, by only a few hundred yards. Jon's disappointment at not completing the descent was acute; but that night, as we sat exhausted around our tiny campfire, I was as happy as I had ever been.

We spent two more days at the head of Mystery Canyon, poking into alcoves guarded by scrub-oak thickets, climbing up to the ridge separating Mystery from the next canyon to the west. We found a pair of rusty old cans, along with a camp table of sandstone slabs, left no doubt by the '59 party. And we found four small Anasazi sites dating from the Pueblo II–III period. In them lay scatterings of potsherds, much of it the black corrugated ware the ancients used for cooking. Christy Turner's team had seen the same sites, dating the potsherds between A.D. 1050 and 1200 and diagnosing them as pure Kayenta in style.

In one alcove, we came across a bighorn sheep skull and horns—apparently an Anasazi kill. One small panel of petroglyphs (mentioned in the fifty-niners' report) centered on a stick-figure anthropomorph etched in a style I had seen nowhere else: horned like a sheep, left hand upraised, penis striking the ground like a third leg. I found a fine, stemless cream-and-red arrowhead, kept it in my pocket for a day and a half as a talisman, then put it back where I found it.

Our push on May 19 down the slots and pourovers to the verge of Lake Powell had cast light on one minor archaeological mystery, only to deepen the fog surrounding another. Before our trip, an expert had pointed out to me that on the map, Mystery Canyon seemed to offer the shortest route between the Colorado River and Navajo Mountain. For today's Navajo, the huge, 10,388-foot mountain is a deeply sacred place, one of the most important topographic features in their cosmos (Anglos are forbidden to trespass on it). It is Naatsis'áán, the Head of the Earth, the place where the culture hero Monster Slayer was born and where he brought back to life all the Navajos killed by the alien gods. Surely the peak had had a kindred prominence in the Anasazi world. And among all the natural boundaries in the Southwest, none was more inescapable than the Colorado River.

Yet the technical difficulty of Jon's and my six-mile push proved that, whether or not a few daring Anasazi pioneers had ventured into the twisting gorge, it could never have served as a trade route between river and mountain. Other canyons, longer but walkable, would have served that purpose far better.

So why had the Anasazi put so much effort into finding ways into Mystery? As evidence, we had not only the tricky quartzite-pounded staircase by which Jon and I had entered the head of the canyon, but the even more difficult hand-and-toe trail at Mystery's mouth, which Norm Nevills had failed to climb. The latter must have given access to the lowest stretches of the canyon, now lost beneath the lake. And Turner's team had found other toe trails in the subsidiary canyons.

The vestiges of the four modest Pueblo II–III sites Turner had documented hardly seemed to justify such toil. I was not convinced that Mystery Canyon had been occupied only during that short stretch from 1050 to 1200 (nor had Turner so claimed). For one thing, at the site where we found the bighorn sheep skull and horns, I had seen several faint petroglyphs with the unmistakable cross-hatched bodies of what Polly Schaafsma calls Glen Canyon Linear style, which she dates to the Archaic, even before Basketmaker II. In 1959, Schaafsma's linking of styles to periods had not yet been formulated, and the dating of rock art was still completely uncertain.

Had Mystery Canyon been a religious sanctum? Or a hideout for the visionary? A sense of something odd, even eccentric, lurked about the four minimalist sites that Turner found and we visited. The glorious logic of Chaco Canyon or Mesa Verde was utterly absent here. One had the sense not of the proud inheritors of a bold civilization, but of furtive hermits, marginal mystics, outlaws and rebels.

For the most part, archaeologists dismiss such out-of-the-way Anasazi lands as Mystery Canyon as peripheral, unimportant. For me, the place evoked an alien Elysium, and during the two days Jon and I prowled about our hidden valley, I mused long and hard on all I had learned and wondered about the Anasazi.

IN the long view, the A.D. 1300 abandonment remains the central puzzle. Jonathan Haas, Winifred Creamer, Bruce Bradley, and other experts had taught me vivid lessons in just how hard life had become on the Colorado Plateau around 1250. A daily fear, the sense of living on the edge, seemed built into the very dwellings I had explored in Grand Gulch, Moqui Canyon, Tsegi Canyon, and a dozen other sandstone gorges. The tree-ring dates were unarguable. Fully half the Anasazi domain had been abandoned around 1295 and never reoccupied.

Eighty years ago, the scholars might have confidently asserted that raiding nomads such as the Utes and Navajos drove the Anasazi south. Only twenty years ago, the archaeologists would have explained the abandonment entirely in terms of drought, famine, arroyo cutting, and other environmental setbacks. Now the cutting edge of research tries to trace the origins of the Kachina Phenomenon, seeing this comprehensive new religion as the pull that, coupled with an environmental push, drew tens of thousands of the Old

Ones southeast toward the Rio Grande and the Little Colorado.

Is this vein of inquiry only the latest abandonment fad? Will future scholars look back at the 1990s and point out why the Kachina Phenomenon hypothesis fails to explain all kinds of data? The kiva mural paintings and the rock art that seem to picture masked dancers may indeed demonstrate kachinas as early as 1325, but those images are susceptible to other explanations. What would clinch the argument would be to find a bona fide early kachina mask. But until four years ago, no mask of any sort dating from before the advent of the Spanish had been unearthed in the Southwest.

At a fourteenth-century pueblo called San Lazaro, a few miles south of Santa Fe, an amateur archaeologist named Forrest Fenn has unleashed a bitter controversy among New Mexico archaeologists. Having made a fortune legally buying and selling prehistoric artifacts, Fenn organized a consortium that bought the land the pueblo stands on. Then he began to excavate it.

However deplorable, Fenn's digging at San Lazaro is legal. In 1992, shoveling dirt out of Room 4, he uncovered a startling cache of objects. Having had some training in archaeology, Fenn knew the find was too big for him to handle alone, so he called in the Museum of New Mexico. Fearful that Fenn's unique find would go undocumented, museum archaeologists helped the collector finish his work in Room 4. Purist scholars regard this as a deal with the devil; pragmatists, such as the museum's Eric Blinman, see it as rescuing a resource that would otherwise be destroyed.

In 1994, I visited Blinman's lab in Santa Fe, where he showed me the cache from Room 4. Tentatively dated to the 1440s or 1450s, the assemblage stunned me. Laid out in immaculate sliding drawers were a pair of wooden staffs, one found with a badger paw attached, the other with a plaster effigy head; doughnut-shaped stone rings used perhaps as altars; six carved and painted wooden corncobs; arrowheads, pendants, and quartz lightning stones (rubbed together, they glow with internal light); worn-out manos still bearing traces of gray, black, and red pigment; and—most astonishing of all—a pair of three-dimensional masks made of gypsum plaster. The masks, which fell into pieces the moment Fenn uncovered them, look vaguely like black-and-yellow football helmets, with weird animalistic snouts and jaws still attached.

"You can't imagine how fragile some of this material is," said Blinman. He had isolated a tiny, featureless fragment of one of the masks as a test piece. Now he brushed it gently with a fingertip, then grimaced as he showed me the smudge of plaster that had come away. "Every time you touch it, you lose something. You can see why we couldn't just stand by and let these things vanish."

Are these fragile objects the oldest kachina masks ever found? Is the whole assemblage paraphernalia from the Kachina Phenomenon? Is this the pull that depopulated the Colorado Plateau? Some archaeologists think so.

At the moment, scholars are divided between seeing the Kachina Phenomenon as a cult indigenous to the Southwest and seeing it as an import from Mexico. The whole question of the Mexican connection is deeply intriguing, as well as completely unsolved. Did Chaco priests know about the Toltecs, whose glorious city-states twelve hundred miles to the south represented the pinnacle of New World civilization in the eleventh century? Another hot field of research is the quest for rock-art images in the Southwest that picture such Toltec deities as Tlaloc, the rain god, and Quetzalcoatl, the Plumed Serpent.

In general, archaeologists are still inclined to see the formative ideas of Anasazi culture as slowly traveling north from Mexico. The Mogollon, directly to the south, made pottery at least two centuries before the Anasazi and may have taught their northern neighbors how to turn clay into vessels.

In central Mexico, corn was gathered and eaten, and maybe deliberately planted, as early as 7000 B.C. Why did it take so long for corn to travel to the American Southwest? The new long chronology for the Basketmaker II period pushes the advent of corn among the Anasazi back from around the time of Christ to 1200 B.C., and one recent finding on Black Mesa in Arizona gives a radiocarbon date as early as 1900 B.C. Even so, this leaves a gulf of five millennia during which corn—and its power to transform culture from nomadic to sedentary—centered the lives of one people after another in

Mesoamerica long before it reached the Southwest.

During the coming decades, Anasazi discoveries will no doubt begin to lift the veil from the shadowy Archaic and Basketmaker II periods, so long neglected by Southwestern archaeologists. It may turn out, as revisionist scholars all over the world increasingly argue, that the old paradigm by which "primitive" hunter-gatherers evolve inevitably into "civilized" farmers simply does not work. Australian archaeologists have demonstrated that early Aborigines, regarded by European explorers as the most "wretched" people on earth, may have led a hunting-gathering life of relative ease and affluence. Perhaps the Anasazi saw corn and rejected it. Certainly they never gave themselves over entirely to the agricultural life.

As I pondered the Anasazi, I thought about Chaco Canyon. Christy Turner's bone collections had convinced me of the reality of Anasazi cannibalism, a truth it is hard to countenance in any form, and if his and David Wilcox's speculations were correct, this dark side of Anasazi life was intimately linked to the rise of Chaco. Yet I had the disposition of a cultural relativist: even so grisly a rite as eating one's enemies, I thought, could be weighed only in terms of how it worked within the Anasazi cosmos. And that was still far from clear. Had the Chaco Phenomenon been a spectacular aberration, a two-hundred-year meteor of bloody and brilliant arrogance flashing and dying across the blank sky of centuries in which the Anasazi coexisted in harmony?

For I had also witnessed the bright side of the Chacoan achievement—nowhere more memorably than at Chimney Rock, near Pagosa Springs, Colorado, in the company of Kim Malville. An archaeoastronomer at the University of Colorado, Malville recently made a discovery that deftly ties ancient sky-watching into Chaco's domination of the Anasazi world.

Of all the seventy-some outliers tied into the Chaco network, Chimney Rock is the northeasternmost yet discovered, as well as the highest, at seventy-six hundred feet. It is also one of the most dramatic of all ancient sites in the Southwest: the pueblo ruins cling to a sharp, narrow ridge that culminates in two soaring rock towers, today the nesting grounds of peregrine falcons.

Malville's discovery had to do with an arcane phenomenon called the lunar standstill. Because of its eccentric orbit around the earth, the full moon rises at a different point on the skyline each month. Those points range from north to south through a cycle that lasts 18.6 years. The northernmost and southernmost risings of all are called lunar standstills.

The standstill is a very subtle phenomenon, of which most prehistoric people were ignorant. (Indeed, there is no evidence that today's Pueblo sky watchers know about the standstill's 18.6-year cycle.) One might even say that it is a useless thing to know: the standstill has nothing to do with weather, climate, or growing seasons. Yet Malville discovered, using carbon 14 dates from roof timbers, that the Chacoan outlier at Chimney Rock was built in two phases, one at A.D. 1075 and one at 1094. These happen to have been the dates of two successive lunar standstills. And if you stand at the outlier and watch the full moon rise at the time of the winter solstice, during those standstill years it comes up exactly in the notch between the rock towers.

Clearly the astronomer-priests who dictated the building of Chimney Rock Pueblo wished to commemorate, perhaps even to worship, the lunar standstill. But of what use could such esoteric lore have been?

Malville further demonstrated that, during the year of a lunar standstill, total eclipses of the sun could occur only in the spring and fall. "Every time you have a full moon," Malville told me, "you have the threat of a solar eclipse. Even today, at Zuni Pueblo, the sun priest is in charge of fixing the date of the winter solstice festival—the most important festival of all. There could be no greater disaster than to have a solar eclipse during that festival."

As far as we know, no prehistoric people ever learned how to predict eclipses precisely. But with their esoteric knowledge of the lunar standstill, acquired over generations of careful sky-watching, the Chacoan priests could have predicted those parts of the year when eclipses were most likely to happen. And they could have guaranteed the winter solstice was a safe time, with no possibility of a solar eclipse, during the standstill year. To the average Anasazi, the Chacoan priests must have seemed to commune directly with the gods.

Yet Chaco had collapsed. Then the abandonment had transformed the Anasazi world. Ever since my visit to Kwanstiyukwa, the lordly pueblo of some two thousand to three thousand rooms on the mesa above Jemez, I had formed a vision of huge, brilliantly organized Anasazi villages flourishing in the fourteenth and fifteenth centuries.

Here lay another deep puzzle. A site such as Kwanstiyukwa conjures up a far more integrated way of life than one finds today among the Pueblos. There may be 4,500 Hopi living on the three mesas in Arizona, but the Hopi tribe is a bureaucratic fiction. No Hopi village can make even the most trifling regulation apply to the village next door. Even within a village, clans make their own rules and decisions. The people of Walpi, Sichomovi, and Hano, the three villages on First Mesa, do not share a common dance plaza or a great kiva, as the villagers of Kwanstiyukwa did in the year 1450. Puebloan life today is far more individual, more locally autonomous, than it seems to have been in the Pueblo IV era.

What happened? The coming of the Spanish after 1539—the second of Jeffrey Dean's great fault lines—transformed Anasazi culture once more. At the time of the *entrada,* we know from Spanish records, the conquistadors found more than one hundred occupied pueblos stretching across what is today New Mexico and Arizona. Only some twenty are still inhabited.

Much of the secrecy and xenophobia that Anglos confront today at Hopi, Zuni, and Acoma, or among the Rio Grande Pueblos derives from the brutal Spanish conquest and from the reconquest after the Pueblo Revolt of 1680. Aiming to wipe out Pueblo culture and religion, the Spanish only drove it underground. Much of that culture thrives underground today.

Here lies another field for future scholars. No single Anasazi archaeologist, no ethnographer of the Pueblos is conversant with the myriad obscure documents in the Spanish record. The most important accounts—those fragmentary and conflicting narratives of Coronado's great adventure, for example—have been published in English. Many others linger unread in archives in Seville, Mexico

City, Chihuahua, and other cities. Taken together, these letters from friars, governors' decrees, and church certificates, blurred though they may be by the cultural myopia of the oppressor, have much to tell us about how the prehistoric Anasazi became the historic Puebloans.

Recently Bill Whatley, the Anglo who serves as Jemez tribal archaeologist, startled me with a revelation. The Pueblos themselves, he said, still keep and guard Spanish documents from the seventeenth century, seized during the Pueblo Revolt. "Not everything was destroyed in 1680," he pointed out. Scholars would give much to see these records.

I had emerged from all my reading and from my occasional visits to the Pueblos as something of a skeptic, after the fashion of Jeffrey Dean, as to the reliability of oral tradition. Yet now and then I had my own preconceptions jolted by some extraordinary story. Perhaps the best one was told me by David Wilcox.

In the 1940s, Wilcox related, digging at the site called Ridge Ruin near Flagstaff, an archaeologist named John McGregor unearthed what he described as "the richest burial ever reported in the Southwest." The Magician, as he came to be called, was a large male buried in an ordinary room of a relatively insignificant pueblo. McGregor dated the site at around A.D. 1125.

With the Magician, McGregor found twenty-five decorated pots, eight remarkable baskets (one of them covered with fifteen hundred pieces of turquoise and shaped orange rodent teeth), four hundred projectile points, beautiful mosaic amulets made of seashell and turquoise, painted and drilled claws and teeth from a mountain lion, a skullcap of beads, and long wooden wands whose heads were carved in the shape of human hands, deer's feet, and the like.

McGregor took some of these grave goods to Hopi. Independently, several elders agreed that the artifacts pertained to a witchcraft ceremony aimed at giving power to a war leader: in a kind of sword-swallowing rite, the celebrants thrust the wooden sticks down their throats until only the figured handle could be seen. Most remarkably, McGregor's informants, shown only a few of the grave goods, specified other objects the archaeologist should have found in the burial. These were precisely the artifacts McGregor had uncovered. Across eight hundred years, fault lines or no, the knowledge of a ceremony no longer performed had been kept intact in the Hopi consciousness.

THE stone-and-mud buildings left by the Old Ones—particularly the cliff dwellings in the national parks and monuments—are our country's most famous ruins. Other edifices—the great platform mounds of the Cahokia culture in the lower Mississippi valley, for example—represent comparable pinnacles of prehistoric civilization. But Cliff Palace and Spruce Tree House and Keet Seel have captured our imagination in a way no other ancient monuments in the United States have. As a friend of mine put it after only a preliminary acquaintance with Mesa Verde, "The Anasazi ruins are America's Stonehenge."

Yet for me the vestigial sites of Mystery Canyon spoke with greater eloquence than Cliff Palace. On our last night in camp, as we stayed up late feeding juniper twigs to our fire on the rippling bedrock, Jon and I felt a deep contentment. We stopped talking, and the silence spread around us like a balm. The moon, two days before full, bathed the valley with silver light. Our campfire flickered out, leaving the coals to pulsate, red dimming to gray. Through the last eight centuries, perhaps only a handful of visitors had entered this refuge in the slickrock before us, but at the moment, the ancients seemed close at hand.

9

The Sucked Orange

"WHICH guys are you going to give us this time?" I asked Jim Hook.

"Thought we'd fix you up with Buck and Muchacho. They've been around the block."

My wife, Sharon, and I were at Recapture Lodge, an oasis of leafy repose in the desert of southeastern Utah. The lodge hugs the western limits of Bluff, once the Mormon stronghold designed to keep the Gentiles from getting a foothold in the region, but now a town gone half over to the counterculture. The well-built red-brick houses of the pioneers still proclaim the mirthless rigor of the Latter Day Saints, but one of them had recently been turned into a Thai restaurant. At a Saturday evening potluck dinner in Bluff, the residents who showed up were more likely to be rafting guides and sculptors than farmers or cowboys. The grocery store even sold 3.2 beer, which you could not purchase in staid and still firmly Mormon Blanding, twenty miles to the north.

And at Recapture Lodge, Jim and Luanne Hook pastured llamas, with which, instead of horses, they outfitted backcountry expeditions. A slender gray-haired fellow in his forties with a sun-creased face and as musical a drawl as any cowpuncher, Jim had been one of the avant-garde in introducing llamas as pack animals to the West. Most of his clients sign up for guided expeditions, with Jim or a hired hand from Recapture Lodge handling the animals, cooking dinner, and reading the maps. But three times before, in Wyoming and Utah, I had rented llamas, taken an hour-long lesson from their owners, and set off on my own into the wilderness for eight to ten days. It was, I knew by now, the way to go.

Commercial llamas range from downright unmanageable to superbly trained. I had rented a pair of the Hooks' animals two years before and sailed with them through a nine-day foray in the wilderness. But only after a woeful struggle with a badly trained llama on a subsequent outing did I fully appreciate the savvy that had gone into Jim Hook's years of llama education.

It was April 1994, and our timing was critical. Sharon's and my objective was to spend eight days poking our way down lower Grand Gulch, from Collins Spring to the San Juan River, and back. This sixteen-mile stretch (adding up, with side canyons, to about a forty-five-mile circuit) was by now the only section of Grand Gulch I had left to explore. Rumor had it that the Bureau of Land Management in Monticello was about to close lower Grand Gulch to pack animals.

The decision was made while we were in the canyon, and as it turned out, May 1 was the cutoff date. Thus Sharon and I enjoyed the luxury of what may have been the last pack trip ever in the lower Gulch.

To many, the decision had a curious logic. The rationale was to protect the canyon from the kinds of abuse—notably overgrazing and the fire rings and log benches of traditional cowboy camps—that pack trains, particularly those made up of horses, tend to inflict. But the BLM had already banned campfires in the Gulch and laid down a codex of responsible camping that most parties scrupulously adhered to. Meanwhile the agency declined to outlaw pack animals in the spectacular heart of Grand Gulch, the thirty-six-mile stretch from Kane Gulch Ranger Station to Collins Canyon, by far the most popular part of the canyon and the hardest hit.

Jim Hook's partner Larry Sanford drove Buck and Muchacho from Bluff to the Collins Spring trailhead, where Sharon and I parked our rental car. It was a hot afternoon, and as we sorted out our gear and organized the complicated packing, the details made me hectic. As I had learned on previous llama outings, it's actually more work breaking and making camp with animals than on one's own. But the rewards are commensurate.

Like all pack llamas, Buck and Muchacho were gelded males (ungelded males are too frisky, females too valuable as breeders). Both five years old, they had been trained from infancy by Jim and Larry and a third wrangler, Diane Jensen. Each weighed about 300 to 325 pounds. In standing position, with their long necks erect, the stately beasts rose to about five and a half feet. Buck was piebald, with black splotches on his rump and throat; Muchacho, bigger and slightly leaner, was virtually white all over but for a black cap on the top of his head that looked like a yarmulke.

You do not ride a llama: you harness him with a padded saddle from which matching panniers dangle on either flank. The balance of loads in these panniers is so crucial to a llama's well-being that we carried a spring scale to equalize them. If the loads don't work quite right, it's better to throw in a five-pound rock than to give a llama forty pounds on the left and forty-five on the right. With all our gear loaded, Buck and Muchacho started off that April day carrying ninety pounds apiece. Some twenty pounds each of that were llama feed, a corn-and-alfalfa mixture that we scattered on the ground morning and night. Llamas, which browse selectively, could easily live off the greenery in the canyon alone, without (unlike horses) making a noticeable dent in the foliage; but the BLM requires the carrying of feed and officially forbids grazing. (But try to stop a llama from chewing his favorite grasses!)

We were off by 3:15 P.M. The joy of llama-packing is that you can loaf along with five pounds in your day pack, holding a short lead hooked to a nylon halter that fits over the llama's head. In the panniers we had all kinds of luxuries: hinged closed-cell-foam camp chairs, for lounging on the slickrock during breakfast and dinner; a big battery-powered lantern; cans of gourmet food, such as hearts of palm and mandarin oranges and a five-pound ham; a bottle of brandy for communing with the night; as many books as we cared to read by headlamp. Often in my mountaineering youth I had lugged seventy pounds on my back into some alpine cirque. The load had always made the journey pure torture; views became mere irritants, the only goal to get to camp and heave the monstrous burden to the ground.

Now we could take our time, pay attention to the scenery, stop and get out the binoculars to check some high alcove in a side wall, and if it proved promising, tie off the llamas to saplings and hike up there to see what we might find. Only an hour into Collins Canyon, we met a group of twelve oldsters, clients of a wilderness school based in Monticello. They had boated down the San Juan to the mouth of Grand Gulch, then spent four days hiking up toward Collins Spring.

As it turned out, they were the last people Sharon and I would see for the next six days. We camped that night only two and a half miles in, near a sharp gateway called the Narrows, where not long before in geologic terms (last century? ten thousand years before?), some cataclysmic flood had broken through a fin of ruddy rock, leaving yet another sweeping bend in the canyon dry and off the track, forming another rincon like Arrow Point, on top of which, a few months later, Bruce Bradley would crawl in his ecstasy after the flint flakes that he knew so much about.

The evening was unseasonably warm. At 9 P.M., we lounged still in T-shirts. Before dark, I had headed around the Narrows rincon and almost at once found the first pictographs. A clean panel in white paint, dating, I thought, from Basketmaker III (roughly A.D. 500 to 750): a chain of anthropomorphs stood facing me, holding hands. One had rabbit ears on his head, another a Martian-looking "space helmet" topped with a bent plume. Beside them, looking away, sat a bird that looked like a duck on water. Was I witnessing the commemoration of some dance? Was the weird headgear some kind of mask, dating from centuries before we detect even the first traces of the Kachina Phenomenon?

Now, in the darkness, a chorus of frogs croaked from the bedrock pools. Unlike most canyons in the Southwest, Grand Gulch seems thronged with frogs, which only begin to sound off at dusk. On a wet spring night, they can keep you awake past your bedtime.

For years, when I went off on my trips to the Southwest, Sharon had declined all invitations. Like me, she had grown up in Colorado, and in the early years of our marriage we had camped a lot in the mountains—perhaps a bit too often in the snow and cold. But when I came back raving about the Anasazi country, she remained indifferent. A single word was her stumbling block. Like many another visitor to the canyonlands, I tended to refer to it as the "desert." (In a town such as Durango today, the locals adhere to the idiom: "Going skiing this weekend?" "Naw, thought I'd head out to the desert.") To Sharon, the desert connoted Saharan wastes.

Then she looked at some of the pictures I brought back and realized that the desert I extolled had junipers and piñons growing in it, and bushes painted blue with indigo blossoms, and cactuses that flowered a brilliant claret, and willows and cottonwoods guarding pools where deer and coyote came to drink. It took only one car-camping trip, during which we touched lightly on Chaco Canyon and Ute Mountain Tribal Park and obscure ruins near Abiquiu, New Mexico, to turn her into a convert.

Grand Gulch is conventionally divided into upper and lower by Collins Canyon, which enters from the right thirty-six miles below the ranger station at Kane Gulch. An easy two-mile trail leads down Collins Canyon from the roadhead at Collins Spring to the junction with Grand Gulch itself. For two reasons, lower Grand Gulch is far more lightly trafficked than upper. The first is that, unless you pull off a logistical trick such as the Monticello school's approach by boat down the San Juan, you must backtrack to Collins Spring, exiting where you entered. In the upper Gulch, one-way jaunts are easily set up by ferrying cars to trailheads. The second reason is that the ruins are fewer and less impressive in the lower Gulch. Yet, as I was to find out, there are only a handful of other canyons in all the Southwest with a comparable wealth of rock art.

That discrepancy itself—a paucity of dwellings where the rock art floresced in magnificent panels—is duplicated along a short stretch of the San Juan River near Butler Wash, some fifty miles upstream from the mouth of Grand Gulch. What accounts for it? Though most often one finds rock art on the walls just above and behind Anasazi cliff dwellings, perhaps the truly visionary outpourings—

especially during Basketmaker II and III—required pilgrimages to shrines set aside for the purpose, far from where the people planted their crops and fired their pots.

I woke the next morning with the hum in my left ear. Ever since I started hiking in the Anasazi canyonlands, I have been assailed, off and on, by the steady drone of a bass note almost as deep as I can hear. It waxes and wanes, and at times I manage to forget it, but in a place like Grand Gulch, for as long as nine or ten days straight, it never goes away entirely.

Nowhere else in the world do I hear the hum—not sitting at home before the word processor, nor even hiking canyons in Europe or Peru or New Zealand. The maddening thing is that the hum is so real I can sing its pitch an octave or two higher; in certain locales, particularly where a parabolic wall curves around my path like a huge satellite dish, the hum suddenly doubles in volume. None of my companions can hear it. With Sharon in Grand Gulch, several times I stopped in midstride to say, "Now. There. In the southeast. Tell me you hear it now." She would cock her head, try to humor me: "I almost hear something. But not really." Once or twice she picked up the distant throb of a 747 cruising from Denver to L.A. "Not that," I would complain. "A much deeper sound."

Twice, however, during my Southwest ramblings, I met men who, when I confessed my affliction, said something like, "That's funny. I've had this buzz in my ears for a while now. Always thought I'd been to too many rock concerts when I was young." Since both men were seasoned veterans of the canyonlands, I took heart at their testimony.

There is, of course, the famous Taos hum—a steady drone, first reported in Taos, then in other Southwestern towns, that aggravates the calm of a substantial portion of the populace, which science is powerless to trace to any source. For a while I toyed with submitting myself to some University of New Mexico researchers who were investigating the Taos hum. The problem was, I've never heard my hum in Taos or in any other town, only in the canyons. The last I heard the scientists concluded that the Taos hum was a psychosomatic delusion.

My current theory is that a canyon acts, for ears like mine, sensitive to the lowest frequencies, like a giant seashell. What is it we hear when we put our ears to a seashell and listen to the roar of the "ocean"? Only the hum of our own blood racing through our veins? In some sense, my hum must be real.

Our first full day in the Gulch was a congeries of rock art and well-crafted granaries. During six miles of leisurely travel, we stopped to inspect ten Anasazi sites. Some could not be missed, for as we walked down the Gulch, wading the slow-trickling stream, they sprang at us from either side; others were hidden on high benches and ledges, and only the probability that something might be up there dictated tying off our llamas and going to look.

After a point, it becomes a hopeless task to describe Anasazi rock art. A taxonomic list of the anthropomorphs and animals and abstract symbols assembled on some stone canvas fails to explicate the thrill of stumbling upon the place. And though the art is stylized, rigid, and canonically limited (in the sense that the same sorts of images—triangle-bodied anthropomorphs, bighorn sheep, spirals, atlatl symbols, and the like—recur again and again), it is the endless variety of its manifestations that beguiles the eye and mind.

That day, among many wonderful things, we saw one panel that consisted of nothing more than about a hundred red handprints, ranging from child-sized to bigger than mine, the highest thirty or forty of them well out of reach of today's passerby. Another panel mingled more than eighty beasts and humans, and though the figures were faded and smudged, the colors were not: white, rose, yellow, brownish orange, deep red, green, dark brown, mud brown, butterscotch, orange, and rust-purple. I had not known the Anasazi palette contained so many hues.

Twice we came upon Richard Wetherill's stylish, spidery *W*—once on a boulder's surface before a site and once, remarkably, carved in the hardened mud of an arroyo bank at the back of a deep alcove, still preserved after a century of floods.

It is only a matter of time before somebody publishes a guidebook to Grand Gulch. Guides to other Utah wilderness areas outside the National Park Service system have appeared: the Escalante, the San Rafael Swell, Paria Canyon. When the book comes out, you will be able to follow instructions such as these: "1.2 miles after Water Canyon enters on the left, climb an old stock trail to the bench on the right (west) wall and look behind a tall leaning slab."

Until then, however, you still have to do your own sleuthing in Grand Gulch. One measure of the richness of the lower Gulch is that on our way back upstream, far from merely plodding past the sites we had discovered on the way down, we came across all sorts of things we had missed. Sometimes just the act of facing the opposite direction does the trick of giving away a likely shelf or cranny. Often I was reminded of one of Fred Blackburn's rules of thumb: to scout a canyon thoroughly for Anasazi remains, you should hope to cover no more than one mile of one side of the canyon per day.

We had hit the Gulch during a rare April heat wave. It stayed hot all the second day, after having scarcely cooled off through the night. As we walked, we sought the shade of the towering canyon walls rather than fleeing it, and we were happy to soak our feet as we waded down the stream. Parched, Sharon and I each drank four liters of water a day. Our llamas, however, barely took a few sips apiece from the pools we led them to. A relative of the camel, the llama can go days without food or water.

At night we tied the llamas on longer leads to trees, and dumped their corn-alfalfa feed and left them to wander within a forty-foot circle as they browsed through their resting hours. Each afternoon we took off their panniers and saddles, then in the morning combed out the matted hair on their backs and flanks with our fingers before packing them up again.

Ecologically, llamas have it all over horses as backcountry pack animals—though don't try to tell that to an old-time horseman. With their soft, padded feet, llamas leave dainty prints where horses chew a wet trail to muck; their droppings are dry pellets, like a deer's. They are surer-footed creatures than horses, and can be led along routes beyond the reach of the boldest equine ambition. Their woolly, long-necked, big-eared look makes everyone who sees a llama want to pet it, yet these South American ruminants are aloof creatures, unimpressed with human affection. They do not like to be touched anywhere near the head, though they will tolerate an arm around the neck or a congratulatory slap on the back. An ill-trained llama, such as one I had been outfitted with the previous year, will buck wildly when you try to saddle him, and even spit on you. The latter is one of the most disgusting experiences in nature, for though llamas are on the whole clean, relatively odorless beasts, their expectorate fluid is like some essence of bile, vomit, and hideous bad breath.

As we led our llamas down the canyon, we got to know their natures. Both Buck and Muchacho were ardent hummers. That snuffling, high-pitched whine is one of the strangest of animal noises, a querulous commentary that seems a cross between "we know something you don't" sagacity and mere old-maidish nattering. A llama's hum can be a sign of anxiety or distress, but in Buck and Muchacho it seemed an old habit, a way of talking to themselves.

At night, Muchacho kept himself clean and sleek, "kushing down" in the llama's economical position of repose, legs tucked under torso. Buck, however, loved to roll in the dirt and grass, and every morning he was as seedy and dusty as a vagrant. Of the two on the trail, Buck was the basher, Muchacho the holder back, who several times balked for ten minutes at a talus pile Buck had just waltzed across.

As you hike and camp with llamas, despite their aloofness, you grow fond of them. Five months after our trip, I was shocked to learn from Jim Hook that Muchacho had died in an entirely preventable accident. Jim had leased the llama to a pair of relatively green outfitters elsewhere in Utah, who hoped Muchacho's good breeding might rub off on their rambunctious youngsters. One day the pair led all their llamas except Muchacho out of their corral and headed up the trail. This is something you do not do, if you know llamas. Frantic at being left behind, the 325-pound animal tried to vault the five-foot-high corral. His trunk smashed hard against the top log, and he spilled on the ground; within hours, Muchacho was dead of internal bleeding.

Our days passed in a blur of delight and solitude. The afternoons stayed hot, the nights mild, and the frogs croaked perpetually in the darkness. The moon waxed from first quarter toward full, turning our campsites silver. Sometimes, for a mile or more at a stretch, the Gulch dried up completely. Just as I began to worry, a muddy pothole would appear, then clearer pools, then the stream itself, emerging from some underground detour dictated by obscure geology.

We saw so many pictographs that our brains overflowed with detail. We found a full, block-capital WETHERILL, instead of his usual shorthand initial. Around us the flowers were bursting into bloom: pale violet and dusky yellow paintbrush, the waxy claret cup cactus, red penstemon, and lots of tiny purple and yellow flowers whose names I did not know.

As we moved south, the surrounding walls towered higher and higher, until they rose eight hundred feet above us. Here, at its very mouth, Grand Gulch achieves its greatest depth. All the way down from Collins Canyon, I had scanned the wall on the right for a route up to the plateau to the west. There was not, so far as I could see, a single place where even a rock acrobat could make his way out. On the east, the canyon's defenses were almost as formidable, although several side canyons offered paths by which game regularly entered and by which the Anasazi must once have exited the lower Gulch. Oddly enough, despite the verticality of the terrain, I had never found much in the way of hand-and-toe trails in Grand Gulch. Here lay another local puzzle in the general conundrum of the prehistoric Southwest.

Two miles above the Gulch's junction with the San Juan, where the last tributary, nicknamed Shangri-La, enters from the east, we set up camp and hitched our llamas for three days. Below this point, the Gulch is not "llamable" (to use Jim Hook's jargon), thanks to boulder-choked defiles and scary arroyo walls, across the faces of which thin foot trails crumbled. We spent a surprisingly arduous day, in the worst heat yet, making our way down this gauntlet to the river.

Never had the encroaching walls looked more savage, arching in pancaked overhangs for as much as seven hundred feet at a stretch, knobbing out in distant hoodoo towers that no one has ever climbed. Yet underfoot, as we sank below four thousand feet above sea level, the flora degenerated into spiny cholla, sotol, yucca, and tumbleweed. Nor, in that two-mile stretch, did I find any trace of Anasazi occupation, despite the fact that here more water ran in the canyon than anywhere upstream (at noon, I bathed in a deep pool just to cool off).

The San Juan was a gray-green flood. Across it loomed the brow of an out-of-the-way plateau, on the northern edge of the Navajo Reservation. I knew the Anasazi had established regular fords of both the San Juan and the Colorado, but this deep canyon looked like an unlikely crossing even in low water. Despite the wildness of the scenery, I felt a vague depression, partly the jittery edge of heat-stroke, partly an uneasy apprehension at having strayed into a bad-lands that even to the Anasazi may have seemed unwelcome.

The next day we made a long, leisurely loop up and down Shangri-La Canyon. The contrast with the lower Gulch was startling. Here everything was on a smaller, gentler scale: the grasses billowed in a heat-cutting breeze, ruddy bedrock gave us miles of easy walking, and we found a clever route up to the rim between the two branches of the valley, skirting hoodoos and linking ledges to complete the traverse. We passed many south-facing alcoves but found little evidence of the Anasazi in them.

It had been five days since we had seen anyone else, and our lives seemed to have adopted a rhythm dictated not by the nagging cares of home and work and the hands of the clock but by the shape of the valley and the angle of the sun. We had wandered far enough out of our normal paths to lapse into a llamalike contentment.

The next morning, under a mackerel sky that portended a change in the weather, we packed up Buck and Muchacho and headed upstream. They seemed eager to work again, and by now, because they had eaten their feed and we our five-pound ham, their loads were down to about seventy pounds apiece—a mere day pack for a fit llama.

A little before noon, as we crossed a low gap that cut off yet another oxbow rincon in the Gulch, I spied a clean panel of creamy sandstone on the right. It had the feel of a good place for rock art, and I hadn't studied the wall on the way down. I handed Muchacho's lead to Sharon, saying, "Let me just check that out."

I strode fast toward the panel, my eyes raised to survey its features, and turned a large boulder and stepped into the shadow behind it. The quickest part of my brain, pure animal reflex, took note of a sudden clicking sound; I jerked my gaze to the earth, saw the coiled yellow snake—rattles raised shaking, forked tongue darting in and out of its flat reptilian head—and managed to arrest my right foot in midair, about eighteen inches short of the snake, on which I would otherwise have stepped.

All the desert handbooks tell you how to behave on encountering a coiled rattlesnake. Back slowly, deliberately away, taking care to avoid sudden, jerky motions or gestures that might be construed as threat. Face the snake, and keep an eye on its reaction.

Instead, I turned and ran as fast as I could. It worked: the snake stayed where he was, still coiled and rattling, having defended his territory. As soon as I reached Sharon, I tasted the adrenaline rush. Whether reacting to the sound of the rattles or to my pell-mell flight, Buck and Muchacho hummed urgently and pawed at the ground.

The rest of the day seemed to pass in a pall. It was no fun to watch my every step, to wonder whether, despite the heat, I would be safer changing from shorts to long pants. It was the closest call I had ever had with a rattler, but I didn't know enough about snakes to know whether it really had been close or merely routine. Greenhorn hikers in Alaska, on seeing a grizzly a hundred yards away, come back with stories of having cheated death. On my climbing expeditions, bears had twice walked right through my camp, and I had learned over the years to fear them no more than they deserved. About rattlers, though, I was still a greenhorn myself.

On our next-to-last night we camped at the Great Arch, where we had spent a too brief hour on the way downcanyon. We had passed directly under it, though it took a fight to persuade Muchacho to make the passage (Buck had no qualms). Unlike the soaring, delicate bridges that give Arches National Park its cachet, this arch, some 50 feet high by 150 feet wide, seemed crushed beneath the massive weight of 250 vertical feet of caprock that topped it. Nonetheless, the wind and the stream had worn it away in the same fashion.

For prehistoric humans all over the world, natural arches seem to have had a special, perhaps a mythical, significance. Even to the late-arriving Navajo, Rainbow Bridge in Utah—the largest natural arch in the world—was a sacred place. A man could not cross under it without special prayers and preparation. After too many Anglos had picnicked beneath the bridge, it lost its supernatural power for the Navajo.

For the Anasazi, it is hard to guess what arches meant. At Rainbow Bridge, the first Anglo explorers found only a heap of stones enclosing a slab-sided bin, perhaps a Basketmaker cist. Yet the whole north side of our Great Arch was covered with pictographs and petroglyphs. On top of a bedrock boulder shellacked with desert varnish, I traced the meandering designs of lizard-men, frog-men, and a hunchbacked flute player. On the right wall, there were handprints galore in white, red, green, and mud brown. A big white rake, as the experts call it for want of a better metaphor—a horizontal white line from which depended twelve white teeth—claimed a panel fifteen feet off the ground. Anthropomorphs stretched hither and yon. One of the strangest sights was a spray of red paint curving upward, for all the world like the ejaculations of pigment Jackson Pollock was wont to spurt upon his canvases.

After hours of staring at the paintings, my mind still thrummed with the tantalizing ache of lost meaning. "We'll never decode it"—Steve Lekson's words mocked in my ear.

There was a time when archaeologists felt more confident of their command of the mysteries of the Anasazi past. Astounding though it seems today, when Alfred V. Kidder, still a Harvard student, was just starting to work in the Southwest in 1907, he was daunted by a warning he learned had been delivered to other potential protégés by his mentor, Edgar Hewett. So well had the ancients been studied during the past several decades, Hewett insisted, that, archaeologically speaking, the Southwest was "a sucked orange." There was little juice left to extract. Near the end of his life, Kidder would remember that phrase with amusement.

A generation later, J. O. Brew, who would conclusively demonstrate the Basketmaker–Pueblo continuum, was similarly warned away from the field. As he wrote in 1946,

> Upon beginning my studies in American archaeology, I was told by some that the Southwest had been "done" and that, if I were wise, I should select a field wherein more problems were to be found. When I disregarded this advice and persisted in the Southwest, I was told that the San Juan, particularly the Mesa Verde division of the San Juan, had been "exhausted."

In 1995, you could not find, even in the smuggest nooks of academe, an Anasazi archaeologist who would offer the palest echo of the assertions that Kidder's and Brew's mentors threw out to cool the ardor of eager acolytes. With respect to the Anasazi, at last we have begun to know just how much we do not know.

Remarkably enough, on our way down the canyon we had missed the finest rock-art site of all in the lower Gulch. Now, on the way back, we tied off our llamas for two hours while we perused a bewildering array of images. For sheer crowded variety, it rivaled Green Mask Spring in upper Grand Gulch in my experience; for visionary power, the Lower Butler Wash petroglyphs of the San Juan.

Informally (and inadequately) known as the Great Panel, its hundreds of figures have been painted above an extensive ledge that rises from right to left as it curves inward on a concave bend. You can reach the ledge only on the extreme right, and the climax of the pictographs comes at the far left, so that to walk slowly beneath the panel is to indulge in a crescendo of imagery. Bird-headed humans, a long row of stick-figure people running in profile, great ravenlike birds, perfect bighorn sheep, small triangle-bodied anthropomorphs carrying shields, a regal couple crowned with shamanistic grids of dots . . . Simply to list the details fails to convey the thronged purposiveness of the Great Panel, its confident aura of disclosing a truth that we, born too late, cannot hope to understand. A single motif runs through the dozens of anthropomorphs: nearly all of them have their right arms raised to the sky. What cry are their souls uttering? What revelation do they salute?

• • •

THROUGHOUT those eight days in the lower Gulch, I thought about the Anasazi, as well as the Puebloans, who have inherited the enigma of the pictographs. During my months of wandering and listening and reading, I felt that I had begun to grasp something of the inner character of the people who had left so many tantalizing ruins scattered across the Southwest.

My ambivalence on visiting a Pueblo village today was not something I was particularly eager to dissolve. As travelers, we Americans betray our insecurities by trying too soon to feel comfortable in some alien milieu. We want to be liked, to shake hands, to make friends—and then leave. But in other countries around the world, I had slowly learned to hang back and watch, to linger in the lacunae of misunderstandings, to look without blinking at some squalid or trivial act that undercut my neat preconceptions. A certain unease at Acoma or Jemez could teach me a lot.

In the backcountry, near the end of my Anasazi travels, I sensed that my itch was insatiable. No other prehistoric civilization anywhere in the world had so gotten under my skin. Even visiting my two hundredth or three hundredth utterly predictable, third-rate Anasazi ruin, I found much to seize my attention. When I tried to analyze what it was that proved so infectious, I came up with a simple—perhaps a simplistic—answer.

Where the Anasazi had chosen to live was, for the most part, a landscape as congenial and yet as challenging to my spirit as any on earth—even more so, I had to confess, than the Alaskan mountains I had campaigned among for thirteen straight years in my climbing youth. But it was not enough that the Anasazi had lived in that landscape; the Navajo live there today, and I have never envied or even seriously tried to comprehend their way of life.

What the Anasazi had done in those canyons was to shape their very lives to the landscape in a way no other people I know had ever done. That fit, that synchronism spoke in the masonry of a wall built to balance on three inches of rim ledge sixty feet above the abyss, in a hand-and-toe trail that solved a headwall, in a burial site deep in the gloomiest recess of a north-facing cave. The Anasazi had not remade the world: the world, in all its sandstone idiosyncrasy, had made them.

Nor could that fit of people to the land be reduced to a formula. Some of my most frustrating—and yet, in the end, illuminating—days in the Southwest had come when I walked for hours up a canyon that looked perfect for the Anasazi, only to find it barren of their remains, each south-facing alcove bearing only mouse droppings for residential debris, each wall of clean-sliced cliff innocent of the pictographs that begged to be painted there. Those hours of ungratified longing prepared me for the moments of sudden discovery for which there was no way deliberately to prepare.

The finest of all those moments—the single most moving hour of all my days in Anasazi country—happened upon me with Sharon in lower Grand Gulch. And I came within a step and a glance of missing it altogether.

The day was an ordinary day, the place an unremarkable stretch of canyon. Almost out of habit, I veered from the creek bed up through a screen of talus and scratchy bushes to walk through a shallow alcove facing north. If it was a Basketmaker II site, it was not a promising one: the breakdown boulders took up too much ground; the slope before the cave shelved too abruptly away.

Starting at one end of the alcove, I slowly walked the back wall, searching for flint flakes underfoot. Sharon searched a few yards behind me. At last I found several scalloped chips of red-brown flint in the dirt. But that was all: not the ghost of a storage cist, not the hint of a petroglyph. We moved on. Near the far end of the alcove, great tabletops of stone had fallen on end, where they leaned against one another, a chaos of broken slabs. It looked messy to hike through, and I almost veered down the hill to exit the alcove at that point. But a vague sense of thoroughness pushed me on, behind the slabs.

I had gone five or six strides when Sharon yelled, "Oh, my God, David, look at this!" She had her hands on her knees and was half bent to stare at something hidden beneath a pair of leaning slabs that had caught in the ground and formed a kind of box around it. Whatever it was, I had walked right past and missed it entirely.

I came back and looked, and the blood sang in my head. In that small, special space between the tilting slabs was a basket, placed facedown. In a glance I saw that it was as perfectly preserved as any museum specimen and that it was a classic Basketmaker II container. Dull tan in color, made of either willow or yucca fiber, woven in so exquisitely tight a pattern I knew it would hold water, the basket evidently lay where someone had left it, at the very minimum fifteen hundred years ago.

The cranny in which it rested was dim. We got on our knees to look closer. I could see how the flat bottom of the basket had been crafted as a coil radiating outward in a spiral. The sides were formed of twigs, around which the fiber snaked at right angles in unfathomably tiny loops—thirty-two rows of weave-wrapped twigs between the base and where the basket rim disappeared in the dirt. Depending on how much fiber was under that dirt, the basket was about the size of a good saucepan—some ten inches in diameter by eight inches in height. In shape it was conical, like a wastebasket.

I allowed myself, with a single fingertip, to tap the basket bottom gently. It rang with a soft thump, indicating dead air beneath. The temptation to overturn the basket was powerful, but I knew that even to try to dig it out along the edges might damage it irrevocably. And, as I kept slapping myself to realize, the basket was perfect: not a strand of fiber appeared broken. Baskets in such condition are usually found only beneath the saving dirt—not exposed to the air for fifteen centuries.

The previous fall, on my solo trip into another Utah canyon, when I had found the intact pot on the ledge, I had been galvanized to the core. Yet how many hundred times more unlikely it was to find an equally pristine basket, so much more fragile and so much older!

Next to the basket lay a pair of light sticks rounded at the ends. I picked them up, saw that the end of one fit neatly into a cup hole worn in the side of the other. I guessed it was a fire-starting kit and laid the sticks back where I had found them.

All our perusal took place in a hush, punctuated by whispered cries of incredulity. Sharon, especially, could not tear herself from staring at the basket.

As I studied the leaning slabs that had guarded the cranny for so long, my astonishment rose a notch. For on one side, a great oval slab weighing maybe forty pounds rested on end atop a slab many times smaller. It looked as though a nudge would break the balance, topple the upper slab, and crush the basket. And on the other side, an even larger slab, weighing maybe a hundred pounds, leaned over the basket at an ominous angle: only the planting of the butt end in packed dirt kept it from collapsing. The slab looked so unstable I refrained from stepping on the ground near its base, for fear the slightest jolt would release it. How could so precarious an assemblage of stones have endured the ages of storm and wind?

With my camera propped on the ground, I took long-exposure photos of the basket. When we projected our slides weeks later, one of these saturated pictures, shot from an awkward cranny on the far side of the basket, revealed something we never saw with the naked eye. The basket was not plain tan. A sophisticated pattern of blue triangles, linked corner to corner in diagonal stripes, had been woven into it. I knew from museums that the pattern had not been painted on the finished basket: each strand of fiber had been painted beforehand, then woven into the master plan.

I thought about the outdoor museum. Had he made the discovery, Fred Blackburn would now have piled stones around the basket to hide and save it, and left a note imploring whoever found it next to leave it where it was.

But that was not my style—or Sharon's. We agreed to leave the basket just as we had found it. It lay in as obscure a place as the canyons of the Southwest could offer, and for the last fifteen hundred years, it was likely that no one had seen it. Perhaps the basket would evade human scrutiny for another fifteen hundred years.

At last we turned to leave. From twenty feet away, we stopped for a final look. Darts of sweet pain swam through my last image of the basket, for I knew that in the rest of my life, I would never see anything quite like it again.

Acknowledgments

WITHOUT the help of many Pueblo people, descendants of the Anasazi, my research would have been far more difficult. In particular, Leigh Jenkins, cultural preservation officer at Hopi, was consistently shrewd with insight and helpful with advice. Tessie Naranjo, of Santa Clara, chairperson for NAGPRA, touched me with her wit and wisdom. At Jemez, a number of tribal officers, including governor Paul Chinana, lieutenant governor Vincent Toya, councilmen Paul Tosa and José Toledo, as well as liaison Roger Fragua and elder Cristobal Loretto, shared with me some of the heritage of their people. So also, with respect to his people, did Brian Vallo, lieutenant governor at Acoma.

Other acquaintances and guides at Zuni, Hopi, Acoma, Cochiti, Santa Clara, Jemez, Zia, and San Ildefonso Pueblos gave generously of their time and knowledge.

A large number of Southwestern archaeologists aided my work. I was astounded at their willingness to take hours and even days out of their hectic schedules to shape my understanding of the Anasazi. A number of these experts guided me on foot to the sites where they had done important work. These included Bill Lipe and Steve Lekson at Woods Canyon, Kristin Kuckelman at Castle Rock, Winston Hurst at Cave 7, Kurt Dongoske at Kawaika'a and Awatovi, Peter McKenna at Aztec Ruins, Kurt Anschuetz in the Oso Valley, Jonathan Haas and Winifred Creamer in the Kayenta and Klethla Valleys, Kim Malville at Chimney Rock, Polly Schaafsma on the San Juan River, Bill Wyatt in Gallina, Bill Whatley at Kwanstiyukwa and other ancestral Jemez sites, and Chris Adams, John Hohmann, and Ned Danson at Casa Malpais.

No less valuable were the hours spent in labs, offices, and homes as I was brought up to speed on recent developments in Southwestern archaeology. In terms of broad overview, I benefited especially from consultations with Steve Lekson, Bill Lipe, David Wilcox, Christy Turner, and Jeffrey Dean. Other experts who enhanced my understanding of Southwest prehistory include Bruce Bradley, Victoria Atkins, Richard Wilshusen, Rick Bell, Art Rohn, Alexander Lindsay, Alfred E. Dittert, Clint Swink, Eric Blinman, Joel Brisbin, George Gumerman, Tim McKuen, Cherie Scheik, Tim Maxwell, Dave Cushman, Mike Taylor, John Ware, Ann Phillips, and Linda Cordell.

Several National Park Service and Bureau of Land Management employees shared their expertise with me. Among these were Kim McLean at Chaco Culture National Historical Park; Linda Martin, Liz Bauer, and Jack Smith at Mesa Verde National Park; and Dale Davidson of the BLM in Monticello, Utah. Alan Downer, historical preservation officer for the Navajo Nation, gave me a perspective on the Navajo attitude toward the Anasazi that I could not otherwise have gained, as did my horsepacking Navajo guide, Eric Atene. Ted Hearne, of Springerville, Arizona, made an eloquent personal case for legal collecting of antiquities on private land. Tom Wetherill, Al Wetherill's grandson, offered vivid insights into the pioneering work of the Wetherill brothers at the turn of the century. Over the years, I have come to regard Jim and Luanne Hook's Recapture Lodge, in Bluff, Utah, as my Southwest haven. The Hooks' hospitality is like a balm, and the expertise they—and partners Diane Jensen and Larry Sanford—have put into their llama training ensured for me three wonderful pack trips into Grand Gulch. Those steady, uncomplaining llamas themselves—especially Boynton, Louie-Louie,

Buck, and the late lamented Muchacho—won my lasting fondness and respect.

Museum personnel also facilitated my research. I am particularly indebted to Anibal Rodriguez and Jaymie Brauer at the American Museum of Natural History in New York. Duane King, Eulie Bonar, and Mark Clark of the National Museum of the American Indian in New York granted access to their important collection. The staffs of other museums and libraries were also helpful: they include the Colorado Historical Society in Denver; the Henderson Museum in Boulder, Colorado; the Museum of Northern Arizona in Flagstaff; the Field Museum in Chicago; the Edge of the Cedars Museum in Blanding, Utah; the Smithsonian Institution Research Branch in Suitland, Maryland; the Mesa Verde National Park Museum; the Anasazi Heritage Center in Dolores, Colorado; the archives of the Chaco Culture National Historical Park; and the Tozzer and Widener Libraries at Harvard.

My deepest gratitude goes out to those friends who shared my trips into the Anasazi backcountry with me, putting their own spark into some of the happiest days of my life. Among these good companions were Tamara Wiggans, Tom Rice, and Milt Haywood of Wild Rivers Expeditions out of Bluff, photographers Terry Moore and Ira Block, self-taught archaeologist-guides Fred Blackburn and Vaughn Hadenfeldt, Ute guide Tommy May, ranger Bruce Mellberg, archaeologists Marietta Davenport and Bruce Bradley, and old friends Irene Spector, Lisa Gieger, Matt Hale, Marie-France Moisi, and Jon Krakauer, as well as my wife, Sharon Roberts.

Three times on solo trips I was haunted by Ernest Shackleton's hallucination (during one of his Antarctic voyages) of the presence of an invisible companion, lurking just behind his shoulder. As it was for Shackleton, that presence was for me a benign one, promising something like safety and peace, deepening my rapport with the Old Ones. By that disembodied companion—there with me during transcendental moments at Batwoman House, Nagashi Bikin, and Poncho House—I felt touched with grace.

Jon Krakauer, Marie-France Moisi, Steve Lekson, and Sharon

Roberts read my book chapter by chapter in manuscript and gave me valuable criticism. My agent, Max Gartenberg, was a faithful support. Johanna Li, at Simon & Schuster, performed many invaluable chores. Finally, my Simon & Schuster editor, Bob Bender, who has become a good friend, mixed guidance and enthusiasm from start to finish with the deftness of a virtuoso.

Appendix

ANASAZI CHRONOLOGY*

DATES	PERIODS	DISTINCTIVE CHARACTERISTICS
6500–1200 B.C.	Archaic	Subsistence based on wild foods; high mobility; low population density; shelters and open sites; atlatl and dart; no pottery.
1200 B.C.–A.D. 50	Basketmaker II (early)	Long-term seasonal (?) use of caves for camping, storage, burial, rock art; camp and limited activity sites in open; no pottery; atlatl and dart; corn and squash but no beans.
A.D. 50–500	Basketmaker II (late)	Habitation is shallow pithouse plus storage pits or cists; no pottery; atlatl and dart; corn and squash but no beans.
A.D. 500–750	Basketmaker III	Habitation is deep pithouse plus surface storage pits, cists, or rooms; plain gray pottery, small frequencies of black-on-white pottery; bow and arrow replaces atlatl; beans added to cultigens.
A.D. 750–900	Pueblo I	Large villages in some areas; unit pueblos of "proto-kiva," plus surface room block of jacal or crude masonry; great kivas; plain and neck-banded gray pottery with low frequencies of black-on-white and decorated red ware.
A.D. 900–1150	Pueblo II	Chacoan florescence; "Great Houses," great kivas, roads, etc., in many but not all regions; "unit pueblos" composed of a kiva and small surface masonry room block; corrugated gray and elaborate black-on-white pottery plus decorated red or orange types in some areas.
A.D. 1150–1350	Pueblo III	Large pueblos; cliff dwellings; towers; corrugated gray and elaborate black-on-white pottery, plus red or orange pottery in some areas; abandonment of the Four Corners by 1300.
A.D. 1350–1600	Pueblo IV	Large plaza-oriented pueblos; Kachina Phenomenon widespread; corrugated pottery replaced by plain utility types; black-on-white pottery declines relative to red, orange, and yellow types.

*Courtesy of William D. Lipe

Glossary

alcove: any natural overhanging shelter in a (usually sandstone) cliff; often misleadingly called a "cave."

anthropomorph: a rock-art figure of human form; the neutral term is used to avoid implying that the figure represents a human being as opposed to a god, spirit, or the like.

Archaic: Anasazi culture before the cultivation of corn, roughly from 6500 to 1200 B.C.; *see* Anasazi Chronology, p. 243.

arroyo: a steep gorge with hardened mud walls formed in a canyon by erosion.

arroyo cutting: a geological process, still imperfectly understood, by which in relatively few years a stream cuts a deep channel in a valley bottom, lowering the water table; probably a contributing factor to the abandonment of the Colorado Plateau in A.D. 1300.

atlatl: a spear-thrower, consisting of a throwing stick fitted with finger loops and a separate dart laid in a groove in the throwing stick; precedes the bow and arrow, which replaced it.

Basketmaker: phases of Anasazi culture numbered II and III, ranging from 1200 B.C. to A.D. 750; *see* Anasazi Chronology, p. 243.

chimney: a gap between two rock walls narrow enough for humans to climb.

cist: a small storage bin, usually from Basketmaker times, typically made of upright stone slabs planted in the ground.

corrugated pottery: ceramic ware whose outer surface is covered with indentations made with a tool or fingernail; such pots were almost always used for cooking.

desert varnish: a black patina naturally formed on sandstone by minerals deposited by seeping water; favored by the Anasazi for petroglyphs (q.v.).

Fremont: a little-understood culture of prehistoric farmers in central Utah, contemporary with the Anasazi and their neighbors to the northwest.

granary: any enclosure used to store corn, beans, squash, *etc.*

hand-and-toe trail: an Anasazi staircase carved in a steep cliff with a handheld pounder made of a hard stone such as quartzite; many Anasazi hand-and-toe trails are almost unclimbable today.

Hohokam: a culture of prehistoric farmers in southern Arizona contemporary with the Anasazi, their neighbors to the southwest.

hoodoo: a natural rock tower with an overhanging, bulbous cap.

jacal: daub and wattle; a wall built of mud and sticks without stone.

kachina: any of several hundred supernatural beings in Pueblo religion, intercessors between the people and their gods, bringers of rain, fertility, and health.

Kachina Phenomenon: a comprehensive religion based on the kachinas, traced by archaeologists back to about A.D. 1325, which might have integrated Anasazi life as never before; by luring tens of thousands of people to the south and east, the Kachina Phenomenon might have contributed crucially to the 1300 abandonment of the Colorado Plateau.

kiva: a common feature of Anasazi sites: a chamber, usually round and subterranean, long thought (by analogy with current-day Hopi kivas) to be of ceremonial or religious use, a view that recent research challenges.

mano: a grinding stone, used principally for corn; *see* metate.

metate: a scalloped stone grinding basin; *see* mano.

Mogollon: a culture of prehistoric farmers contemporary with the Anasazi and neighboring them to the south, from southern Arizona and New Mexico into northern Sonora and Chihuahua.

petroglyph: rock art made by pecking the surface; *see* pictograph.

pictograph: rock art made by painting the surface; *see* petroglyph.

pithouse: an underground living chamber used by the Anasazi throughout Basketmaker times; some scholars see the pithouse as the precursor to the kiva (q.v.).

plunge pool: any deep pool in a narrow canyon, usually caused by water spilling from a pourover (q.v.).

pourover: an overhanging lip of stone in a canyon streambed, which when it rains creates a waterfall that deposits a plunge pool (q.v.) beneath it.

projectile point: any arrowhead or atlatl dart point.

provenience: the context of an artifact in its original site; crucial to archaeological interpretation.

pueblo (archaeological site): any Anasazi village.

Pueblo (village and people): any of the present-day villages in Arizona and New Mexico peopled by the descendants of the Anasazi, including Hopi, Zuni, Acoma, Laguna, Jemez, Zia, and fourteen villages ranging along the Rio Grande from Taos to Isleta; also, the people of those villages.

Pueblo (versus Basketmaker phase of Anasazi): phases numbered I through IV in the Pecos classification, ranging from A.D. 750 to 1600; *see* Anasazi Chronology, p. 243.

rincon: an oxbow in a canyon, or the elevated island formed therein by the cutoff bend of the river.

slot: an exceptionally narrow canyon.

Selected Bibliography

Abbey, Edward. *Desert Solitaire: A Season in the Wilderness.* New York: 1968.

Adams, E. Charles. *The Origin and Development of the Pueblo Katsina Cult.* Tucson: 1991.

Adams, William Y., Alexander J. Lindsay, Jr., and Christy G. Turner II. *Survey and Excavations in Lower Glen Canyon, 1952–1958.* Flagstaff, Arizona: 1961.

Adler, Michael, ed. *Pueblos in Transition: The Anasazi World,* A.D. *1100–1400.* Tucson: in press.

Ambler, J. Richard, and Mark Q. Sutton. "The Anasazi Abandonment of the San Juan Drainage and the Numic Expansion." *North American Archaeologist* 10, no. 1 (1989).

Anschuetz, Kurt F. "Earning a Living in the Cool, High Desert: Transformations of the Northern Rio Grande Landscape by Anasazi Farmers to Harvest and Conserve Water." Typescript, Ann Arbor, Michigan: 1994.

Atkins, Victoria M., ed. *Anasazi Basketmaker: Papers from the 1990 Wetherill–Grand Gulch Symposium.* Salt Lake City: 1993.

Babbitt, James E., ed. *Rainbow Trails: Early-Day Adventures in Rainbow Bridge Country.* Page, Arizona: 1990.

Bandelier, Adolf F. *The Delight Makers.* New York: 1971.

Baker, Shane A. "The Question of Cannibalism and Violence in the Anasazi Culture." *Blue Mountain Shadows* 13 (Summer 1994).

Bean, Lowell John, ed. *Seasons of the Kachina.* Hayward, California: 1989.

Benedek, Emily. *The Wind Won't Know Me: A History of the Navajo-Hopi Land Dispute.* New York: 1992.

Benedict, Ruth. *Patterns of Culture.* Boston: 1934.

Bernheimer, Charles L. *Rainbow Bridge.* New York: 1924.

Blackburn, Fred. *Save the Signatures* (pamphlet). Moab, Utah: n.d.

Blinman, Eric. "Anasazi Pottery: Evolution of a Technology." *Expedition* 35, no. 1 (1993).

Bourke, John G. *The Snake Dance of the Moquis of Arizona.* New York: 1884.

Bradley, Bruce A. "Pitchers to Mugs: Chacoan Revival and the Demise of the Mesa Verde Tradition." Typescript, Crow Canyon Archaeological Center (Cortez, Colorado): 1994.

Brew, John Otis. *Archaeology of Alkali Ridge, Southeastern Utah.* Cambridge, Massachusetts: 1946.

Brisbin, Joel. "Preliminary Report on Excavations of Prehistoric Kilns at Mesa Verde National Park." Typescript, Mesa Verde, Colorado: 1993.

Brugge, David. "A History of the Chaco Navajos." Typescript, Santa Fe: 1977.

Bullock, Peter Y. "A Reappraisal of Anasazi Cannibalism." *Kiva* 57, no. 1 (1991).

———. "A Return to the Question of Cannibalism." *Kiva* 58, no. 2 (1992).

Bunte, Pamela A., and Robert J. Franklin. *From the Sands to the Mountain: Change and Persistence in a Southern Paiute Community.* Lincoln, Nebraska: 1987.

Canby, Thomas Y. "The Anasazi: Riddles in the Ruins." *National Geographic* 162, no. 5 (November 1982).

Carlson, John B., and W. James Judge, eds. *Astronomy and Ceremony in the Prehistoric Southwest.* Albuquerque: 1983.

Chapin, Frederick. *Land of the Cliff Dwellers.* Tucson: 1988.

Christenson, Andrew L. *The Last of the Great Expeditions: The Rainbow Bridge/Monument Valley Expedition 1933–38.* Flagstaff, Arizona: 1987.

Cole, Sally J. *Legacy on Stone: Rock Art of the Colorado Plateau and Four Corners Region.* Boulder, Colorado: 1990.

Cordell, Linda S. "How Were Precolumbian Southwestern Polities Organized?" Typescript, Boulder, Colorado: n.d.

———. *Prehistory of the Southwest.* Orlando, Florida: 1984.

———. "Tracing Migration Pathways from the Receiving End." Typescript, Boulder, Colorado: 1994.

Cordell, Linda S., and Mindy H. Halpern. "Anasazi Nucleation for Defense: Reasons to Doubt an Obvious Solution." *The Rocky Mountain Science Journal* 12, no. 2 (April 1975).

Cordell, Linda S., and George J. Gumerman, eds. *Dynamics of Southwest Prehistory.* Washington, D.C.: 1989.

Courlander, Harold. *The Fourth World of the Hopis.* Albuquerque: 1971.

Crampton, C. Gregory. *Standing Up Country: The Canyon Lands of Utah and Arizona.* Salt Lake City: 1983.

Crown, Patricia L., and W. James Judge, eds. *Chaco & Hohokam: Prehistoric Regional Systems in the American Southwest.* Santa Fe: 1991.

Dean, Jeffrey S. *Chronological Analysis of Tsegi Phase Sites in Northeastern Arizona.* Tucson: 1969.

Dean, Jeffrey S., Alexander J. Lindsay, Jr., and William J. Robinson. "Prehistoric Settlement in Long House Valley, Northeastern Arizona." In *Investigations of the Southwestern Anthropological Research Group: The Proceedings of the 1976 Conference.* Flagstaff, Arizona: 1978.

Dittert, Alfred E., Jr., and Fred Plog. *Generations in Clay: Pueblo Pottery of the American Southwest.* Flagstaff, Arizona: 1980.

Dongoske, Kurt E., Leigh Jenkins, and T. J. Ferguson. "Issues Relating to the Use and Preservation of Hopi Sacred Sites." *Historic Preservation Forum* 8, no. 2 (March/April 1994).

Dongoske, Kurt, Natalie Garnett, Martin Stoney, and Jonathan Terry. "Kawaika'a Mapping Project." Typescript, Kykotsmovi, Arizona: 1994.

Dyk, Walter, ed. *Son of Old Man Hat: A Navaho Autobiography.* Lincoln, Nebraska: 1967.

Ellis, Florence Hawley. "Patterns of Aggression and the War Cult in Southwestern Pueblos." *Southwestern Journal of Anthropology* 7, no. 2 (Summer 1951).

———. *A Reconstruction of the Basic Jemez Pattern of Social Organization, with Comparisons to Other Tanoan Social Structures.* Albuquerque: 1964.

Faunce, Hilda. *Desert Wife.* Lincoln, Nebraska: 1981.

Ferguson, William M., and Arthur H. Rohn. *Anasazi Ruins of the Southwest in Color.* Albuquerque: 1987.

Fewkes, Jesse W. "A-Wa'Tobi: An Archaeological Verification of a Tusayan Legend." *American Anthropologist* 6 (1893).

Frazier, Kendrick. *People of Chaco: A Canyon and Its Culture.* New York: 1986.

Frost, Kent. *My Canyonlands.* London: 1971.

Gabriel, Kathryn, ed. *Marietta Wetherill: Reflections on Life with the Navajos in Chaco Canyon.* Boulder, Colorado: 1992.

Gaede, Marnie, ed. *Camera, Spade and Pen: An Inside View of Southwestern Archaeology.* Tucson: 1980.

Gillmor, Frances, and Louisa Wade Wetherill. *Traders to the Navajos: The Wetherills of Kayenta.* Albuquerque: 1953.

Givens, Douglas R. *Alfred Vincent Kidder and the Development of Americanist Archaeology.* Albuquerque: 1992.

Grant, Campbell. *Canyon de Chelly: Its People and Rock Art.* Tucson: 1978.

Grey, Zane. *The Rainbow Trail.* New York: 1994.

Guernsey, Samuel James. *Explorations in Northeastern Arizona: Report on the Archaeological Fieldwork of 1920–1923.* Cambridge, Massachusetts: 1931.

Gumerman, George J. *A View from Black Mesa: The Changing Face of Archaeology.* Tucson: 1984.

Haas, Jonathan, and Winifred Creamer. "The Role of Warfare in the Pueblo III Period." In *Pueblos in Transition: The Anasazi World, A.D. 1100–1400,* edited by Michael Adler. Tucson: in press.

———. *Stress and Warfare among the Kayenta Anasazi of the Thirteenth Century A.D.* Chicago: 1993.

Hall, Edward T. *West of the Thirties: Discoveries Among the Navajo and Hopi.* New York: 1994.

Haury, Emil W. "Recent Thoughts on the Mogollon." *Kiva* 53, no. 2 (1988).

Hayes, Alden C., David M. Brugge, and W. James Judge. *Archaeological Surveys of Chaco Canyon, New Mexico.* Albuquerque: 1981.

Hughte, Phil. *A Zuni Artist Looks at Frank Hamilton Cushing.* Zuni, New Mexico: 1994.

Hurst, Winston B., and Christy G. Turner II. "Rediscovering the 'Great Discovery': Wetherill's First Cave 7 and Its Record of Basketmaker Violence." In *Anasazi Basketmaker: Papers from the 1990 Wetherill–Grand Gulch Symposium,* edited by Victoria M. Atkins. Salt Lake City: 1993.

Hutchinson, Art, and Jack E. Smith, eds. *Proceedings of the Anasazi Symposium 1991.* Mesa Verde, Colorado: [1992].

James, Harry C. *Pages from Hopi History.* Tucson: 1974.

Jennings, Jesse D. *Glen Canyon: A Summary.* Salt Lake City: 1966.

Judd, Neil M. "Beyond the Clay Hills." *National Geographic* 45, no. 3 (March 1924).

———. *Men Met Along the Trail: Adventures in Archaeology.* Norman, Oklahoma: 1968.

Kidder, Alfred Vincent. *An Introduction to the Study of Southwestern Archaeology with a Preliminary Account of the Excavations at Pecos, and a Summary of Southwestern Archaeology Today.* New Haven: 1962.

———. "Speculations on New World Prehistory." In *Essays in Anthropology Presented to A. L. Kroeber.* Berkeley: 1936.

Kluckhohn, Clyde. *Beyond the Rainbow.* Boston: 1933.

———. *To the Foot of the Rainbow.* Albuquerque: 1992.

Lange, Frederick W., and Diana Leonard, eds. *Among Ancient Ruins: The Legacy of Earl H. Morris.* Boulder, Colorado: 1985.

Lekson, Stephen H. "Archaeology and Traditional Knowledge." *Contact* 14 (January–March 1992).

———. "Chaco, Cahokia, and Complexity." Typescript, Crow Canyon Archaeological Center (Cortez, Colorado): 1994.

———. "Chaco, Hohokam and Mimbres." *Expedition* 35, no. 1 (1993).

———. "The Idea of the Kiva in Anasazi Archaeology." *Kiva* 53, no. 2 (1988).

———. "Mimbres Art and Archaeology." In *Archaeology, Art and Anthropology: Papers in Honor of J. J. Brody,* edited by Meliha S. Duran and David T. Kirkpatrick. Albuquerque: 1992.

———. "The Museum and the Antiquities Market." Typescript, Santa Fe: 1992.

———. "The Pueblo Southwest After A.D. 1150." Typescript, Crow Canyon Archaeological Center (Cortez, Colorado): 1994.

———. "Sedentism and Aggregation in Anasazi Archaeology." In *The Sociopolitical Structure of Prehistoric Southwestern Societies,* ed. Steadman Upham, Kent G. Lightfoot, and Roberta A. Jewett. Boulder, Colorado: 1989.

Lekson, Stephen H., and Rina Swenzell. *Ancient Land, Ancestral Places: Paul Logsdon in the Pueblo Southwest.* Santa Fe: 1993.

Lekson, Stephen H., Thomas C. Windes, John R. Stein, and W. James Judge. "The Chaco Canyon Community." *Scientific American* 259, no. 1 (July 1988).

Lindsay, Alexander J., Jr., J. Richard Ambler, Mary Anne Stein, and Philip M. Hobler. *Survey and Excavations North and East of Navajo Mountain, Utah, 1959–1962.* Flagstaff, Arizona: 1968.

Lipe, William D. "The Depopulation of the Northern San Juan: Conditions in the Turbulent 1200s." Typescript, Crow Canyon Archaeological Center (Cortez, Colorado): 1994.

———. "Grand Gulch: Three Days on the Road from Bluff." In *Camera, Spade and Pen: An Inside View of Southwestern Archaeology*, ed. Marnie Gaede. Tucson: 1980.

———. "Man and the Plateau: An Archaeologist's View." *Plateau* 49, no. 1 (Summer 1976).

———. "Material Expression of Social Power in the Northern San Juan, A.D. 1150–1300." Typescript, Crow Canyon Archaeological Center (Cortez, Colorado): 1994.

———. *The Sand Canyon Archaeological Project: A Progress Report*. Cortez, Colorado: 1992.

——— "The Southwest." In *Ancient Native Americans*, ed. Jesse D. Jennings. San Francisco: 1978.

Lipe, William D., and R. G. Matson. "Human Settlement and Resources in the Cedar Mesa Area, SE Utah." In *The Distribution of Prehistoric Population Aggregates: Proceedings of the Southwestern Anthropological Group*, ed. George J. Gumerman. Prescott, Arizona: 1971.

Lipe, William D., and Michelle Hegmon, eds. *The Architecture of Social Integration in Prehistoric Pueblos*. Cortez, Colorado: 1989.

Lister, Florence C. *In the Shadow of the Rocks: Archaeology of the Chimney Rock District in Southern Colorado*. Boulder, Colorado: 1993.

———. *Kaiparowits Plateau and Glen Canyon Prehistory*. Salt Lake City: 1964.

Lister, Florence C., and Robert H. Lister. *Earl Morris & Southwestern Archaeology*. Albuquerque: 1968.

Lister, Robert H., and Florence C. Lister. *Aztec Ruins on the Animas Excavated, Preserved, and Interpreted*. Albuquerque: 1987.

———. *Chaco Canyon: Archaeology and Archaeologists*. Albuquerque: 1981.

———. *Those Who Came Before: Southwestern Archaeology in the National Park System*. Tucson: 1983.

Lumholtz, Carl. *Unknown Mexico: Explorations in the Sierra Madre and Other Regions, 1890–1898*, 2 vols. New York: 1987.

Lummis, Charles. "The Enchanted Mesa." In *Mesa, Cañon and Pueblo*. New York: 1925.

———. *The Land of Poco Tiempo*. Albuquerque: 1952.

McGregor, John C. "Burial of an Early American Magician." *Proceedings of the American Philosophical Society* 86, no. 2 (February 1943).

McKenna, Peter J. "Late Bonito Phase Developments at the Aztec Ruins, New Mexico." Typescript, Santa Fe: 1988.

McNitt, Frank. *Richard Wetherill: Anasazi*. Albuquerque: 1957.

McPherson, Robert S. *Sacred Land, Sacred View: Navajo Perceptions of the Four Corners Region*. Provo, Utah: 1992.

Madsen, David B. *Exploring the Fremont*. Salt Lake City: 1989.

Malotki, Ekkehart, ed. *Hopi Ruin Legends: Kiqötutuwutsi*. Lincoln, Nebraska: 1993.

Malville, J. McKim. "Prehistoric Astronomy in the American Southwest." *The Astronomy Quarterly* 8 (1991).

Malville, J. McKim, and Claudia Putnam. *Prehistoric Astronomy in the Southwest*. Boulder, Colorado: 1989.

Malville, J. McKim, Frank Eddy, and Carol Ambruster. "Lunar Standstills at Chimney Rock." *Archaeoastronomy* no. 16 (1991).

Malville, J. McKim, and W. James Judge. "The Uses of Esoteric Astronomical Knowledge in the Chaco Regional System." Typescript, Boulder, Colorado: 1993.

Malville, J. McKim, and Gary Matlock, eds. *The Chimney Rock Archaeological Symposium*. Fort Collins, Colorado: 1993.

Martin, Russell. *A Story That Stands Like a Dam: Glen Canyon and the Struggle for the Soul of the West*. New York: 1989.

Masland, F. E., Jr. "Anasazi." Typescript, n.p.: n.d.

Matheny, Ray T. *An Archaeological Survey of Upper Montezuma Canyon, San Juan County, Utah*. Master's thesis, Brigham Young University, Provo, Utah: 1962.

Matson, R. G., and W. D. Lipe. "Settlement Patterns on Cedar Mesa: Boom and Bust on the Northern Periphery." In *Investigations of the Southwestern Anthropological Research Group: Proceedings of the 1976 Conference*. Flagstaff, Arizona: 1978.

Mays, Buddy. *Indian Villages of the Southwest*. San Francisco: 1985.

"Mesa Verde Region Prehistoric Pottery Firing Kilns." Typescript, Mesa Verde, Colorado: n.d.

Minge, Ward Alan. *Acoma: Pueblo in the Sky*. Albuquerque: 1991.

Naranjo, Tessie. "Guest Essay." *Native Peoples* 7, no. 3 (Spring 1994).

———. "Thoughts on Migration by Santa Clara Pueblo." Typescript, Santa Clara, New Mexico: n.d.

Nordenskiöld, Gustaf. *The Cliff Dwellers of the Mesa Verde*. Mesa Verde, Colorado: 1990.

Nusbaum, Rosemary. *Tierra Dulce: Reminiscences from the Jesse Nusbaum Papers.* Santa Fe: 1980.

Olson, Alan P. "A Mass Secondary Burial from Northern Arizona." *American Antiquity* 31, no. 6 (1966).

Oppelt, Norman T. *Earth, Water and Fire: The Prehistoric Pottery of Mesa Verde.* Boulder, Colorado: 1991.

Ortiz, Alfonso. *The Tewa World: Space, Time, Being, and Becoming in a Pueblo Society.* Chicago: 1969.

Parsons, Elsie Clews. "The Scalp Ceremonial of Zuñi." *Memoirs of the American Anthropological Association* 31 (1924).

Pattison, N. D., and L. D. Potter. *Prehistoric and Historic Steps and Trails of Glen Canyon–Lake Powell.* Washington, D.C.: 1977.

Pepper, George H. "The Museum of the American Indian Heye Foundation." *The Geographical Review* 2 (December 1916).

Poling-Kempes, Lesley. *The Harvey Girls: Women Who Opened the West.* New York: 1989.

Potter, Loren D., and Charles L. Drake. *Lake Powell: Virgin Flow to Dynamo.* Albuquerque: 1989.

Powell, Shirley, and George J. Gumerman. *People of the Mesa: The Archaeology of Black Mesa, Arizona.* Tucson: 1987.

Preston, Douglas. *Talking to the Ground: One Family's Journey on Horseback Across the Sacred Land of the Navajo.* New York: 1995.

Reid, J. Jefferson, and David E. Doyel, eds. *Emil Haury's Prehistory of the American Southwest.* Tucson: 1986.

Roberts, David. "Ghosts in the Sandstone." *Men's Journal* 3, no. 1 (February 1994).

———. "Going After Geronimo." *Outside* 15, no. 6 (June 1990).

———. "In the Canyon Incognita." *Outside* 20, no. 6 (June 1995).

———. *Once They Moved Like the Wind: Cochise, Geronimo, and the Apache Wars.* New York: 1993.

———. "'Reverse Archaeologists' Are Tracing the Footsteps of a Cowboy-Explorer." *Smithsonian* 24, no. 9 (December 1993).

———. "Together, Scientists and Indians Explore the Conundrums of Casa Malpais." *Smithsonian* 22, no. 12 (March 1992).

Rothman, Hal K. *Navajo National Monument: A Place and Its People.* Santa Fe: 1991.

Sando, Joe S. *Nee Hemish: A History of Jemez Pueblo.* Albuquerque: 1982.

Schaafsma, Polly. *Indian Rock Art of the Southwest.* Santa Fe: 1980.

———. "The Prehistoric Kachina Cult and Its Origins as Suggested by Southwestern Rock Art." In *Kachinas in the Pueblo World*. Albuquerque: 1994.

Schaafsma, Polly, ed. *Kachinas in the Pueblo World*. Albuquerque: 1994.

Sharrock, Floyd W., Kent C. Day, and David S. Dibble. *1961 Excavations, Glen Canyon Area*. Salt Lake City: 1963.

Simmons, Marc. *Witchcraft in the Southwest: Spanish and Indian Supernaturalism on the Rio Grande*. Lincoln, Nebraska: 1980.

Smith, Duane A. *Mesa Verde National Park: Shadows of the Centuries*. Lawrence, Kansas: 1988.

Smith, Jack E., ed. *Proceedings of the Anasazi Symposium 1981*. Mesa Verde, Colorado: 1983.

Smith, Watson. *When Is a Kiva? and Other Questions About Southwestern Archaeology*. Tucson: 1990.

Steen, Charlie R. "The San Juan Anasazi in the 13th Century." In *Proceedings of the Anasazi Symposium 1981,* ed. Jack E. Smith. Mesa Verde, Colorado: 1983.

Stein, John R., and Peter J. McKenna. "An Archaeological Reconnaissance of a Late Bonito Phase Occupation Near Aztec Ruins National Monument, New Mexico." Typescript, Santa Fe: 1988.

Stein, John R., and Stephen H. Lekson. "Anasazi Ritual Landscapes." In *Anasazi Regional Organization and the Chaco System,* ed. David E. Doyel. Albuquerque: 1992.

Stevenson, Matilda Coxe. *The Sia*. Washington, D.C.: 1894.

———. *The Zuni Indians: Their Mythology, Esoteric Fraternities, and Ceremonies*. Washington, D.C.: 1887.

Swink, Clint. "Limited Oxidation Firing of Organic Painted Pottery in Anasazi-Style Trench Kilns." *Pottery Southwest* 20, nos. 1–4 (1993).

Tedlock, Barbara. *The Beautiful and the Dangerous: Encounters with the Zuni Indians*. New York: 1992.

Trimble, Stephen. *The People: Indians of the American Southwest*. Santa Fe: 1993.

Trombold, Charles R., ed. *Ancient Road Networks and Settlement Hierarchies in the New World*. Cambridge, England: 1991.

Turner, Christy G., II. "Taphonomic Reconstructions of Prehistoric Violence and Cannibalism Based on Mass Burials in the American Southwest." In *Carnivores, Human Scavengers and Predators: A Question of Bone Technology,* ed. Genevieve M. LeMoine and A. Scott MacEachern. Calgary: 1983.

———. "Teec Nos Pos: More Possible Cannibalism in Northeastern Arizona." *Kiva* 54, no. 2 (1989).

Turner, Christy G., II, and Nancy T. Morris. "A Massacre at Hopi." *American Antiquity* 35, no. 3 (1970).

Turner, Christy G., II, and Jacqueline A. Turner. "The First Claim for Cannibalism in the Southwest: Walter Hough's 1901 Discovery at Canyon Butte Ruin 3, Northeastern Arizona." *American Antiquity* 57, no. 4 (1992).

———. "On Peter Y. Bullock's 'A Reappraisal of Anasazi Cannibalism.'" *Kiva* 58, no. 2 (1992).

———. "Perimortem Damage to Human Skeletal Remains from Wupatki National Monument, Northern Arizona." *Kiva* 55, no. 3 (1990).

Tyler, Hamilton A. *Pueblo Gods and Myths.* Norman, Oklahoma: 1964.

Wallace, Kevin. "A Reporter at Large: Slim-Shin's Monument." *The New Yorker,* 19 November 1960.

Waters, Frank. *Book of the Hopi.* New York: 1963.

Wetherill, Benjamin Alfred. *The Wetherills of Mesa Verde: Autobiography of Benjamin Alfred Wetherill,* ed. Maurine S. Fletcher. Lincoln, Nebraska: 1977.

Wetherill, Tom O. "A Personal Assessment of the Wetherills." Typescript, Farmington, New Mexico: 1989.

White, Tim D. *Prehistoric Cannibalism at Mancos 5MTUMR-2346.* Princeton, New Jersey: 1992.

Whitely, Peter. *Bacavi: Journey to Reed Springs.* Flagstaff, Arizona: 1988.

Widdison, Jerold G., ed. *The Anasazi: Why Did They Leave? Where Did They Go?* Albuquerque: 1991.

Wilcox, David R. "Pueblo III People and Polity in Regional Context." In *Pueblos in Transition: The Anasazi World,* A.D. *1100–1400,* ed. Michael Adler. Tucson: in press.

Wilcox, David R., and Jonathan Haas. "The Scream of the Butterfly." In *Themes in Southwest Prehistory,* ed. George J. Gumerman. Santa Fe: 1994.

Williamson, Ray A. *Living the Sky: The Cosmos of the American Indian.* Norman, Oklahoma: 1984.

Woodbury, Richard B. *Sixty Years of Southwestern Archaeology: A History of the Pecos Conference.* Albuquerque: 1993.

Yava, Albert. *Big Falling Snow: A Tewa-Hopi Indian's Life and Times and the History and Traditions of His People.* Albuquerque: 1981.

Young, M. Jane. *Signs from the Ancestors: Zuni Cultural Symbolism and Perceptions of Rock Art*. Albuquerque: 1988.

Zwinger, Ann. *Wind in the Rock: The Canyonlands of Southeastern Utah*. Tucson: 1978.

Index

Photo Credits

Matt Hale: 7, 9–11, 14, 20, 21
Jon Krakauer: 5, 23–29
Terrence Moore: 3
David Roberts: 1, 2, 4, 6, 8, 12, 13, 15–19, 22, 30